THE TRIVIUM

IN

College Composition and Reading

Third Edition Revised

BY

SISTER MIRIAM JOSEPH, C.S.C.

Martino Publishing
Mansfield Centre, CT
2014

Martino Publishing
P.O. Box 373,
Mansfield Centre, CT 06250 USA

ISBN   978-1-61427-686-9

© *2014 Martino Publishing*

Cover design by T. Matarazzo

Printed in the United States of America On 100% Acid-Free Paper

THE TRIVIUM

IN

College Composition and Reading

Third Edition Revised

BY

SISTER MIRIAM JOSEPH, C.S.C.

McClave Printing Company
South Bend, Indiana
1948

Cum permissu superiorum

Nihil obstat

Sister Mary Annice, C.S.C., Ph.D.

Imprimatur

John Francis Noll, D.D.
+Bishop of Fort Wayne

August 4, 1947

PREFACE

This book, together with a collection of Western World literature, provides matter for a coordinated course in introductory English re-establishing the trivium in the study of composition and literature, somewhat as it was exercised in the grammar schools of sixteenth-century England and continental Europe. A detailed exposition of the Renaissance trivium and illustration of Shakespeare's use of it are available in the author's book *Shakespeare's Use of the Arts of Language* (New York: Columbia University Press, 1947).

The present course in introductory English is designed for a class of college freshmen meeting five days a week for two semesters. It combines a complete course in logic with the study of composition and literature. That man is a rational animal is not merely an abstract definition. Rationality is daily observable even in the talk of small children. As the child speaks sentences without knowing formal grammar, so he also uses propositions, enthymemes, and syllogisms without knowing formal logic. Both formal grammar and formal logic, learned in school, satisfy the natural desire to know "the reason why." *The Trivium* explains "the reason why" through the relation of formal logic to formal grammar and rhetoric, giving special emphasis to the practical nature of these arts by the use of illustrations drawn from everyday life and from literature. It emphasizes the fact that thinking is inseparable from writing, reading, speaking, and listening.

Although the course may seem formidable, it has proved interesting, satisfying, and successful in freshman classes in a number of colleges for twelve years. As Bishop John Lancaster Spalding once remarked, teachers are inclined to underestimate their pupils' intelligence and to overestimate their experience. Abstracting the ideas from the large number of concrete examples throughout this book provides experience. The method of learning through the examples and exercises must be continually stressed. The exercises are more numerous than a class is likely to use, but the instructor can readily select what is desired.

The material in Chapter XI is to be used throughout the course for critical theory and for composition.

An abridgment of *The Trivium* entitled *Everyday Logic*, with parts of the first three chapters and all of Chapter XI omitted, is printed separately as a textbook for classes in logic. Chapter XI, preceded by the preliminary pages and four pages of Chapter I, is printed separately as a textbook or a supplement for classes in college composition.

This work owes its inception to Sister M. Madeleva, C.S.C., President of Saint Mary's College, Notre Dame, who authorized it, and to Professor Mortimer J. Adler of the University of Chicago, whose inspiration and instruction gave it initial impulse. To Dr. Adler is due, in particular, the treatment of mediated opposition.

Some of the material in Chapter III is derived from *Hermes: a Philosophical Inquiry into Universal Grammar* by James Harris (London, 1751). Of great aid have been the works of Aristotle on logic, rhetoric, and poetic, and texts on logic or rhetoric or both by sixteenth-century writers, by Milton, Blaisdell, Coffey, Creighton, Crumley, Hartman, Joyce Loomis, Maritain, and Pence.

For their courtesy in permitting the inclusion in this book of copyrighted material I wish to thank the following publishers: Little, Brown and Company for Francis W. Bourdillon's poem, "The Night Has a Thousand Eyes"; Alfred A. Knopf, Incorporated, for Adelaide Crapsey's poems; Dr. John McCrae Kilgour for John McCrae's "In Flanders Fields"; Harcourt, Brace and Company for Carl Sandburg's "Moonlight and Maggots."

I wish to thank my colleague Sister M. Annice, C.S.C., for advice and helpful comment and for acting as censor; and my colleague Sister Maria Teresa, C.S.C., for her cooperation in initiating and continuing this work at Saint Mary's College and for constructive criticism.

S. M. J.

Saint Mary's College, Notre Dame
August 11, 1947

Contents

A COURSE IN READING, WRITING, AND THINKING
(Five hours a week)

First Semester

I. COMPOSITION (See Chapter XI, pages 280-286.)

A. Narration

1. Autobiography (six to eight chapters; two in detail; synopsis of others)
2. Missing scene (350-600 words)
3. Scenes for original story (350-600 words)
4. Short story (1000-3000 words)

B. Description

C. Verse-writing

D. Composition based on literature (writing for reading): analysis, interpretation, comparison, criticism

II. READING: poetic, applying *The Trivium*, pages 247-273

A. Epic: substantial selections from the *Iliad* and *Odyssey*; *Aeneid*, Book II

B. Satire: Lucian

C. Drama: Aeschylus, Euripides, Aristophanes, Plautus, *Everyman*, Shakespeare, Calderón, Racine, Molière, Sheridan, Goethe Ibsen

D. Romance: *Aucassin and Nicolette*

E. Short story (reading for writing): Poe, O. Henry, Hawthorne, Boccaccio, Maupassant, Alarcón, Dostoevski, Turgenev, Gogol

F. Lyric poetry: Gray, Blake, Burns, Wordsworth, Shelley, Keats, Browning, Rossetti, Thompson, Masefield, Noyes, E. Dickinson, E. A. Robinson, Frost, Sandburg, etc.

III. THINKING: *The Trivium*, Chapters I-VI

Second Semester

I. COMPOSITION (See Chapter XI, pages 286-299.)
   A. Exposition
      1. Familiar essay (350-700 words)
      2. Definition (200-450 words. See question 37, page 102.)
      3. Preliminary research paper (300-450 words) requiring exercise in the use of library facilities
      4. Longer research paper (1000-1750 words)
   B. Argumentation: brief for debate
   C. Composition based on literature: analysis, interpretation, comparison, criticism

II. READING: mainly expository
   A. Literary essay: Bacon, Addison, Steele, Goldsmith, Johnson, Lamb, Hazlitt, De Quincey, Ruskin, Carlyle, Irving, Holmes, Thoreau, Emerson
   B. Essays on education and culture: Milton, Huxley, Schopenhauer, Newman, Arnold
   C. Autobiography and biography: Plutarch, Pepys, Boswell, Strachey
   D. Satire: Horace, Juvenal
   E. Criticism: Horace, Dryden, Lessing, Whitman, Tolstoy
   F. Narrative: Ovid, Dante, La Fontaine, Lessing, Goethe, O'Neill
   G. Philosophical exposition: Plato, Aristotle, Cicero, Marcus Aurelius, Boethius, Machiavelli, Pascal, Rousseau, Marx, Schopenhauer, Nietzsche

III. THINKING: *The Trivium,* Chapters VII-X

FUNDAMENTALS OF COMPOSITION

I. Relations of the arts of language

Impressions of { Nature, Man, Books } ——————observing——————
 ——————————reading literature——————→

 Composition,   { Content —— Logic —— thought ————
 Expression   { Form

NORMS

Correctness—Truth { of statement: proposition
 { of reasoning: syllogism

A. Language

 Oral { Phonetics (forming symbols) — Correctness of pronunciation
 { Grammar (relating symbols) — Correctness of sentence structure
 { Rhetoric (choosing symbols) — Effectiveness in reaching other minds (adaptation)

 Written { Spelling (forming symbols) — Correctness
 { Grammar (relating symbols) — Correctness
 { Rhetoric (choosing symbols) — Effectiveness

B. Color: painting, tapestry, etc.
C. Shape: sculpture
D. Sound: music
E. Stone: architecture

II. The function of language: communication

A. What { Thought—logical dimension
 { Emotion—psychological dimension (beauty, ugliness; delight, distaste)

B. How { Imitation—sensible object having meaning from resemblance to nature (photograph, painting, statue, picture-writing. A very few words are onomatopoeic, like boom)
 { Symbol—sensible sign, word, having meaning arbitrarily imposed on it (impositions)

III. The nature of language: a system of symbols

A. Matter { Sound—phonetics—spoken language
 { Mark—spelling—written language

B. Form: Meaning (semantics)

REAL BEING	LOGIC	GRAMMAR
Essence of species or genus	General term	Common name / General description
Individual	Empirical term	Proper name / Empirical description

CHAPTER I

The Liberal Arts

A college student entering upon a course of study leading to the degree bachelor of arts may reasonably wish to know what the seven liberal arts are.

I. The liberal arts
  A. The trivium: the three arts of language (pertaining to mind)
    1. Logic, the art of thinking
    2. Grammar, the art of inventing symbols and combining them to express thought
    3. Rhetoric, the art of communicating thought from one mind to another, the adaptation of language to circumstance
  B. The quadrivium: the four arts of quantity (pertaining to matter)
    1. Discrete quantity, or number
      a. Arithmetic, the theory of number
      b. Music, an application of the theory of number, the measurement of discrete quantities in motion
    2. Continuous quantity (extension, or space)
      a. Geometry, the theory of space
      b. Astronomy, an application of the theory of space

These arts of reading, writing, and reckoning have formed the traditional basis of liberal education, each constituting both a field of knowledge and the technique to acquire that knowledge. The degree bachelor of arts is awarded to those who demonstrate the requisite proficiency in these arts, and the degree master of arts to those who have demonstrated a greater proficiency.

Today, as in centuries past, a mastery of the liberal arts is widely recognized as the best preparation for work in professional schools, such as those of medicine, law, engineering, or theology. A man who first perfects his own faculties through liberal education is thereby better prepared to serve his fellow men in a professional or other capacity.

The seven liberal arts differ essentially from (1) the many utilitarian arts (such as carpentry, masonry, plumbing, stenography, salesmanship, printing, editing, banking, law, medicine, or even the care of souls and (2) from the seven fine arts (architecture, instrumental music, sculpture, painting, literature of *belles lettres* quality, the drama, and the dance), for both the utilitarian arts and the fine arts are transitive activities, whereas the essential characteristic of the liberal arts is that they are immanent or intransitive activities.

The utilitarian artist produces utilities that serve the wants of man; the fine artist, if he is of the highest order, produces a work that is "a thing of beauty and a joy forever" and that has the power to elevate the spirit of man. In the exercise of both the utilitarian and the fine arts, although the action begins in the agent, it goes out from him and ends in the object produced, which usually has a commercial value; and therefore the artist is paid for his work. In the exercise of the liberal arts, however, the action begins in the agent and ends in the agent, who is perfected by the action; consequently the liberal artist, far from being paid for his hard work, of which he receives the sole and full benefit, usually pays a teacher to give him needed instruction and guidance in the practice of the liberal arts. A student who realizes that he is working for his own good and not for his teachers (who, in fact, are working for him) has a true conception of his work and will do it gladly, with alacrity and a sense of freedom.

The intransitive character of the liberal arts may be better understood from two analogies:

1. Transitive and intransitive verbs compared
   a. The stenographer types the letters.
   b. The rose blooms.

   The action of a transitive verb (like *types*) begins in the agent, but "goes across" and ends in the object (the letters, which serve the interests of the employer by promoting his business). The action of an intransitive verb (like *blooms*) begins in the agent and ends in the agent (the rose, which is perfected by blooming).

2. The active and the contemplative Christian life compared. The primary purpose of both is the glory of God, but they differ in means and in secondary purpose. The purpose of the active life is transitive: to do good to others by preaching the word of God, by teaching, or by relieving the distress of the sick or needy. The purpose of the contemplative

life is intransitive: to perfect the agent, the soul that contemplates. Since the perfecting of the soul by increasing its participation in the life of God, who dwells in it by grace, is in itself the higher work, contemplation is in itself superior to action.

Three classes of goods may be distinguished.

1. Valuable goods are those which are not only desired for their own sake but which increase the intrinsic worth of their possessor. Such are knowledge, virtue, health, etc.

2. Useful goods are those which are desired because they enable one to acquire valuable goods. Such are food, medicine, money, tools, books, etc.

3. Pleasurable goods are those which are desired for their own sake because of the satisfaction they give their possessor. Such are happiness, an honorable reputation, social prestige, a gorgeous sunset, flowers, tasty food etc. They do not add to the intrinsic worth of their possessor, nor are they desired as means, yet they may be associated with valuable goods or useful goods. For example, knowledge, which increases worth, may at the same time be pleasurable; ice cream, which is nourishing food, promotes health, and is, at the same time, enjoyable.

The utilitarian or servile arts enable a man to be a servant— of another man, of the state, of a corporation, or of a business enterprise of his own—and so to earn a living. The liberal arts, in contrast, teach him how to live; they train his faculties and bring them to perfection; they enable him to rise above his material environment to live an intellectual, a rational, and therefore a free life in gaining truth. The Word Himself said, "You shall know the truth; and the truth shall make you free" (St. John 8:32).

The new motto of Saint John's College, Annapolis, Maryland, expresses the purpose of a liberal arts college with an interesting play on the etymology of *liberal*: "Facio liberos ex liberis libris libraque." "I make free men of children by means of books and balances [laboratory experiments]."

Each of the liberal arts is both a science and an art in the sense that in the province of each there is something to know (science) and something to do (art). An art may be used successfully before one has a formal knowledge of its precepts. For example, a child of three may use correct grammar even though he knows nothing of formal grammar. Similarly, logic and rhetoric may be effectively used by those who do not know the precepts of these arts. It is, however, desirable and satisfying to acquire a clear knowledge of the precepts, and to know why certain expressions are right or wrong.

The trivium is the organon, or instrument, of all education at all levels, because the arts of logic, grammar, and rhetoric are the arts of communication itself in that they govern the means of communicating—namely, reading, writing, speaking, and listening. Thinking is inherent in these four activities. Reading and listening, for example, although relatively passive, involve active thinking, for we agree or disagree with what we read or hear.

The present course in freshman English is a course specifically in reading, writing, and thinking—in literature, composition, and logic. The trivium is used vitally when it is exercised in reading and composition. It was systematically and intensively exercised in the reading of the Latin classics and in the composition of Latin prose and verse by boys in the grammar schools of England and the continent during the sixteenth century. This was the training that formed the intellectual habits of Shakespeare and other Renaissance writers. The result of it appears in their work. (See T. W. Baldwin, *William Shakspere's Small Latine and Lesse Greeke*. Urbana: The University of Illinois Press, 1944.) The trivium was basic also in the curriculum of classical times, the Middle Ages, and the post-Renaissance.

In the Greek grammar of Dionysius Thrax (*ca.* 166 B. C.), the oldest extant book on grammar and the basis for grammatical texts for at least thirteen centuries, grammar is defined in so comprehensive a manner that it includes versification, rhetoric, and literary criticism:

Grammar is an experimental 'knowledge of the usages of languages as generally current among poets and prose writers. It is divided into six parts: (1) trained reading with due regard to prosody [versification]; (2) exposition, according to poetic figures [rhetoric]; (3) ready statement of dialectical peculiarities and allusions; (4) discovery of etymologies; (5) accurate account of analogies; (6) criticism of poetical productions, which is the noblest part of grammatical art.

Because communication involves the simultaneous exercise of logic, grammar, and rhetoric, these three arts are the fundamental arts of education, of teaching and of being taught. Accordingly, they must be practiced simultaneously by both teacher and pupil. The pupil must cooperate with the teacher; he must be active, not passive. The teacher may be present either directly or indirectly. When one studies a book, the author is a teacher indirectly present through the book. Communication, as the etymology of the word signifies, results in something possessed in common; it is a one-ness shared. Communication takes place only when two minds really meet. If the reader or listener receives in his mind the same ideas and emotions that the writer or speaker wished to convey, he understands (although he may disagree); if he receives no idea, he does not understand; if different ideas, he misunderstands. The same principles of logic, grammar, and rhetoric guide writer, reader, speaker, and listener.

[Education is the highest of arts in the sense that it imposes forms (ideas and ideals) not on matter, as do other arts, for instance, carpentry or sculpture, but on mind; and these forms are received by the pupil not passively but through active cooperation. In true liberal education, as Newman explained, the essential activity of the student is to relate the facts he learns into a unified organic whole, to assimilate them as the body assimilates food, or as the rose assimilates matter from the soil and thereby increases in size, vitality, and beauty. He must continually get out his mental hooks and eyes and join the facts together to form a significant whole. This makes learning easier, more interesting, and much more valuable. The accumulation of facts not so related is mere information and is not worthy to be called education, since it burdens the mind and stultifies it instead of developing, enlightening, and perfecting it. Even if one forgets many of the facts once learned and related, the mind retains the vigor and perfection gained by its exercise upon them. It can do this, however, only by grappling with facts and ideas. Moreover, more knowledge is retained when ideas are related than when they are not.]

Each of the liberal arts has come to be understood not in the narrow sense of a single subject but rather of a group of related subjects. The trivium, in itself a tool or a skill, has become associated with its most appropriate subject matter—the languages, oratory, literature, history, philosophy. The quadrivium comprises not only mathematics but many branches of science: (1) the theory of number includes not merely arithmetic, but also algebra, calculus, the theory of equations, and other branches of higher mathematics; (2) applications of the theory of number include not only music (here understood as musical principles, like those of harmony, which constitute the liberal art of music and must be distinguished from applied instrumental music, which is a fine art) but also physics, much of chemistry, and other forms of scientific measurement of discrete quantities; (3) the theory of space includes analytic geometry and trigonometry; (4) applications of the theory of space include principles of architecture, geography, surveying, engineering.

The three R's—reading, writing, and reckoning—constitute the core not only of elementary education but also of higher education. Competence in the use of language and competence in handling abstractions, particularly mathematical quantities, are regarded as the most reliable indexes to a student's intellectual caliber. Accordingly, tests have been devised to measure these skills, and guidance programs in colleges and in the armed forces have been based on the results of such tests.

The three arts of language provide discipline of mind inasmuch as mind finds expression in language. The four arts of quantity provide means for the study of matter inasmuch as quantity, or, more precisely, extension, is the outstanding characteristic of matter. (Extension is a characteristic of matter only, whereas number is a characteristic of both matter and spirit.) The function of the trivium is the training of mind for the study of matter and spirit, which together constitute the sum of reality. The fruit of education is culture, which Matthew Arnold defined as "the knowledge of ourselves [mind] and the world [matter]." In the "sweetness and light" of Christian culture, which adds to the knowledge of the world and ourselves the knowledge of God and of other spirits, we are enabled truly to "see life steadily and see it whole."

II. Relations of the arts of language
    A. Relations to reality (with which metaphysics, or ontology, the science of being, is concerned).
       Metaphysics is concerned with the thing-as-it-exists, (with real being).
       1. Logic is concerned with the thing-as-it-is-known.
       2. Grammar is concerned with the thing-as-it-is-symbolized.

3. Rhetoric is concerned with the thing-as-it-is-communicated from one mind to another by means of symbols.

Illustration: In 1930, the planet Pluto was discovered at the observatory in Flagstaff, Arizona. This planet had been a real entity, traveling in its orbit about our sun, for centuries; its discovery in 1930 did not create it. But by being discovered it became in 1930 for the first time a logical entity. When it was named Pluto, it became a grammatical entity. When by its name knowledge of it was communicated to others through the spoken word and also through the written word in newspapers and magazines, the planet Pluto became a rhetorical entity.

Love this format

Rhetoric is the master art of the trivium, for it presupposes and makes use of grammar and logic; it is the art of communicating through symbols ideas about reality.

B. A comparison of the materials, functions, and norms of the arts of language (including phonetics and spelling which are subsidiary to grammar).

1. Phonetics prescribes how to combine sounds so as to form spoken words correctly.
2. Spelling prescribes how to combine letters so as to form written words correctly.
3. Grammar prescribes how to combine words so as to form sentences correctly.
4. Rhetoric prescribes how to combine sentences into paragraphs and paragraphs into a whole composition having unity, coherence, and the desired emphasis, as well as clearness, force, and beauty. Furthermore, since the norm of rhetoric is not correctness but effectiveness of expression, it deals not only with the paragraph and the whole composition but also with the word and the sentence, for it prescribes that diction be clear and appropriate and that sentences be varied in structure and rhythm. It recognizes various levels of discourse, such as the literary (maiden or damsel, steed), the common (girl, horse), the illiterate (gal, hoss), the slang (skirt, plug), the technical (*homo sapiens, equus caballus*), each with its appropriate use. The adaptation of lan-

guage to circumstance, which is a function of rhetoric, requires the choice of a certain style and diction in speaking to adults; of one style in presenting scientific ideas to the general public and of another in presenting them to a group of scientists. Since rhetoric is the master art of the trivium, it may even enjoin the use of bad grammar or bad logic, as in the portrayal of an illiterate or stupid character in a story.

5. Logic prescribes how to combine concepts into judgments and judgments into syllogisms and chains of reasoning so as to achieve truth. Its function is to determine the laws of correct thinking.

In the preface to his *Art of Logic* the poet Milton remarks:

The general matter of the general arts is either reason or speech. They are employed either in perfecting reason for the sake of proper thinking, as in logic, or in perfecting speech, and that either for the sake of the correct use of words, as in grammar, or the effective use of words, as in rhetoric. Of all the arts the first and most general is logic, then grammar, and last of all rhetoric, since there can be much use of reason without speech, but no use of speech without reason. We give the second place to grammar because correct speech can be unadorned; but it can hardly be adorned before it is correct.

Because the arts of language are normative, they are practical studies as contrasted with speculative.

A speculative study is one that merely seeks to know; e. g., astronomy. We can merely know about the heavenly bodies. We cannot influence their movements.

A practical, normative study is one that seeks to regulate, to bring into conformity with a norm, or standard; e. g., ethics. The norm of ethics is the good, and its purpose is to bring human conduct into conformity with goodness.

Correctness is the norm of phonetics, spelling, and grammar. Effectiveness is the norm of rhetoric.

Truth is the norm of logic. Correctness in thinking is the normal means to reach truth, which is the conformity of thought with things as they are—with reality.

QUESTIONS AND EXERCISES

1. Name the seven liberal arts. Briefly describe each.
2. Name the arts that constitute the trivium; the quadrivium; the arts of discrete quantity; of continuous quantity.
3. Name some of the utilitarian arts. Name the seven fine arts.

4. What is the essential difference between the liberal arts and the utilitarian and fine arts? Make this distinction clear with the aid of two analogies.

5. Why should you pay for your college education while some of your former high school classmates, now employed in an office or store, are doing less work than you and are getting paid for it?

6. Distinguish between valuable goods, useful goods, and pleasurable goods. Give examples of each. May the same good be classified in more than one of these divisions at the same time? In which of these classes of goods do the liberal arts primarily belong? the utilitarian arts? the fine arts?

7. Classify as goods primarily either valuable, useful, or pleasurable: shoes, education, jewelry, skill in playing basketball, hair naturally curly, bobby-pins, an aptitude for science, an automobile, charitableness, mild weather, art appreciation, chocolate cake, quinine, absolute pitch, a sewing machine, skill in writing stories, religion, a typewriter, generosity, a rainbow, courage, a lawnmower.

8. Which studies primarily fit you to know the truth which will make you free—those that directly prepare you for a job, or those that aim principally at intellectual and cultural growth? Do some studies do both at once?

9. State the purpose of a liberal arts college as expressed in the motto of Saint John's College, Annapolis, Maryland.

10. In what sense is each of the liberal arts a science? an art? Which character predominates? Can one use an art before he has made a formal study of it?

11. Show that the trivium must be the instrument of education at all levels. Name the four activities involved in communication and explain why thinking is inherent in each of them.

12. Was the trivium systematically exercised in reading and composition in any school curriculum of the past?

13. In what sense is a book a teacher?

14. State three possible reactions of a reader or listener to what he reads or hears.

15. In what sense is education the highest of the arts?

16. Distinguish between one who is acquiring a true liberal education and one who is merely amassing information. Which method of learning is more enjoyable?

17. How much of what you learn do you think you will know ten years from now? If little, will that prove your education futile? How many pounds of food will you consume in the next ten years? If your weight does not increase by that amount, will that prove your meals futile? Why do you eat? Why do you study? What constitutes physical perfection? intellectual perfection?

18. Explain how the following may serve as mottoes for a college student: "The rose blooms." "Get out your hooks and eyes."

19. What subject matter is associated with the trivium? with each of the arts of the quadrivium?

20. What part of the psychological examination, designed to discover the intellectual caliber of students, is based on the trivium? on the quadrivium?

21. Explain how the arts of the trivium are related to mind; those of the quadrivium to matter.

22. State Matthew Arnold's definition of culture. What does the Christian concept of culture add to this definition?

23. State the relation of the arts of language to reality. Illustrate.

24. Why is rhetoric the master art of the trivium?

25. Compare in material, function, and norm: phonetics, spelling, grammar, rhetoric, logic. Mention four levels of discourse.

26. What is a speculative study? a practical, normative study? Classify as speculative or practical: literary criticism, history, biology, costume design, editorial writing, news writing, chemistry, ethics, psychology, play production, statistics, geography, orchestra conducting, advertising, physics, nursing education, aesthetics, physiology, hygiene, politics.

CHAPTER II

The Nature and Function of Language

I. The function of language is threefold: to communicate thought, volition, and emotion.

A. Emotion

Man, like other animals, may communicate emotions, such as fright, anger, or satisfaction, by means of cries or exclamations which in human language are called interjections. Dumb animals use different kinds of cries to express different emotions. A dog barks in one way when he is angry; in another, when he is pleased. So also the mews of a cat and the neighs of a horse vary in order to express various feelings.

Although they may be repeated, animal cries can never be united to form a sentence; they are always mere interjections, and interjections, even in human speech, cannot be assimilated into the structure of a sentence. Man, however, is not limited, as other animals are, to expressing his feelings by interjections; he may use sentences.

B. Volition or appetition

The most elemental appetites and desires may be expressed by cries or exclamations, as when a baby cries, or a dog barks, for food. Since, however, desires multiply as knowledge increases, man usually expresses his desires, choices, and commands in sentences.

C. Thought

Only man can utter sounds which unite in a sentence to express thought, because he alone among animals has the power to think. Consequently, man alone has language in the proper sense of the word. This follows from his very nature, for he is:

1. Rational, and therefore has something to say
2. Social, and therefore has someone to say it to
3. Animal, and therefore requires a physical mode of communicating ideas from his mind, which is isolated from all others in his body, to another mind likewise isolated

Pure spirits, such as angels, communicate thought, but their communication is not properly called language because it does not employ a physical medium.

II. Means of communication

There are possible only two modes of communicating ideas through a physical or material medium: by imitation or by symbol.

A. An imitation is an artificial likeness; for example, a painting, photograph, cartoon, statue, pantomime, a gesture such as threatening with a clenched fist or rejecting by pushing away with the hands, picture-writing. There is no mistaking the meaning of a picture; it means what it resembles. The picture of a horse or a tree cannot represent a man or a dog.

Imitation, as a mode of communication is:

1. Limited
2. Difficult
3. Slow
4. Utterly unable to express the essences of things.

Try picture-writing your next letter home. See what success you will have in (1) telling what you are doing; (2) asking for what you want.

Within limits, however, imitation is a vivid and effective mode of communication. For this reason pictures are used to supplement news stories.

B. A symbol is an arbitrary sensible sign having a meaning imposed on it by convention.

A sign is sensible, for it can be perceived by the senses.

Every sign has meaning either from nature or from convention. A cloud, which is a sign of rain, and smoke, which is a sign of fire, have meaning from nature. A green light, which is a sign that traffic should move, has meaning from convention.

1. By convention, or arbitrary agreement, symbols are devised that are either temporary or permanent.

a. Examples of temporary symbols: the signals adopted by a football team, or by children for a game of "Run, sheep, run"; the password necessary to get through military lines or into an exclusive meeting; class colors.

b. Examples of permanent symbols: traffic lights, flags, a soldier's salute, a nod of affirmation, the cross, the crescent, heraldry, hieroglyphics, chemical formulas, numbers. All words are symbols, with the exception of a very few imitative, or onomatopoeic words, such as *boom, buzz, hiss, plop, tick-tock*. The symbols of heraldry have an interesting history and significance. See the article on heraldry in the *Encyclopedia Britannica*. Acquaint yourself with the coat of arms of the United States, Great Britain, your bishop, your school.

We are likely to undervalue our precious heritage of symbols and to underestimate their convenience. Some symbols are less convenient than others invented for the same purpose. For example, Roman numerals are less convenient for computation than Arabic numerals. In a work by Alcuin (735-804), CCXXXV is multiplied by IV in this manner.

CC x IV — DCCC
XXX x IV —   CXX
 V x IV —   XX

Roman numerals were used in all computations necessary in carrying on the business of the vast Roman empire.

2. Symbols may be designed for special or for common communication.

   a. Special symbols are designed by experts to express with precision ideas in a special field of knowledge, for example, mathematics, chemistry, music. Such special languages are international and do not require translation, for their symbols are understood by peoples of all nationalities, each in his own language. The multiplication table is a set of symbols understood by a Frenchman in French, by a German in German, etc. The same is true of chemical formulas and equations and of music.

   b. Common symbols or words, such as French, German, Polish, or Greek words, constitute the common languages. A common language is one invented by the common people to meet all their needs of communication in the course of life. Accordingly, it is a more adequate mode of communication than the special languages, although it is less precise and more ambiguous in the sense that one word may have either of two or more meanings. The common languages are not understood internationally but require translation.

   Two attempts to provide an international language may be mentioned: (1) Esperanto, an artificial amalgam, based on words common to the chief European languages; (2) Basic English, a careful selection of 850 English words, which through paraphrase are designed to do duty for a wider vocabulary.

A common language may be:

1) According to place, either native or foreign

2) According to usage, either living or dead

Every dead language, such as Latin, was at one time a living common language. It may be serviceable for special uses, such as embodying liturgy or doctrine, from the very fact that it is a dead language and therefore not subject to changes or to variety of interpretation, as a living language is. A dead language is more likely to be understood exactly the same in all times and places.

3) According to mode of expression, a system either of spoken symbols or of other signs

The spoken language is the original and fundamental system of symbols for which all other signs are merely substitutes. The written language is the most important substitute and the only one ordinarily understood. Among other substitute signs are: shorthand, braille, deaf and dumb signs, the Morse telegraphic code of dots and dashes, or long and short clicks (outmoded now by teletype), the semaphore code. Each of these substitutes merely renders into its own system of signs words of a common language.

III. The nature of language: a means of communication through symbols

A language is a system of symbols for expressing our thought, volitions, and emotions.

A. A word, like every other physical reality, is constituted of matter and form. A word is a symbol. Its matter is the sensible sign; its form is the meaning imposed upon it by convention. Matter and form are metaphysical concepts necessary to the philosophical understanding of any material whole, for together they constitute every such whole.

Hylomorphism

Matter is defined as the first intrinsic and purely potential principle of a corporeal essence; as such, it cannot actually exist without form, for it is not a body, but a principle of a body, intrinsically constituting it. Form is the first intrinsic and actual principle of a corporeal essence. These definitions will probably seem very difficult to you now.

You will gain a sufficient understanding of matter and form for your present needs from the following examples: (1) In man, the body is the matter and the soul is the form; together they constitute man. (2) In every sacrament, we distinguish the matter and the form; for instance, in baptism, the matter is water, and the form consists of the words to be spoken while pouring the water. (3) In water, the matter consists of hydrogen and oxygen; the form is the precise mode of their union in a molecule of water and may be expressed by the chemical formula H_2O.

The matter of words in spoken language is the sound. This aspect of language is treated in phonetics. The matter of words in written language is the mark, or notation. It is treated in orthography, or spelling. The form of words is their meaning and it is treated in semantics.

1. Matter: sound

Voice is the sound uttered by an animal. The voice of irrational animals has meaning from nature, from the tone of the utterance. The voice of man alone is symbolic, having a meaning imposed upon it by convention.

Man has articulate voice, by which he adds to his simple voice modifications that are produced by the organs of speech: tongue, palate, teeth, lips. The capacity of the articulate voice to produce such modifications in almost limitless variety makes possible the many symbols needed to communicate the wide range of human thought.

Note. The alphabet of the International Phonetic Association (see p. viii of *Webster's Collegiate Dictionary*, Fifth Edition) is a system of written symbols aiming at an accurate and uniform representation of the sounds of speech. It distinguishes twenty vowel sounds, six diphthongs, and twenty-seven consonant sounds. The English language lacks three of the vowel sounds (those present in German *grün* and schön and in French *seul*) and two of the consonant sounds (those present in German *ich* and Scottish *loch*).

2. Form: meaning

Words can symbolize both individuals and essences.

a. In metaphysics, or ontology, the science of being, we distinguish the individual and the essence.

1) The individual is any physical being that exists.

Only the individual exists, in the sense that every material being that exists or has existed is an individual, is itself and not another, and is therefore in its individuality unique. Every man, tree, stone, or grain of sand is an individual. Bucephalus, the horse which belonged to Alexander the Great, was an individual horse.

2) Essence is that which makes a being what it is and without which it would not be the kind of being it is.

Essence is that in an individual which makes it like others in its class, whereas its individuality is that which makes it different from others in its class.

Inasmuch as every individual belongs to a class which in turn belongs to a wider class, we distinguish these classes as species and genus.

a) A species is a class made up of individuals that have in common the same specific essence or nature.

Examples: Man is the species or class to which Dwight Eisenhower, William Shakespeare, Queen Victoria, and every other man and woman belongs, because the essence or nature of man is common to all of them. Horse is the species or class to which Bucephalus and every other horse belongs, because the essence or nature of horse is common to all horses.

b) A genus is a wider class made up of two or more different species that have in common the same generic essence or nature.

Examples: Animal is the genus or class to which man, horse, rabbit, oyster, and every other species of animal belongs, because the essence or nature of animal is the same in all of them. Flower is the genus to which rose, violet, tulip, and every species of flower belongs, because the essence or nature of flower is the same in all of them.

An individual animal or flower belongs to a genus only by being a member of a species within that genus. The abstract character of genus is such that one cannot draw a picture, for example, of animal, but only of a particular kind, or species, of animal, such as a horse or a dog. Yet, even species is abstract, for one cannot photograph the species horse or dog; one can photograph only an individual horse or dog, since every horse or dog that exists is an individual.

In every individual is the specific essence or class nature which it has in common with every other member of its species and also the generic essence or class nature which it has in common with every member of the genus to which its species belongs. The generic essence is merely the specific essence with the more definite characteristics of the latter omitted. In addition to the essence which makes it like other members of its species and its genus, the individual has individuating characteristics which make it different from every other individual in its species or its genus.

An aggregate, or group of individuals, must be clearly distinguished from a species or a genus. An aggregate is merely a particular group of individuals, such as the trees on this campus, the inhabitants of Chicago, the Notre Dame football team, the articles on this desk, the furniture in your home.

A species or a genus always signifies a class nature or essence and includes all the individuals of every place and time having that nature or essence. For example, man is a species and includes all men of every place and time—past, present, and future. Tree is a genus and includes every tree. On the other hand, an aggregate is a particular group of individuals that may or may not have the same essence or class nature; but in either case, the aggregate does not include all the members that have that nature. For example, the men of the nineteenth century constitute an aggregate of individuals belonging to the same species; but they are only a part of the species, namely, those who existed at a particular time. The things in this room constitute an aggregate of individuals belonging to different species, such as chair, desk, book, pencil, pen, chalk, blackboard, window, radiator, etc., but they are only a small part of each species.

An individual is one. An aggregate is simply a group consisting of two or more individuals.

b. Language employs four important kinds of symbols to represent reality: two to symbolize the individual, two to symbolize the essence which is common to all the individual members of a class.

1) Language can symbolize an individual or an aggregate by either of two kinds of symbols:

a) By a proper name, for example, Abraham Lincoln, the Mississippi River, Christmas, London, the United States Senate, the Rotarians, the Great Lakes.

b) By a particular, or empirical, description, that is, by a common name to which is joined a definitive which limits its application to a particular individual or group; for example, this eraser, the man who emancipated the slaves, the present manager, the chairs in this room, the starch now turning blue in the test tube.

Note. Empirical means founded on experience. Since only individuals exist, our experience is directly concerned with them. Throughout this book, the word *empirical* is used with reference to our knowledge of individuals as such.

If language could not symbolize the individual, we could not designate particular persons, places, or times. This would be extremely inconvenient. For example, you could not then direct a friend to go to your room and bring you your glasses, or key, or purse, or a particular book.

On the other hand, if language could symbolize only the individual, we should be in a worse plight for then:

a) Every word would be a proper name and it would therefore be necessary to give a different proper name to every object of which we wished to speak —not only to persons and places but to everything —to every tree, blade of grass, chair, fork, potato, coat, shoe, pencil, etc.

b) No one could understand us except those who had

shared with us, through simultaneous sense-expe-
rience, acquaintance with the identical individual
objects of which we spoke. Hence the language of
every town, even of every home, would be different
and would be unintelligible to outsiders. You may
have had the experience of being present when three
or four former classmates were reminiscing about
their earlier school days and absent classmates, all
of them totally unknown to you. As an outsider,
you took little or no interest in the conversation because, even though there were many words you did
understand, the proper names of the absentees sprin-
kled plentifully through the conversation had no
meaning for you. But if every word were a proper
name, unless you had personal experience of the
very objects being spoken of, you would be not only
bored but completely baffled in an attempt to understand the conversation.

c) Words, being all proper names, would become
meaningless on the destruction of the objects they
symbolized. They could not even be explained, as
proper names are now explained in the biographical
and geographical supplements to the dictionary, by
means of common names (e. g., William Caxton,
1422?-1491, first English printer; translator), for
there would be no common names. Therefore there
could be no history, no literature. What men wrote
would be as dead as their voices in their graves.

d) General, or universal, ideas could not be expressed
in language. Therefore there could be no books on
science or philosophy.

2) Language can symbolize essence by either of two kinds
of symbols, both of which are applicable to all the
members of a class:

a) By a common name, for example, man, horse, tree,
chair, square, circle, hour.

With very few exceptions, all the words listed in
the dictionary, except those in the biographical and
geographical supplements, are common names. Obviously then, the bulk of language is made up of

common .names; they symbolize either species or genus. Examples: *jump* names a species of movement; *move* names the genus of jump, fly, creep, walk.

b) By a general, or universal, description. This is always a group of words; for example, a rational animal, an equilateral rectangle, an organ of sight, a period of sixty minutes.

The definitions given in the dictionary are general descriptions of the single-word entries. They clarify the meanings of the common names. A general description is itself made up wholly of common names.

c. Words that represent no reality are not symbols; they are only empty words devoid of meaning.

1) A proper name or an empirical description must symbolize an individual or an aggregate existing in fact (past or present) or in fiction (wherein are characters, places, etc. created by the imagination). Otherwise it is devoid of meaning, as, for example, the present King of France, the Emperor of Iowa. The following, however, are truly symbols: Hamlet, Sidney Carton, Jack the Giant Killer, Nathan Hale, King Henry IV of France. So also are all the symbols given above as examples of an individual or an aggregate.

2) A common name or a general description must represent an essence or class nature which is intrinsically possible, although it need not actually exist. Otherwise it is devoid of meaning, as, for example, a square circle, a triangular square. The following, however, are truly symbols, because they express something conceivable: a mermaid, a purple cow, an inhabitant of another planet, a regular polygon with one hundred sides, an elephant, a rose. So also are all the symbols given above as examples of the essence, or class nature, of either a species or a genus.

B. Since words are symbols of ideas about reality, it is relevant to inquire how we derive ideas from reality and how we classify them.

1. The generation of a universal idea, or concept, involves the

following steps, which are treated more fully in psychology:

a. The operation of our external senses in perceiving an object present before us (for example, a tree or a chair) produces a percept. The external senses are sight, hearing, touch, smell, taste.

b. The operation of the internal senses, primarily the imagination, produces a phantasm, or mental image, of the individual object perceived, and this phantasm is retained and can be reproduced at will in the absence of the object.

Analogy: A percept is like a portrait being painted by the artist while he looks at the model. A phantasm is like that same portrait possessed and looked at whenever one wishes for years afterward, although the person painted is absent or even dead.

There are four internal senses in men and other animals: the imagination, the sensuous memory, the common or central or synthesizing sense, and instinct.

c. The operation of the intellect in the process of abstraction produces the concept. The imagination is the meeting ground between the senses and the intellect. From the phantasms in the imagination the intellect abstracts that which is common and necessary to all the phantasms of similar objects (for example, trees or chairs); this is the essence (that which makes a tree to be a tree, or that which makes a chair to be a chair). The intellectual apprehension of this essence is the general, or universal, concept (of a tree or a chair).

A general concept is a universal idea existing only in the mind but having its foundation outside the mind in the essence which exists in the individual and makes it the kind of thing it is.

A general concept is universal because the knowledge of the essence is present equally in every member of the class, regardless of time, place, or individual differences. For example, the concept chair is the knowledge of the essence chair, which must be in every chair at all times and in all places, regardless of size, weight, color, material, and other individual differences.

Only man has the power of intellectual abstraction; therefore only man can form a general, or universal, concept. Irrational animals have the external and internal senses, sometimes keener than those of man. But because they lack the rational powers (intellect, intellectual memory, and free will) they are incapable of progress or of culture. Despite their remarkable intelligence (their instinct, which is the intelligence given them by their Maker) their productions, intricate though they may be, remain the same through the centuries; for example, beaver dams, bird nests, ant hills, bee hives.

Analogy: Flowers contain honey. Butterflies, ants, bees, mosquitoes and other insects, may light upon the flower; but only bees can abstract the honey, for only bees have the power to do so. As the bee abstracts honey from the flowers and ignores everything else in them, so the intellect abstracts from the phantasms of similar objects the essence, that which is common and necessary to them, and ignores everything else, namely, the individual differences.

Axiom: There is nothing in the intellect that was not first in the senses except the intellect itself.

Man's intellectual powers need material to work upon. This comes from nature through the senses. Nature provides the material, and man's intellect conceives and constructs works of civilization which harness nature to his purposes and supplement and increase its value and its services to the human race.

Analogy: There is nothing in fine cotton lace or organdie or heavy muslin that was not in the raw cotton from which they were made; but there is greater variety and value. To produce these, the manufacturer requires raw material obtained from nature by cotton planters. Likewise the intellect requires for thought the raw material obtained from nature through the senses.

Abstract, or intellectual, knowledge is clearer although less vivid than concrete, or sense, knowledge. For example, circles and squares of various sizes and colors can be perceived by the senses and can, consequently, be perceived by a pony as well as by a man. A pony in a circus act might be trained to respond in various ways to colored discs and squares. Only a man, however, can derive from these various circles and squares the definition of a circle and of a square. He can also know by abstraction the properties of these figures, such as the relation of the circumference of a circle to its radius, which he expresses in the abstract formula $C = 2\pi R$. Such abstract knowledge is clearer, although it is less vivid, than the sense apprehension of the colored figures, which the pony can share with man.

Saint Thomas More, in his defense of the use of statues and pictures, contrasts them with words as means of instruction. He points out that words are symbols of phantasms and concepts, as has been explained above:

> Images are necessary books for the uneducated and good books for the learned, too. For all words be but images representing the things that the writer or speaker conceives in his mind, just as the figure of the thing framed with imagination, and so conceived in the mind, is but an image representing the very thing itself that a man thinks of.
>
> As for example, if I tell you a tale of my good friend, the imagination that I have of him in my mind is not himself but an image that represents him. And when I name him, his name is neither himself nor yet the figure of him in my imagination, but only an image representing to you the imagination of my mind. If I be too far from you to tell it to you, then is the writing not the name itself but an image representing the name. And yet all these names spoken, and all these words written, be no natural signs or images but only made by consent and agreement of men, to betoken and signify such thing, whereas images painted, graven, or carved, may be so well wrought, and so near to the quick and the truth, that they shall naturally, and much more effectually represent the thing than shall the name either spoken or written. For he that never heard the name of my friend, shall if ever he saw him be brought in a rightful remembrance of him by his image.

—The Dialogue concerning Tyndale

2. The ten categories of being were devised by Aristotle to classify being, and these metaphysical categories have their exact counterpart in the ten categories, or *praedicamenta*, of logic, which classify our concepts, our knowledge of being.

Every being exists either in itself or in another. If it exists in itself, it is a substance. If it exists in another, it is an accident. We distinguish nine categories of accident; these, with substance, constitute the ten categories of being.

a. Substance is that which exists in itself; e. g., man.

b. Quantity is a determination of the matter of substance, giving it parts distinct from parts; e. g., tall.

c. Quality is a determination of the nature, or form, of a substance; e. g., dark, handsome, intelligent, athletic, chivalrous.

d. Relation is the reference which a substance or accident bears to another; e. g., friend, near.

e. Action is the exercise of the faculties or power of a substance so as to produce an effect in something else or in itself; e. g., clicking a camera, standing up, smiling.

f. Passion is the reception by a substance of an effect produced by some agent, e. g., being invited to return, being campused.

g. *When* is position in relation to the course of extrinsic events which measure the duration of a substance; e. g., Sunday afternoon.

h. *Where* is position in relation to bodies which surround a substance and measure and determine its place; e. g., on a bench, beside the lake.

i. Posture is the relative position which the parts of a substance have toward each other; e. g., sitting, leaning forward.

j. Habiliment consists of clothing, ornaments, or weapons with which man, by his own art, complements his nature in order to conserve his own being or that of the community (his other self); e. g., in grey tweeds.

The categories are more clearly understood when they are organized as follows:

There are three ways of predicating something of a subject:

(1) If the predicate is that which *is* the subject itself, and does not exist *in* the subject, the predicate is a substance. (John is a man.)

(2) If the predicate exists *in* the subject,

    a) absolutely, as flowing from

        1) matter, the predicate is a quantity. (John is tall.)

        2) form, the predicate is a quality. (John is handsome.)

    b) relatively, with respect to another (*ad aliquid*), the predicate is in the category relation. (John is your brother.)

(3) If the predicate exists in something extrinsic to the subject, and is
    a) partially extrinsic, as
        1) a principle of action in the subject, the predicate is an action. (John pitched the ball.)
        2) a terminus of action in the subject, the predicate is a passion. (John was injured.)
    b) wholly extrinsic, as
        1) a measure of the subject, according to
            i) time, the predicate is in the category *when*. (John was late.)
            ii) place, either
                (a) simple, the predicate is in the category *where*. (John is here.)
                (b) according to the order of parts, the predicate is in the category posture. (John is sitting.)
        2) merely adjacent to the subject, the predicate is is in the category habiliment. (John is in overalls.)

3. The following seven important definitions emerge from these considerations:
    a. The essence is that which makes a being what it is and without which it would not be the kind of being it is.
    b. Nature is essence viewed as the source of activity.
    c. The individual is constituted of essence existent in quantified matter plus other accidents.

    This definition is more clearly understood from the following:
    1) Essence is that which makes the individual like other members of its class.
    2) Quantified matter is that which makes the individual different from other individuals in its class, because matter, extended by reason of its quantity, must be this or that matter, which, by limiting the form, individuates it.
    3) Accidents are those notes (shape, color, weight, size, etc.) by which we perceive the difference between the individuals of a class.
    The individuals within a species (for example, all

men) are essentially the same. But they are not merely accidentally different; they are individually different. Even should individuals be as alike in essence and
in accidents as the matches in a box of matches or the
pins in a paper of pins, they are nonetheless individually different, because the matter in one is not the matter
in the other, but is a different quantity or part, even
though of the same kind and amount.

d. A percept is the sense-apprehension of an individual reality (in its presence).

e. A phantasm is the mental image of an individual reality
(in its absence).

f. A general concept is the intellectual apprehension of
essence.

g. An empirical concept is the indirect intellectual apprehension of an individual. The intellect can know individual objects only indirectly, in the phantasms, because individuals are material, with but one exception, the intellect
itself; because it is a spiritual individual, the intellect
can know itself directly and reflexively. (See Saint Thomas, *Summa Theologica*, Part 1, Question 86, Articles 1
and 3. Also Maher, *Psychology*, p. 159, note.)

In a natural object the following are similar, but distinct:
substance, essence, nature, form, species. The knowledge of
these is the concept, which is expressed fully in the definition
and symbolized by the common name.

Since man cannot create substance but can merely fashion
substances that are furnished by nature, an artificial object,
such as a chair, has two essences: the essence of its matter
(wood, iron marble, etc.) and the essence of its form (chair).
The essence of the form is expressed in the definition (of
chair).

Frequently, a common name symbolizes a concept that is
not simple, nor equivalent to the essence of a natural species,
like man, but composite, like lawyer or athlete, including
in its definition certain accidents which determine not natural
species, but classes that differ only accidentally. A composite
concept may be called a construct. Lawyer and athlete are
constructs, for their definition adds to the simple concept
man, certain accidents, such as knowledge of law, or physical

agility, which are essential to the definition of lawyer or of athlete, although not essential to the definition of man. On the other hand, other accidents, although they may be present, are not essential to the definition of a construct. For example, a particular lawyer may be tall, dark, irritable, generous, etc., but these accidents are no more essential to being a lawyer than they are to being a man.

A construct may be analyzed into its component parts by showing in what categories its essential meanings lie:

(1) Carpenter
   Substance—man
   Quality—skill in building with wood
(2) Ruler
   Substance—man
   Action—exercising authority
   Relation—to a subject
(3) Blizzard
   Substance—water
   Quality—cold
   Passion—vaporized, frozen into snow, and blown about by a high wind

In the English language a construct is usually symbolized by a single word which does not make explicit the composite character of the construct. In an agglutinated language, like German, however, a construct is more commonly symbolized by a compound word which does make explicit its composite character; for example, *Abwehrflammenwerfer* (defensive flame-thrower). Also, the English word *tank* in German is *Raupenschlepperpanzerkampfwagen* (a caterpillar-like, self-moving, armored war wagon). This has been shortened to *panzer*, which gained currency in English during World War II, when newspapers frequently mentioned panzer divisions.

C. The logical and psychological dimensions of language

The total meaning of a word may be represented thus:

house *a*   *b*
home *a*   *b*   *x*

Objectively, the definition (the logical dimension) of *house* and *home* are similar, and may be represented by the lines *ab*; but subjectively, *home* is a much richer word, for to its logical content is added an emotional content (the psychological dimension) associated with the word and represented by the line *bx*.

The fact that *house* has practically no psychological dimension while *home* has much accounts for the different effects produced by the following lines, which are equivalent in the logical dimension:

House, house, loved, loved house!
There's no place like my house! There's no place like my house!

"Home, Home, sweet, sweet Home!
There's no place like Home! There's no place like Home!"
—*John Howard Payne*

Analogy: The logical dimension of language may be compared to the incandescent electrified wire in a transparent bulb; the wire is obvious and its limits are perfectly defined. The psychological dimension may be compared to a frosted bulb, in which all the light, it is true, comes from the incandescent wire within, but the light is softened and diffused by the bulb, which gives it a more beautiful and psychologically warmer glow.

1. The logical, or intellectual, dimension of a word is its thought content, which may be expressed in its definition, given in the dictionary. In rhetoric this is called the denotation of the word.

   Language with a purely logical dimension is desirable in legal documents and in scientific and philosophical treatises, where clearness, precision, and singleness of meaning are requisite. Consequently, synonyms, which usually vary in shades of meaning, ought to be avoided, and the same word should be employed throughout to convey the same meaning; or if it is used with a different meaning, that fact should be made clear. Abstract words are usually clearer and more precise than concrete words, for abstract knowledge is clearer, although less vivid, than sense knowledge (see p. 22). Yet to communicate abstract knowledge, one should employ concrete illustrations from which the reader or hearer can make the abstraction for himself, since by so doing he grasps the abstract ideas much better than if the writer or speaker gave them to him ready-made.

Accordingly, in studying this book, carefully consider the examples, abstract the ideas from them, and then you will really understand the definitions and principles much more readily than you will otherwise.

2. The psychological dimension of language is its emotional content—the related images, nuances, and emotions spontaneously associated with words. In rhetoric this is called the connotation of the word.

Language with a rich psychological dimension is desirable in poetry and other literature of the *belles lettres* level, where humor, pathos, grandeur, sublimity, or the like are to be communicated. (Compare the distinction between the logical and psychological dimensions of language with De Quincey's distinction in his essay "Literature of Knowledge and Literature of Power." Also compare in psychological dimension the essays of Bacon with those of Emerson.)

In literary composition, one should employ words that are concrete rather than abstract, that are rich in imagery, and idiomatic. Synonyms should be used in order to avoid monotony of sound and to convey subtle shades of meaning that vary in both the logical and the psychological dimension. The fine shades of difference between synonyms are explained not only in the dictionary but also, in greater detail, in such books as *Webster's Dictionary of Synonyms*, Roget's *Thesaurus*, Soule's *Dictionary of English Synonyms*, and Crabbe's *English Synonyms*.

A sensitive awareness of the subtleties of language, particularly in its psychological dimension, enables one to recognize good style in the speech and writing of others and to cultivate good style in one's own composition, both oral and written.

The substance of a given composition may be translated almost perfectly from one language to another, in the logical dimension. Translation is seldom satisfactory, however, in the psychological dimension. That is why poetry in translalation is usually less pleasing than in the original.

Various characteristics of words affect the psychological dimension of language:

a. The mere sound of a word may produce a pleasing effect which another word of the same meaning lacks.

Example: *Silver* and *argent* have the same meaning.
Read Walter de la Mare's poem "Silver," substituting
argent for *silver*, and note the difference in the psychological effect.

b. A pedantic or pompous style is psychologically displeasing.
For example, compare these sentences, identical in logical
content.
   1) Behold! The inhabitants have all retired to their dom-
   iciles.
   Look! The people have all gone home.
   2) The vaulted dome of heaven is cerulean.
   The sky is blue.
   3) Compare the style of the abdication speech of King
   Edward VIII with what it might have been (*Reader's
   Digest*, March, 1937, condensed from a version by
   Arthur H. Little in *Printer's Ink*, December 17, 1936).

c. The emotional effect of a word, often a by-product of its
historical development, belongs to the idiom of language
and would often be lost in translation.
   The following are alike in the logical dimension, unlike
in the psychological dimension, and therefore unlike in
effect.
   1) A young man tells a girl, "Time stands still when I
   look into your eyes." Another tells her, "You have a
   face that would stop a clock."
   2) A boy tells a girl, "You are a vision." Another, "You
   are a sight."
   3) Mr. X and Mr. Y. had dinner together. Being asked
   by Mr. Z, "What kind of meat did you have for dinner?" Mr. X replied, "I had roast pork." Mr. Y replied, "I had roast swine meat."
      We find Mr. Y's answer revolting because *swine*
   has been regarded as a word unfit for polite discourse
   in English, certainly unfit to name meat, ever since the
   Norman Conquest in 1066. After that, the conquered
   and despised Anglo-Saxon tended the live animal and
   called it *swine;* but the aristocratic Norman to whom
   it was served at the banquet table called it *pork*, a word
   derived from the Latin through the French, and in
   those languages applied to the live animal as well as

to the meat. The associations built into the word *swine*
in the history of the race (by such events as are portrayed in part in *Robin Hood* and in *Ivanhoe*) are felt
by modern English-speaking persons who do not even
know the occasion of the emotional response which
they, nonetheless, experience.

4) At a meeting of the assembly of the United Nations,
an American produced bewilderment among the
translators by speaking of a proposal as "a pork bar-
rel floating on a pink cloud." A fellow American
might understand this as "an impractical plan to be
financed by public funds designed to gain local
political patronage."

d. An allusion is a passing reference to phrases or longer
passages which the writer takes for granted will be
familiar to the reader. Sometimes the writer changes
the phrases somewhat, but, whether the same or modified, they depend for their effect on reminding the
reader of the original; for instance, *With Malice Toward Some* is a title deliberately intended to remind
the reader of the phrase in Lincoln's Second Inaugural
Address, "with malice toward none."

An allusion depends for much of its effect on the
psychological dimension of language, for it enriches
the passage in which it occurs with emotional overtones
and associated ideas derived from the context in which
it originally appeared. Examples:

1) The exclusionist scans the too, too solid flesh of his draft
manuscript and thinks how to melt out of it just an ounce
more or fat . . . No dramatist can have added more cubits
than Sardou (simply by taking thought about technical
matters) to a somewhat low artistic stature. He had brought
himself to resemble a house swept and garnished, all ready
for the spirit of genius to enter in if ever it should care to.
. . . In the bosom of Ibsen; the original nucleus of the thing
seems to have continuously waxed in stature as well as in
grace.—C. E. Montague, "Putting in and Leaving Out"

2) Most of the paper is as blank as Modred's shield.
—Rudyard Kipling, "The Man Who Would Be King"

3) Bores make cowards of us all.   —E. V. Lucas, "Bores"

For those whose literary background is inadequate
and who therefore are unfamiliar with the source of

the allusion a work such as the concordance to the Bible or to Shakespeare, both frequent sources of allusion, will prove helpful. Words from the selections above, such as *solid, flesh, melt,* and *cowards,* appearing in their alphabetical places in the concordance to Shakespeare, will lead the investigator to the passages in Shakespeare alluded to. Similarly, *cubits, stature, swept, garnished, waxed, grace* are listed in the concordance to the Bible, with passages quoted and exact references given. A collegiate dictionary will serve to identify Modred. A dictionary of persons and places mentioned in Greek and Latin literature will explain classical allusions.

The writers who make allusions expect, of course, that their readers will be familiar at first hand with the literature to which they refer. One of the rewards of literary study is the possession of a heritage of poetry and story which causes many names and phrases to echo with rich reverberations down the centuries. The language of allusion often provides a sort of shorthand which links and communicates in few words experiences shared by men facing similar situations in all periods of human history.

e. The psychological dimension of words is especially affected by their combination.

   1) Some combinations, particularly of adjectives and nouns and of nouns and verbs, are "just right," for example, the following combinations in Milton: "dappled dawn," "checkered shade," "leaden-stepping hours," "disproportioned sin jarred against nature's chime." It is fitting to speak of azure light or the azure sky or an azure evening gown, but not of an azure apron, because azure and apron clash in the psychological dimension. The combination is disharmonious. It is certainly not "just right."

   2) Certain combinations of words and thoughts produce a vivid concentration of meaning rich in the psychological dimension. Examples:

      a) We ought not to subject ourselves to the oligarchy of the living.—Chesterton

b) Water is a creature and this commonplace fact is its first title to nobility. For to be a creature is to be in the thought and love of God. . . . The entire universe tends to become a sacrament, as it were a vast monstrance filled with God's Presence.—Zundel, *The Splendour of the Liturgy*

c) For there is no more irresistible call to virtue in the world than the eyes of a child asking its father and mother a silent question, serenely confident that the answer admits of but one reply: "You do yourselves, don't you, what you tell me to do?" It is in this way that souls often reveal to us the splendour of the Face for which they look in us.

—Ibid.

d) In His will is our peace.—Dante, *The Divine Comedy*

e) I have stained the image of God in my soul.

—Saint Catherine of Siena, *Dialogue*

f) Death is no foeman, we were born together;
He dwells between the places of my breath.

—Sister M. Madeleva, "Knights Errant"

g) Brave Sea-Captain, Norse Sea-King—Columbus . . . it is no friendly environment this of thine in the waste deep waters; around thee mutinous discouraged souls, behind thee disgrace and ruin, before thee the unpenetrated veil of Night.—Carlyle, *Past and Present*

f. What is false when taken literally in the purely logical dimension may be true when understood imaginatively, or figuratively, in the psychological dimension. Example:

The night has a thousand eyes,
  And the day but one;
Yet the light of the bright world dies
  With the dying sun.

The mind has a thousand eyes,
  And the heart but one;
Yet the light of a whole life dies
  When love is done.

—Francis W. Bourdillon

This poem, understood literally, that is, in its logical dimension, is false and even ridiculous. But understood imaginatively, as it is meant to be, since it is metaphorical, the poem has emotional truth. The very sound and movement of the words, and the symmetry—the parallel grammatical and logical structure — of the two stanzas contribute to the pleasing effect.

D. The ambiguity of language

Since a word is a symbol, an arbitrary sign whose meaning is imposed on it, not by nature, not by resemblance, but by convention, it is by its very nature subject to ambiguity; for, obviously, more than one meaning may be imposed on a given symbol. In a living language, the common people from time to time under changing conditions impose new meanings on the same word, and therefore words are more subject to ambiguity than are the symbols of mathematics, chemistry, or music, whose meaning is imposed on them by experts.

The ambiguity of a word may arise from: (1) the various meanings imposed on it in the course of time, constituting the history of the word; (2) the nature of a symbol, from which arise the three impositions of a word and the two intentions of a term; (3) the nature of the phantasm for which the word is originally a substitute. (See pages 21 and 40.)

1. The various meanings imposed upon the symbol (the sound or the notation) in the course of time

   a. A given sound is ambiguous when it symbolizes different meanings. Such words are homonyms, ambiguous to the ear, and they may or may not differ in spelling when written. The ambiguous sound may be:

      1) Within the same language; e. g., *road, rode; right, wright, rite, write; sound* "that which is heard," and *sound* "a body of water"

      2) In different languages; e. g.,

         a) *pax* (Latin, "peace") and *pox* (English, "eruption.)

         b) *hell* (German, "bright"; English, "abode of wicked spirits")

         c) *nix* (Latin, "snow"; English slang, "nothing") and *nicks* (English, "notches")

         d) *bright* (English, "shining") and *breit* (German, "broad")

         e) *bower* (English, "a leafy shelter") and *Bauer* (German, "farmer")

        Note. The above pairs of words would be spelled alike if written in the alphabet of the International Phonetic Association (IPA) whereby one can write such directions as "Spell [tu] three ways" without giving away the answer: "two, too, to."

   b. A given notation is ambiguous when it symbolizes different meanings, whether in the same or in different languages.

Some homonyms lose their ambiguity when they are written; e. g., *road, rode; bright, breit.* Some retain it; e. g., *sound, hell.*

Some words, unambiguous when spoken, become ambiguous when written; e. g., *tear* "rend," and *tear* "a drop from the lachrymal gland."

The dictionary records the meanings that have been imposed on a given notation in the history of the language. The dictionary does not legislate, but merely records good usage. Works like Fowler's *A Dictionary of Modern English Usage* and Perrin's *An Index to English* concentrate particularly on present usage.

The Oxford English Dictionary and *A Dictionary of American English* undertake to give the dates, if possible, when new meanings were imposed on a word and to cite passages illustrating that particular use.

An instance of a new imposition is that on *swastika,* both the word and the graphic symbol. After the revolution of 1918 in Germany, the swastika, which was an ancient symbol of good luck, was adopted by the Nazi Party; in 1935, it was officially adopted as a symbol on the German flag.

Another instance is the imposition, since the advent of radio, of the new meaning "atmospheric disturbances" on *static,* which, of course, retains its older meanings.

Still another instance is the imposition of the meaning "treasonous group, working from within" on *fifth column.* In 1936, during the Spanish civil war, General Emilio Mola declared that he would capture Madrid, since in addition to his four columns of troops outside the city he had a fifth column of sympathizers within the city.

The relationship between the various meanings that have been imposed on a given notation may be:

1) Equivocal, having nothing in common; e. g., *sound* "a body of water" and *sound* "that which is heard"

2) Analogical, having something in common; e. g., *march* "a regular measured step" and *march* "a musical composition to accompany marching"

2. The very nature of a symbol, from which arise the three impositions of a word and two intentions of a term

The ultimate purpose of words and terms is to convey to another mind my ideas about reality. But between the reality as it exists and as I apprehend it and express it are a number of intermediate steps which have been described on page 21. If I use a word or a term to refer directly to a reality not itself, to *what* we know, it is used predicatively (that is, said of another, or referring to another, to the reality which it symbolizes). This is the ordinary use of a word or a term, and it is then used in first imposition and in first intention. If, however, I use a word or a term to refer to *itself as an instrument* in any one of the intermediate steps *by which* we know or *by which* we symbolize what we know, it is used reflexively (that it, referring to itself, as a concept, a sound, a mark, a noun, etc.) This is the peculiar use of a word or a term in an imposition or an intention different from the ordinary use, as may be seen in the following examples:

a. Jane married a man (Here the word *man* refers to another, a real man who exists; therefore *man* is here used in first imposition and first intention.)

b. *Man* is a monosyllable. (Here the word *man* refers to itself as a mere sound. One can know *man* is a monosyllable without even knowing its meaning; therefore *man* is here used in zero imposition. It is false to say, "A man is a monosyllable," because *when the article is added* the word *man* refers to a real man, not to a mere sound. Jane did not marry a monosyllable.)

c. *Man* has three letters. (Here *man* refers to itself as a mere notation or mark. One can see that *man*, when written or printed, has three letters without knowing its meaning; therefore *man* is here used in zero imposition. It is false to say, "A man has three letters," because, *with the article*, *man* refers to a real man, not a mere notation. Jane did not marry three letters.)

d. *Man* is a noun. *Man* is the direct object of *married*. (Here *man*—and *married* also—refers to itself as a word, a sign with meaning. One cannot classify a word grammatically as a part of speech or as subject, object, or the like, without knowing its meaning; man is here used precisely as a word, as a sign with meaning, and is said to be used in second imposition. It is false to say, "A man is a noun," or "A man is the direct object of *married*," because, *with the article, man* refers to a real man, not to a word. Jane did not marry a noun or a direct object.)

e. Man is a concept. Man is a term. Man is a species. (Here the term man refers to itself as an idea in the mind, or an idea communicated, or a class nature—all of which are logical abstractions; man is a term used here in second intention to refer to itself, not to a real man. It is false to say, "A man is a concept"—or a term or a species—because, *with the article, man* refers to a real man, a physical entity, not a logical entity. Jane did not marry a concept or a term or a species.)

f. Man is a substance. (Here the word or term *man* refers to another, a real man, who is a substance. The categories are primarily metaphysical classifications of real being; man is here used in first intention and in first imposition. It is true to say, "A man is a substance." Jane did marry a substance.)

After considering the preceding examples, you can more readily understand the following generalizations.

a. Since a word is a symbol, that is, a sensible sign with meaning, it may be used in any one of three impositions:

1) First imposition is the ordinary predicative use of a word with reference only to its meaning, the reality which it symbolizes (its reference to another, e. g., a real man, dog, tree) without adverting to the word itself as a sensible sign.

   The word is then used like a window or like eyeglasses *through* which we see objects, but *of* which we are unaware.

2) Zero imposition is the reflexive use of a word with reference only to itself as a sensible sign (a sound or a notation) without adverting to its meaning, which need not even be known.

   When a word is used in zero imposition, it is like a window or like eyeglasses *at* which we look instead of *through* which we look to see something else. This is not the ordinary use of words or windows or eyeglasses.

   Phonetics is concerned with the word as a sound, for it deals with its correct pronunciation, with the likeness of terminal sounds in words that rime, etc. Spelling, or orthography, is concerned with the word as a notation.

The use of a word in zero imposition is confined to phonetics and spelling, that is, to remarks about a word regarded as a sound or a notation. Examples:

a) *Exquisite* is often mispronounced.

b) *Ally* is accented on the second syllable.

c) *Hamora* has three syllables.

d) Do not mispronounce *fire;* it is not a dissyllable.

e) You use too many *and's* in your themes.

f) Erase *much* and substitute *many.*

g) *Similes* has seven letters, not eight.

Zero imposition is the basis of a certain type of conundrum. Examples:

a) Nebuchodonosor, King of the Jews!
   Spell *that* with four letters and I'll tell you the news.

b) Which word in the English language is most often pronounced *incorrectly?* Answer: *Incorrectly.*

3) Second imposition is the reflexive use of a word, referring to itself precisely as a word, with advertence both to the sensible sign and to the meaning. This use of the word is confined to grammar; a word cannot be classified in grammar if its meaning is not known.

Grammar is therefore the science of second impositions. Examples:

a) *Jump* is a verb.

b) *Hamora* is a noun, genitive plural (Old English).

c) *On the hill* is a phrase.

d) *Cake* is the direct object of *is eating.*

e) *When is stops raining* is an adverbial clause.

Any word, phrase, or clause, no matter what part of speech it is in ordinary usage, becomes a noun when used in second imposition or in zero imposition, because then it names itself.

Words in zero or in second imposition should be italicized (in manuscript, underlined); and they form their plural by adding the apostrophe and *s;* e. g., *and's, 2's, p's,* and *q's.*

Words of the science of grammar and words of the sciences of phonetics and spelling, like all other words, can be used in each of the three impositions. Examples:

a) *Coldly* is an adverb. (*Coldly* is in second imposition; *adverb* is in first imposition, because it refers to another word, to *coldly*, not to itself.)

b) *Adverb* is a noun. (*Adverb* is in second imposition.)

c) An adverb is not a noun. (*Adverb* is in first imposition, and *noun* is in first imposition, because both refer to other words, not to themselves.)

d) *Adverb* has two syllables. (*Adverb* is in zero imposition; *syllables* is in first imposition, because it refers to another word, to *adverb*, not to itself.)

e) *Syllables* is a plural noun. (*Syllables* is in second imposition; noun is in first imposition.)

f) Write *syllables* on the board. (*Syllables* is in zero imposition, referring to itself as a mere notation.)

b. Since a term is a word, or symbol, conveying a particular meaning, it may be used in either of two intentions:

1) First intention is the ordinary predicative use of a term to refer to a reality. This is its reference to another, to a reality (an individual or an essence). A term used in first intention corresponds exactly to a word used in first imposition. The term is then used like eyeglasses *through which* we see objects and *of* which we are unaware.

2) Second intention is the reflexive use of a term to refer to itself as a term or a concept, that *by which* we know, not *what* we know.

Examples: Chair is a concept. Chair is a term. Chair is a species of furniture. (We cannot sit on a concept or a term or a species, or any merely logical entity. We can sit on a real chair, which is a physical entity.) The term is here used like eyeglasses *at which* we look instead of *through which* we see something else.

The use of a term in second intention is confined to logic; therefore logic is the science of second intentions, just as grammar is the science of second impositions.

The terms peculiar to the science of logic, like other

terms, may be used in each of the two intentions. Examples:

  a) Square is a concept. (Square is in second intention, because it refers to itself as a concept; concept is in first intention, because it refers to square, not to itself.)

  b) A square is a concept. (Square is in first intention; concept is in first intention. Neither refers to itself, and the statement is false.)

  c) A concept should be clear. (Concept is a term used in first intention, because it refers predicatively to other concepts, not reflexively to itself.)

  d) A horse cannot form a concept. (Concept is in first intention.)

  e) Concept is a term. (Concept is in second intention, referring to itself as a term.)

3. The nature of the phantasm, for which the word is originally a substitute (as a child's learning of language and also the direct method of teaching a foreign language illustrate)

The phantasm is (1) a mental image of (2) an object or objects outside the mind (the designation, or extension, of the term); from this image the intellect abstracts (3) the concept (the meaning, or intension, of the term) within the mind.

Because of this threefold character of the phantasm, for which it is originally a substitute, the word is subject to three kinds of ambiguity:

a. In the image it evokes

The word *dog* spontaneously evokes a different image in, for instance, a Swiss mountaineer, an Arctic explorer, a British hunter, an Illinois farmer, a New York society woman.

The power of words thus to evoke images affects the psychological dimension of language and is especially important in literary composition.

b. In its extension, or designation—the object or the objects to which the term can be applied—its external reference.

  1) The primary purpose of a proper name is to designate a particular individual or aggregate; yet a proper name is sometimes ambiguous in designation, because the

same name has been given to more than one individual or aggregate within the same species. For example, William Shakespeare, dramatic poet, 1564-1616, and William Shakespeare, a halfback on the Notre Dame football team of 1935.

To make proper names unambiguous is a special problem in drawing up legal documents, such as wills, deeds, contracts. If a man were to leave $10,000 of his estate to Tom Jones, many claimants would appear, unless the heir were designated with less ambiguity, so as to exclude every person except the Tom Jones whom the testator had in mind.

Telephone books add addresses, empirical descriptions, to proper names in an effort to make them unambiguous in their reference. The identification cards of criminals are attempts to make a proper name unambiguous by supplementing it with an empirical description, a photograph, and fingerprints, which are regarded as unique in the truest sense of the word, because no two are exactly alike.

An empirical description is less ambiguous in designation than a proper name; e. g., the first president of this country.

2) A common name, such as *man, ship, house, hill,* is meant to be applicable to every object of the class named, and therefore to be general, or universal, in its designation. For example, the full extension, or designation, of *ocean* is five; of *friend,* with reference to you, is the number of your friends; of *mountain, tree, book* is the total number of objects past, present, or future, to which the term can be applied.

c. In intension—the meaning of the word, the concept—its internal reference.

1) The primary purpose of a common name is to be precise in meaning, or intension; yet a common name is often ambiguous in intension because a number of meanings have been imposed on it; e. g., *sound* may mean "that which is heard" or "a body of water." Each of these explanations of *sound* is called a general, or universal, description.

The general description is less ambiguous in meaning than is the common name. A definition is a perfect general description.

The dictionary lists the various meanings that constitute the intensional ambiguity of words. The words defined are common names; the definitions are general, or universal, descriptions. A common name is used primarily in intension (although it has extension) in contrast to a proper name, which is used primarily in extension (although it has intension.)

2) A proper name, like *George Washington*, although used primarily to designate an individual, must designate an individual of some particular species, e. g., a man, a bridge, a ship, a hotel, a university, because every individual is a member of some class. Inasmuch as the individual designated may be one of various different species, a proper name may be ambiguous in intension.

Other examples: *Bryn Mawr* may designate a college, a district in Chicago, a Pullman car. Madeira may designate a group of islands in the Atlantic Ocean near Morocco, or a river in Brazil.

The geographical and biographical supplements to the dictionary show the ambiguity (both extensional and intensional) of proper names.

4. Deliberate ambiguity

Although ambiguity is a fault to be carefully guarded against in purely intellectual communication, it is sometimes deliberately sought in aesthetic, or literary, communication.

a. Irony is the use of words to convey a meaning just the contrary of the one normally conveyed by the words. (It is a form of deliberate ambiguity in intension.)

b. A pun is the use of a word simultaneously in two or more meanings. (It, too, is a form of deliberate ambiguity in intension.)

The pun is commonly regarded in our time as a trivial form of humor. It was, however, held in esteem by Aristotle, Cicero, and Renaissance rhetoricians (who classified puns among four different figures of speech.) It was used by Plato, the Greek dramatists, and Renaissance preachers and writers, often in a serious way. Examples:

1) Death is most *fit* before you do
   Deeds that would make death *fit* for you.
   —Quoted from Anaxandrides in Aristotle's *Rhetoric*

2)   . . . having both the *key*
   Of officer and office, set all hearts in the state
   To what *tune* pleased his ear.
   —Shakespeare, *The Tempest*, 1.2.83

3) Vex not his ghost. O, let him pass! He hates him
   That would upon the rack of this tough world
   Stretch him out *longer*.
   —Shakespeare, *King Lear*, 5.5.313

4)   If he do bleed,
   I'll *gild* the faces of the grooms withal,
   For it must seem their *guilt*.
   —Shakespeare, *Macbeth*, 2.2.55

5) Now is it *Rome* indeed, and *room* enough
   When there is in it but one only man!
   —Shakespeare, *Julius Caesar*, 1.2.156

6) *Falstaff*. My honest lads, I will tell you what I am about.
   Pistol. Two yards, and more.
   Falstaff. No quips now, Pistol! Indeed I am in the *waist* two
   yards about; but I am now about no *waste;* I am about thrift.
   —Shakespeare, *The Merry Wives of Windsor*, 1.3.42

7) William Somer, King Henry VIII's fool, seeing that the king
   lacked money, said: "You have so many Frauditors, so many
   Conveyors, and so many Deceivers to get up your money, that
   they get all to themselves" (playing on *Auditors, Surveyors,*
   and *Receivers*).
   —Thomas Wilson, *The Arte of Rhetorique* (1553)

8) *Care* for those things which may discharge you from all *care*.
   —Henry Peacham, *The Garden of Eloquence* (1593)

c. Metaphor is the use of a word or a phrase so as to evoke simultaneously two images, one literal and the other figurative. (It is deliberate ambiguity of images.)

The metaphor is of great value in poetry and in all imaginative writing, including the best scientific and philosophical writing.

Aristotle regarded the metaphor as a compressed proportion. The full proportion may be represented thus: $a:b::c:d$. The compressed proportion is *a* is *c*. Illustrations:

1) O Wild West Wind, thou breath of Autumn's being. (*a* is *c*)
   —Shelley

The West Wind is to Autumn as breath is to a human being. (*a:b::c:d*)

2) Love . . . is a star to every wandering bark. (*a* is *c*)
—Shaksepeare

Love guides a wandering soul as a star guides a wandering bark. (*a:b::c:d*)

3) The moon is a boat. (*a* is *c*)
The moon moves through the sky as a boat sails over the sea. (*a:b::c:d*)

A dead metaphor is one which at one time evoked two images, but which now fails to do so, usually because the one-time figurative meaning has completely supplanted what was once the literal meaning. Examples:

a) Your sorrows are the tribulations of your soul.

At one time *tribulum* meant threshing flail. The full proportion then was: Your sorrows are to your soul as a threshing flail is to wheat. (*a:b::c:d*)

This metaphor, first used by an early Christian writer, was so good that *tribulation* came to mean sorrow and lost its original meaning, threshing. Its metaphorical use has become its ordinary use. We do not recognize the one-time metaphor. *Tribulation* now evokes only one image; the sentence is, therefore, a dead metaphor.

b) *Man-of-war* is a dead metaphor. Originally it had the force of the following proportion:

A ship is to a sea battle as a warrior is to a land battle. (*a:b::c:d*)
A battleship is a man of war. (*a* is *c*).

The figurative meaning has become the literal meaning; for *man-of-war* now means only a battleship.

Candidate "clothed in white" and *skyscraper* are other dead metaphors that have lost their original picturesque meaning.

In the series of meanings attached to a word, one can observe how new meanings derived from the fundamental one by figurative use later became ordinary meanings, having lost their figurative quality. For example, the following meanings of *spring*:
(1) To leap, bound

      (2) To shoot, up, out, or forth; to issue as a plant from seed, a stream from its source, etc.

      (3) An issue of water from the earth

      (4) An elastic device that recovers its original shape when released after being distorted

      (5) A season when plants begin to grow

      (6) Time of growth and progress. (Although the dictionary lists this as an ordinary meaning of *spring,* to say "Youth is the spring of life" is still felt, at least mildly, as a metaphor.)

IV. After the preceding considerations we can better understand the comparative scope of the three arts of the trivium, logic, grammar, and rhetoric, which were discussed in the preceding chapter.

    We may first represent the powers of the mind by diagram, and distinguish:

1. Cognition. This includes:
   a. The lower or sensuous cognition, which produces percepts.
   b. The higher or rational cognition, which produces concepts.
2. Appetition. This includes:
   a. The lower or sense appetites, which seek primarily food, clothing, and shelter.
   b. The higher or rational appetite, the will, which seeks the good, and unity, truth, and beauty under the aspect of good.
3. Emotion. This is a pleasurable or painful tone which may accompany the exercise of both sensuous and rational powers.
   a. Pleasure is the concomitant of the healthy and normal exercise of any of our powers.
   b. Pain is the concomitant of either the excessive or the inadequate or inhibited exercise of any of our powers.

A. Logic is concerned only with operations of the intellect, with rational cognition, not with volition, nor with the emotions.

B. Grammar gives expression to all states of mind or soul—cognitive, volitive, emotional — in sentences that are statements, questions, wishes, prayers, commands, exclamations. In this sense, grammar has a wider scope than logic; and so does rhetoric, which communicates all these to other minds.

C. Rhetoric judges which one of a number of equivalent grammatical symbols for one idea is best for communication in the given circumstance; e. g., steed, horse; silver, argent.

D. Grammar deals only with the sentence, with one thought; logic and rhetoric deal with extended discourse, with relations and combinations of thoughts.

E. Logic is addressed only to the intellect; rhetoric, including poetry, is addressed, not only to the intellect, but also to the imagination and the affections in order to communicate the pleasant, the comic, the pathetic, the sublime.

F. Logic may function without rhetoric or poetry; but these without logic are shallow. Grammar is requisite to all.

If the imperfections of a common language, especially its ambiguity, are realized, we can more readily understand the value of rules of grammar, logic, and rhetoric as means of interpretation. For example, the rules of grammar direct us to the correct reading of these lines from Gray, which are often misread. What is the subject of the first sentence? the predicate?

> The boast of heraldry, the pomp of power,
> And all that beauty, all that wealth e'er gave
> Awaits alike the inevitable hour:—
> The paths of glory lead but to the grave.

It is true that the correct use of grammar, rhetoric, and logic (often based on implicit knowledge only) is most important. Habits of daily thought and expression at home and in school measure our practical, personal mastery over language. Nevertheless, formal knowledge of grammar, rhetoric, and logic explicit knowledge) is valuable also, for we should know why certain reasonings and expressions are correct or ineffective, and others just the opposite, and should be able to apply the rules in speaking, writing, listening, and reading.

V. Key ideas in this chapter

A. Being is either the being of the whole individual or of the essence which is common to the individuals of either a species or a genus.

B. The phantasm is (1) a mental image of (2) an object outside the mind (its extensional reference); from this image the intellect abstracts (3) the concept within the mind (its intensional reference.)

C. A symbol is an arbitrary sensible sign having meaning imposed on it by convention.

D. Langauge has a logical and a psychological dimension.

QUESTIONS AND EXERCISES

Note to the student: It is very important for you to use the right methods in studying this book. Do not write out or memorize the answers to the questions. That kind of study is worthless. First study the examples. Then you will understand the definitions, ideas, or principles which they illustrate. (See p. 28.) Understanding, not memory, will bring you success and satisfaction in this work.

1. State the threefold function of language.
2. Explain why man alone has language in the proper sense of the word.
3. Which of the three kinds of communication are animals capable of?
4. Name the only two modes of communication possible between material beings.
5. Cite examples of imitation as a mode of communication. What are its disadvantages? its advantages?
6. Define symbol. Name some symbols that are temporary; some that are permanent; some that are very limited in meaning.
7. How does a symbol differ from a natural sign, such as clouds, or smoke?
8. What is a common language? a dead language? Is a dead language, such as Latin, a common language? Describe Basic English.
9. Name three systems of special symbols. How does such a special language differ from a common language in origin, adequacy, precision, need of translation?
10. Classify each of the following as a common, a special, or a substitute language: Danish, shorthand, Spanish, the multiplication table, German, braille, Greek, algebra, Italian, Sanskrit, the Morse code, music, Russian, deaf and dumb signs, Hebrew, chemical equations, Egyptian, the semaphore code, French.
11. Briefly explain the philosophical concepts of matter and form. Illustrate by two examples.
12. Define language. What constitutes the matter of a word? the form?
13. What is voice? Explain the essential difference between the voice of a dog and the voice of a man.
14. Distinguish: individual and essence; species, genus, and aggregate. Which of these could you photograph? Which could you represent by a drawing?
15. Name two kinds of symbols by which language can symbolize an individual or an aggregate; two by which it can symbolize essence.
16. Classify each of the following as a symbol of either an individual, an aggregate, a specific essence, or a generic essence: United States postmen, Christopher Columbus, an insect, a grasshopper, the sheriff of this county, an agreement, a treaty, the Treaty of Versailles, the fruit in that dish, Florida,

the rivers of America, the *Iliad*, a mountain, Mount Shasta, a tool, a hammer, the forks on that table, Easter.

17. What great difficulties would we experience if language could symbolize only individuals? only essences?

18. Classify the following as either genuine symbols or no symbols: a triangular cylinder, the King of Alaska, a bungalow, the present Emperor of Mexico, Emperor Maximilian of Mexico, a satyr, citrus fruit, the executioner of Marie Antoinette, your brothers, the Wizard of Oz, the inhabitants of London, a stick with one end, the president of this college, snow, the snows of yesteryear, a centaur, your grandparents, Madame Defarge, a cubical sphere, Robinson Crusoe, an island, Napoleon Bonaparte.

19. Explain in detail the threefold process by which we derive general concepts, or universal ideas, from reality.

20. Name the five external senses; the four internal senses; the three rational powers. Which of these does a horse have? Which of them does he lack?

21. Explain by analogy that man alone among animals has the power to abstract ideas from reality. Why does man show progress through the ages while irrational animals do not?

22. Explain by analogy the axiom: There is nothing in the intellect that was not first in the senses except the intellect itself.

23. Which is clearer, abstract knowledge or concrete knowledge? Which is more vivid?

24. Name and define the ten categories of being. Illustrate each. Why do the ten categories of concepts correspond exactly to the ten categories of being?

25. Define substance; accident. Which of the categories of accident are absolutely intrinsic to the subject? relatively intrinsic? partially extrinsic? wholly extrinsic?

26. Classify in the categories: daisy, succession, here, frozen, shoot, hour, loud, sticky, long, leaning over a desk, in armor, pumpkin, dance, eaten, simultaneous, honest, broad, hatless, now, chosen, cousin, in Europe, swift, on tiptoe, in football togs, tomorrow, mile, slanting, grass, gentle, beaten, autumn, aproned, July, speak, rabbit, tiny, earlier, reclining, graceful, insipid, with gun and bayonet, bee, triangular, location, nude, century, wheat, with hat and gloves, swim, on the table, distant, daughter, speed, foppish, fragrant.

27. Define: essence, nature, individual, percept, phantasm, general concept, empirical concept.

28. What constitutes the difference between individuals in a class? By what means do we perceive the difference between them?

29. Explain in what sense an artificial object has two essences.

30. Analyze each of the following constructs by showing in what categories its essential meaning lies: parade, geyser, soldier, battle, giant.

31. What is the logical dimension of language? the psychological dimension? Explain by examples and by an analogy. Which should predominate in contracts and wills? in poetry? in a textbook on chemistry? in a novel? Why can poetry seldom be translated satisfactorily?

32. By what means should abstract knowledge be communicated? Why is it worthless to memorize definitions which you do not understand?

33. Mention six characteristics of words that affect the psychological dimension of language. Give examples of each.

34. What is an allusion? Point out the allusions in each of the following and state the source of each. The concordances to the Bible and to Shakespeare, and *The Oxford Companion to Classical Literature,* or *Harper's Dictionary of Classical Literature and Antiquities* will help you to trace most of them.

(1) It's the kind of thing you prudent people never give. That is what was in the box of precious ointment.
—Willa Cather, *Youth and the Bright Medusa*

(2) The night the blizzard hit Milwaukee it was going sixty miles an hour, spitting lightning and roaring like Aeolus.
—*Time,* February 10, 1947, p. 22

(3) He reached old age with its well-earned surroundings of "honor, troops of friends."—T. Huxley, "Science and Culture"

(4) It is the official monthly review of the best that has been thought and said by French Communists.—*Tmie,* October 7, 1946, p. 33

(5) "Ye shall know the truth," said this same Mr. Aldous Huxley, summing it all up, "and the truth shall make you mad."
—C. A. Bennett, "The Cult of the Seamy Side"

(6) The face [of Groucho Marx] that launched a thousand quips is a keen one.—*Time,* June 16, 1947, p. 64

(7) The groom was a man of Atlantean shoulders.
—De Quincey, *Confessions of an English Opium Eater*

(8) A crowd is not company, and faces are but a gallery of pictures, and talk but a tinkling cymbal, where there is no love.
—Francis Bacon, "Of Friendship"

(9) Shall I keep your hogs and eat husks with them? What prodigal portion have I spent that I should come to such penury?
—Shakespeare, *As You Like It,* 1.1.40

(10) That made everything all right with the world.
—Ring Lardner, "I Can't Breathe"

(11) Under the care of Teacher, his liege lady, he had grown in wisdom and love and happiness, but the greatest of these was love.
—Myra Kelly, "A Christmas Present for a Lady"

(12) One single day of the plague would enrich Pluto's ferryman.
—La Fontaine, *Fables*

(13) There is no doubt that Isabel Markley was beginning to find her mess of pottage bitter.—W. A. White, "By the Rod of His Wrath"

(14) It was at the theatre and at Carnegie Hall that Paul really lived; the rest was but a sleep and a forgetting. —Willa Cather, "Paul's Case"

(15) There is, sure, another flood toward, and these couples are coming to the ark.—Shakespeare, *As You Like It,* 5.4.35

(16) For the last year and a half this room had been my "pensive citadel."
—De Quincey, *Confessions of an English Opium Eater*

(17) Culwin had fished him out of a fog of family dullness and pulled him up to a peak in Darien.—Edith Wharton, "The Eyes"

(18) She spent a lonesome afternoon reading *Home Sweet Homicide* by Craig Rice.

(19) The lover . . . sees Helen's beauty in a brow of Egypt.
    —Shakespeare, *A Midsummer Night's Dream,* 5.1.10

(20) Leave your theory, as Joseph his coat in the hand of the harlot, and flee.—Emerson, "Self-Reliance

(21) What I had done I had done. I would wear forever on my conscience the white rose of theft and the red rose of arson.
    —Max Beerbohm, *And Even Now*

(22) In its campaign to win customers and influence other railroads, Chesapeake & Ohio announced another innovation.
    —*Time,* January 19, 1948, p. 92

(23) One year the orchard had its Forbidden Tree.
    —Mansfield, "The Apple Tree"

(24) Dark sentences are for Apollo's priests; I am not Oedipus.
    —John Ford, *The Broken Heart*

(25) I went to the hotel in a tumbril. It required strong self-repression for me to keep from climbing to the top of it and giving an imitation of Sidney Carton.—O Henry, "A Municipal Report"

(26) Our candidate has his undipped heel.

35. In your reading of literature, both prose and poetry, mark allusions and also words and combinations of words that are vivid and effective.

36. Explain why a word is by its very nature subject to ambiguity. Name the three fundamental sources of ambiguity in a word.

37. Classify the following words as ambiguous to the ear (homonyms), to the eye, or to both, and explain the various meanings: wrote, rote; mine, mein; hike, haec; air, er, ere, e'er, heir; wound; refuse; conjure; object; sum; is; pair, pear; scale; heart, hart; read; crop; close; tick; bark; craft.

38. Tell what new meanings have been imposed on the following words, mainly during World War II: ceiling, freeze, floor, mopping up.

39. In the *Oxford English Dictionary,* find the etymology and the earliest meanings of any two of the following: lord, lady, villain, dunce, gossip, lewd, wit, humor, pecuniary, hussy, silly, courage, nostril, naughty, wed, stench, nice.

40. In Fowler's *A Dictionary of Modern English Usage,* read the article on one of the following: hackneyed phrases, vogue words, incongruous vocabulary, metaphor, working and stylish words.

41. When is a word or a term used predicatively? When is it used reflexively? In which imposition is a word when it is used predicatively? In which intention is a term when it is used predicatively? In which intention is a term when it is used reflexively? In which impositions may a word be when it is used reflexively? To which study or studies is the use of a word in second imposition confined? in zero imposition? in second intention?

42. In which imposition is each solidly capitalized word in the following sentences?

    (1) DEFINITE is often misspelled.
    (2) She mispronounced ERR; it rimes with FUR, not with BEAR.
    (3) ADJECTIVE is a NOUN.
    (4) An ADJECTIVE is a noun.
    (5) He wrote BLOOD on the WALL.

(6) The RED SQUIRREL ran UP the tree.

(7) UP is a preposition in the sentence above; but in this SENTENCE, UP is used as a noun, because it is the SUBJECT.

(8) LEAVES does not rime with TREES; RUNS does not rime with FUN.

(9) BURY and BERRY are homonyms—ambiguous to the ear.

(10) BURY is a VERB; BERRY is a noun.

43. In which intention is each solidly capitalized term in the following sentences?

(1) JOHN CUT the GRASS.

(2) The GRASS is GREEN.

(3) GRASS is a concept.

(4) GRASS is a substance.

(5) GREEN is a species of color.

44. Explain three forms of ambiguity resulting from the nature of the phantasm for which the word is originally a substitute.

45. What spontaneous image does each of the following words evoke in your mind: magazine, holiday, lake, picnic grounds, grocer, horse, football star, movie star, department store, park, river. Compare your image with those of your friends.

46. Show the ambiquity of the following in extension: Portland, Ottawa, Lima, Toledo, Pope Pius, King Charles, Winston Churchill, President Roosevelt.

47. Show the ambiguity of the following in intension: Mercury, Chesterfield, Napoleon, Lincoln, Pontiac, Atlantic, LaSalle.

48. Mention means by which proper names are made unambiguous.

49. Show the ambiguity of the following common names in intension: bat, court, base, column, seal, ball, wing, bank, peck, rose.

50. Name three kinds of deliberate ambiguity. Describe each and tell whether its ambiguity is in intension or in the image evoked.

51. Express in full proportion the following metaphors:

(1) Your mind is a very opal.—Shakespeare

(2) My words shall be as sparks among mankind.—Shelley

(3) Sleep is sore labour's bath.—Shakespeare

(4) The view from my door was pasture enough for my imagination.

—Thoreau

(5) The inquiry of truth is the love-making or wooing of it.—Bacon

52. What is a dead metaphor? Give an example.

53. Draw four circles, each symbolizing the mind. By a horizontal line divide the first to indicate sensuous and rational powers. By a vertical line divide the second to indicate cognitive and appetitive powers. In the third circle combine the distinctions of the first two. In the fourth circle indicate by lines the relation of the emotions to the faculties. With how many of the sectors is grammar concerned? logic? rhetoric? From this point of view, which of these three arts is narrowest in its scope?

54. What does cognition include? What do our sense appetites seek? What is our rational appetite? What does it seek? What is pleasure? pain? How are they related to our rational and sensuous powers? Why do pleasure seekers seldom find pleasure?

55. Show by an illustration that the rules of grammar direct us to the correct reading of passages that might otherwise be misunderstood. Interpret: And all at once their foes, break, spoil and slay.

56. What are the key ideas in this chapter?

CHAPTER III

GENERAL GRAMMAR

I. General grammar distinguished from the special grammars

General grammar is concerned with the relation of words to ideas and to realities, whereas a special grammar, such as English grammar, or Latin or French or Spanish grammar, is concerned principally with the relation of words to words, as, for example, with the agreement of subject and verb in person and number, or the agreement of adjective and noun in number, gender, and case.

General grammar is more philosophic than the special grammars because it is more directly related to logic and to metaphysics, or ontology. Consequently, it differs somewhat from the special grammars in point of view and in resulting classification both in the part-of-speech analysis and in the syntactical analysis.

II. The parts of speech in general grammar

From the point of view of general grammar, the essential distinction between words is that between categorematic words and syncategorematic words.

Categorematic words are those which symbolize some form of being and which may accordingly be classified in the ten categories of being—substance and the nine accidents. Categorematic words are therefore of two great classes: (1) substantives, which primarily symbolize substance; (2) attributives, which symbolize accidents. From this point of view, verbs and adjectives are properly classified together as attributives, as accidents existing in substance, because action as well as quality or quantity must exist in substance. This is an outstanding illustration of the difference in point of view between general grammar and the special grammars.

Syncategorematic words are those which have meaning only along with other words, for, taken by themselves, they cannot be classified in the categories. They do not symbolize being. Rather, they are mere grammatical cement by means of which we relate in a sentence the categorematic words which do symbolize being. For that reason they are sometimes called form words. Syncategorematic words are of two classes: (1) definitives, which point out substances; (2) connectives, which join either words or sentences, or subject and predicate.

Analogy: In music the notes are categorematic symbols, while marks of time, of phrasing, of staccato or legato, etc. are syncategorematic symbols of operation. In mathematics, the numbers, figures, angles, etc. are categorematic symbols, while $+, -, \times, \div, =$, etc. are syncategorematic symbols of operation indicating how the categorematic symbols are related.

Accordingly, in general grammar we distinguish four fundamental parts of speech: substantives, attributives, definitives, and connectives.

We may subdivide these, however, and distinguish nine true parts of speech; and, if we add the interjection, which, for reasons stated below cannot be regarded precisely as a part of speech, we list ten, as follows: nouns, pronouns, verbs, adjectives, adverbs, definitives, prepositions, conjunctions, the pure copula, and interjections.

A. Words significant by themselves—categorematic
    1. Substantives
        a. Nouns
        b. Pronouns
    2. Attributives
        a. Primary—attributes of substances
            1) Verbs (and verbals)
            2) Adjectives
        b. Secondary—attributes of attributes: Adverbs

B. Words significant only along with other words—syncategorematic
    1. Definitives, associated to one word
    2. Connectives, associated to many words
        a. Prepositions, which connect words
        b. Conjunctions, which connect sentences (either expressed or implied)
        c. The pure copula, which connects subject and predicate

Note. Interjections are named with the parts of speech only because it is desirable that there be a name for every class of words. Interjections are not, however, true parts of speech: (1) Because they cannot be assimilated into the structure of a sentence and therefore have no grammatical import. (2) Because they express emotion, not thought, and therefore have no logical import.

III. Detailed consideration of the parts of speech in general grammar
    A. Substantives: nouns and pronouns

1. According to the kind of reality it refers to, a substantive symbolizes either a concrete substance, or an abstraction.
   a. A concrete substance is an object as it exists in itself, whether natural or artificial. Examples:
      1) Natural substance: tree, stone, horse
      2) Artificial substance: chair, glass, clock
   b. An abstraction is either (1) an accident conceived by the mind, for the sake of emphasis, as if it existed by itself apart from the concrete substance in which alone it can really exist, e. g., smoothness, quantity, shape, prudence; or (2) substance regarded in its essence, for the sake of emphasis, apart from its concrete existence, e. g., humanity, corporeity, womanhood, chairness, treeness.

      Abstract substantives symbolize ideas in every one of the ten categories; for example, animality, length, whiteness, similarity, motion, sensitivity, futurity, ubiquity, erectness, accouteredness. In fact, the very names of seven of the nine categories of accident are examples of abstract substantives.

      Man's ability thus to distinguish, to select, to abstract one aspect of reality and to make it the object of his thought has been the indispensable means whereby his limited mind has been able to advance in his search for truth. Each of the various sciences and branches of philosophy abstracts from reality a selected aspect; for instance, mathematics deals only with quantity; physics with motion; metaphysics, with being. Man's power thus to abstract and to study a selected aspect of reality is the measure of his intellectual progress which contrasts strikingly with the utter absence of such progress among irrational animals, despite their wonderful instincts, which are often superior to the instincts of man. As man advances in civilization, the proportion of abstract substantives in his language increases.

2. According to its logical classification a substantive symbolizes either an individual, a species, or a genus. Examples:

a. *Individual*	b. *Species*	c. *Genus*
Nathan Hale	man	animal
Excalibur	sword	weapon
Atlantic	ocean	body of water

3. Grammatical characteristics of substantives
   a. Number. A substantive naming a species or a genus has number; that is, it may be either singular or plural, because it may designate either one or more than one of the individuals that constitute the species or the genus. Such a substantive is either a common name or a general description.

   A substantive naming an individual, strictly speaking, has no number, because an individual is unique and cannot be pluralized in respect to that which makes it individual, but only in respect to that which makes it a member of its species or its genus. A substantive that names an individual is either a proper name or an empirical description.

   b. Gender. A substantive may be masculine, feminine, neuter, or common in gender.

   The nouns in modern English have natural gender; the nouns in French, Latin, German, and many other languages have grammatical gender.

   c. Person. This is a characteristic much more important to pronouns than to nouns. It has its natural origin in conversation, for first person is the speaker; second person the one spoken to; and third person, the one spoken of.

   A pronoun agrees in person, as well as in number and gender, with its antecedent, the noun to which it refers; its case, however, is determined by its use in its own clause.

   The relative pronoun simultaneously performs three functions:
   1) It stands for a noun.
   2) It connects clauses.
   3) It subordinates one clause to another.

   d. Case. This is the relationship of a noun or a pronoun to other words in the sentence.
   1) Four cases of substantives are distinguished in general grammar, for these are the relationships necessary in every language, although not in every sentence.
      a) Nominative. This is the case of the subject. It is the only case necessary to every sentence.
      b) Genitive. This names the possessor.
      c) Dative. This names the term to which the action proceeds.

d) Accusative. This names the object which receives the action.

The special grammar of a particular language may distinguish fewer or more cases than these four, the number usually depending on inflectional forms, rather than on the underlying relationships of ideas and words. Thus, modern English grammar distinguishes only three cases, nominative, genitive, and accusative. It is obvious, however, that the uses of the dative case are present in the English language as clearly as in the Latin language; moreover, the dative case and the instrumental, which is analogous to the ablative in Latin, had inflectional forms and distinctive uses in the Old English period of our language (before 1150 A.D.)

2) Cases of nouns may be expressed by:

a) Word-order. Example: John killed the snake. The snake killed John.

b) Prepositions. Examples: Mother is in the garden. The decision of the umpire was applauded.

c) Case endings. Examples: Father's, him, my, puero, noctis.

4. The grammatical functions of substantives are ten:

Subject, subjective complement, direct object of a verb or verbal, indirect object of a verb or verbal, objective complement, object of a preposition, possessive modifier, nominative absolute, nominative of direct address, an appositive of any of these.

These functions are illustrated in the following sentences:

a. Cobb whacked the ball into the outfield and gave the spectators a thrill by making a home run, thereby tying the score.

1) *Cobb* is the subject.

2) *Ball* is the direct object of *whacked; thrill* is the direct object of *gave; home run* is the direct object of the gerund *making; score* is the direct object of the participle *tying*.

3) *Spectators* is the indirect object of *gave*.

4) *Outfield* is the object of the preposition *into; making*, a gerund, is the object of the preposition *by*.

b. Jane, my uncle's law partner considers that man to be a
scoundrel.

   1) *Jane* is nominative of direct address.

   2) *Uncle's* is a possessive modifier of *partner*.

   3) *Scoundrel* is a subjective complement, or predicate
   noun, for it completes the copula *to be* and refers to
   the subject *man;* it agrees in case with *man*, which is
   here accusative because it is the subject of an infinitive
   in indirect discourse.

c. The class elected John president.

   President is an objective complement, for it completes
   the verb *elected* and refers to *John*, the direct object of
   elected. (*Elected* is one of a group of words including
   choose, name, painted, which take two accusatives to complete their meaning.)

   The sentence is really a condensed combination of these
   two: The class elected John. John is president. In the second of these two sentences, *president* is a subjective complement, for it completes the copula *is* and refers to the
   subject *John;* its relation to John is the same as in the
   combined statement above, but there it is called an objective complement because it refers to the object of the verb.

d. The audience insistently applauding, Lawrence Tibbett,
noted baritone, graciously consented to sing the song "Edward" again.

   1) *Audience* is the nominative absolute, for the phrase of
   which it is a part has no grammatical relation to any
   word in the rest of the sentence. In Latin, the absolute
   construction is expressed by the ablative case; in English, by the nominative.

   2) *Song* is the direct object of the infinitive to *sing.*

   3) *Baritone* is in apposition with the subject *Lawrence Tibbett.* *"Edward"* is in apposition with the direct object
   song.

B. Attributives. These words express the accidents that exist in substance.

1. Primary attributives include verbs, verbals, and adjectives.

   a. Verbs

      1) Functions of the verb. These are four:

a) A verb expresses an attribute along with the notion of time.

This is the essential function of a verb and constitutes its definition. Aristotle, in the *Organon*, defines a verb as that which, in addition to its proper meaning, carries with it the notion of time. It is by this characteristic of carrying with it the notion of time or change that he distinguishes it from the adjective and from every other part of speech.

To understand this definition it is necessary to understand what is meant by time. Time is the measure of change. The year measures a change, the movement of the earth around the sun. The day measures a change, the movement of the earth turning on its axis. The hour measures an artificial movement such as that of sand from the upper to the lower half of an hour-glass, or of the minute hand around a clock.

Since action is change, and change involves time, a verb, which expresses action, necessarily involves time. The particular action expressed varies from verb to verb, as in *jump, speak, sing, swim*. Each of these has its own proper meaning, but since change is common to all of them, every verb carries with it the notion of time. The verb *exist*, when predicated of contingent beings, involves having been moved from potency to actuality, and continuance in that actuality. Therefore it involves duration, or time. The verb *exists*, when predicated of God, is used analogically. The language of man, invented by him to express his own thoughts, is applied to the discussion of God's perfections in an analogical sense.

Thus, time is a concomitant of the meaning of verbs, not their principal meaning. When we wish to make time the principal meaning, we do so by means of abstract nouns, like *year, day, hour* or by means of adverbs, like *yearly, daily, hourly, instantly, gradually*.

b) A verb indicates tense.

Tense is the relation between the time of the act spoken of and the time of speaking of it. If I speak of an action while it occurs, I use present tense (The bird flies); if after it occurs, past tense (The bird flew); if before it occurs, future tense (The bird will fly). In addition to these, there are the present perfect, past perfect, and future perfect tenses.

In English grammar there are two forms for every tense: the simple (I think) and the progressive (I am thinking). In the present and past tenses there is a third form, the emphatic (I do think, I did think).

We must be careful not to confuse tense with time. Time is essential to the verb. Tense is not essential. It is a mere accidental variation. Aristotle likens the tenses of verbs to the cases of nouns.

In the statement of a general truth there is, strictly speaking, no tense at all. Examples: Fire burns. Acids contain hydrogen. Man acquires knowledge by reasoning. Good ought to be done. Evil ought to be avoided. A triangle has three sides. Fishes live in water. Planets move around the sun.

Such a general statement expresses a relation which, so far as our observation goes, does not cease to be, nor come to be; it is continuous. Therefore the relation between the time of the act spoken of and the time of speaking of it never varies. The use of the past or future tense would violate the truth of such general statements. Nor can one truly say that the present tense is used, for that has a temporal signification not here intended. Although the grammatical form of the present tense is used, the statements of general truths are really tenseless.

c) A verb expresses mode, or mood; that is, it asserts the manner in which the subject and predicate are related as certain, possible, conditional, etc.

   i. The indicative mood asserts the relation as a matter of fact, with certainty. Examples: The car raced past. He wished me success.

   ii. The potential mood asserts the relation as possible, or contingent. If the contingent part is subordinate, the relation is not only potential but also subjunctive. Examples: It may rain tomorrow. If I were you, I would refuse the invitation.

iii. The interrogative mood requests information, and it requires a response in words. Example: Who spoke?

English idiom requires that either the progressive or the emphatic form be used in asking questions about matters of fact in the present or past tense active, unless the question has as subject an interrogative pronoun, and then the simple form may be used. Examples: Is she coming? Where did you find that? Who thinks so?

The following are not idiomatic: Comes she? Where found you that?

iv. The volitive mood seeks the gratification of volitions, and it requires a response, usually in deeds. It has direct reference to the future only. So true is this that the future indicative often has the force of command, as in the Decalogue: Thou shalt not steal.

The tone of the volitive may be:

(1) Imperative—a command, issued usually to inferiors. Example: John, close the door.

(2) Optative or hortatory — a wish, expressed usually to equals or to superiors. Examples: May you be successful. Would that I had the means to help them!

Here again, in distinguishing the moods of verbs, we see a difference in the points of view of general grammar and the special grammars. The special grammars, which are principally concerned with the relations of words to words, distinguish (in English, Latin, etc.) three moods marked by a difference in grammatical form: (1) the indicative mood, which expresses the relation as a matter of fact, whether in statement or question; (2) the subjunctive mood, which expresses the potential, the subjunctive, and the optative relations, and sometimes the interrogative, as in asking permissions; (3) the imperative mood, which expresses a command.

It is reasonable in English grammar, or in Latin or French or Spanish grammar, not to distinguish between the interrogative and the indicative moods, but to treat them as one, because the same grammatical forms of the verb are ordinarily used for both question and answer. In general grammar, however, it is reasonable and even necessary to distinguish between these two moods because from the point of view of logic, to which general grammar is intimately related, these two moods differ essentially: the indicative mood expresses a statement which must be either true or false; the interrogative mood expresses a question which is incapable of being either true or false.

Only the indicative and the potential moods are capable of expressing either truth or falsity; the interrogative and the volitive moods are not. The potential mood asserts, not a fact, but a possibility, or contingency; therefore its truth or falsity depends on conformity, not to fact, as that of the indicative mood does, but to possibility, or contingency. For example, "It may rain tomorrow" is a true assertion of a possibility. Its truth is not dependent on whether it actually does or does not rain the day after the statement is made.

d) A verb asserts. This function is necessary to form a sentence, which must express a complete thought.

2) Classes of verbs

A verb is either transitive or intransitive.

a) The transitive verb expresses action that begins in the subject (agent) and "goes across" (*trans* + *ire*) to the object (patient). The object may be the same as the subject; e. g., He cut himself. But it need not be the same; e. g., He cut the cake. He rowed the boat.

A transitive verb always requires a complement, that is, a word which completes the meaning of the predicate. Every transitive verb requires at least one complement, the direct object; some transitive verbs, like *give*, require both a direct and an indirect object; others, like *elect*, require two accusatives to complete their meaning, one the direct object, the other the objective complement. (See the examples on page 57.)

b) The intransitive verb expresses action that begins and ends in the agent, the subject; consequently, the subject must be both agent and patient; e. g., The bird flies.

There are two classes of instransitive verbs: (1) Some express action complete in itself, e. g., *blooms*, *withers*. (2) Some require a complement, a word to complete the meaning of the predicate, e. g., *becomes*. An intransitive verb which requires a complement is a copulative verb.

A copula is a word that links an attributive or a substantive to the subject. Such an attributive (adjective or verbal) or substantive is variously named by grammarians the predicate adjective or predicate noun, the predicate complement, the attribute complement, the subjective complement (meaning that it completes the predicate and modifies the subject).

The pure copula, *is*, is not a verb, because it does not express an attribute along with the notion of time. It is a syncategorematic word of operation, and it will be discussed in its proper place below.

Note. The intransitive verb *is*, which is a categorematic word and a synonym for the verb *exists* but which is not a copulative verb, must be distinguished from the copula *is*. Like other verbs, the verb *is* is capable of having an adverbial modifier, which it could not have unless the verb *is* expressed an attribute, for an adverb is an attribute of an attribute, as will be explained more fully below. Examples of the verb *is*:

John is (i. e., John exists).

John is in the garden (i. e., John exists in the garden).

A copulative verb is one which **performs** simultaneously the functions of a copula and of a verb.

Classes of copulative verbs:

i. The true copula and true verb, like *becomes*
Example: The green leaves become yellow.

(a) *Becomes* is a true verb because it expresses an attribute along with the notion of time. It involves change. In fact, it expresses change itself.

(b) *Becomes* is a true copula because it links an attributive or a substantive to the subject; it links the *before* and the *after* of change.

ii. The pseudo-copula, which is a true verb, expresses sense-perception; e. g., *looks, sounds, tastes, smells, feels.* Example: The apple tastes sour.

Here *tastes* acts as a copula in linking *sour* to *apple.* The sentence represents good English idiom, even though it is illogical and literally false, for the apple cannot taste at all. In its primary meaning, the pseudo-copula is a transitive verb. The sentence is a grammatical condensation of these two: I taste the apple. The apple is sour. Here *taste* is a transitive verb.

b. Verbals. There are three classes of verbals: the infinitive, the participle, the gerund.

Like the verb, the verbal (1) expresses an attribute along with the notion of time; (2) indicates tense.

Unlike the verb, the verbal (1) does not assert; (2) does not express mood.

Note. Because the verbal does not assert, it is a frequent occasion of the fragmentary sentence error.

1) The infinitive is an abstract substantive and can therefore perform all the grammatical functions of a substantive.

2) The gerund is a verbal which, like the infinitive, may perform all the functions of a substantive. The gerund has the same form as the participle, but it differs in function. Example: Thinking is conversing with oneself.

3) The participle is a verbal functioning gramatically as an adjective, for it modifies a substantive.

Example: John, thinking clearly, solved the problem.

c. Adjectives. The essential difference between the adjective

and the verb or verbal is that the verb or verbal **expresses**
an attribute of substance along with the notion **of time,**
and hence involves change, whereas the adjective expresses
an attribute simply.

2. Secondary attributives—attributes of attributes—namely, adverbs. Example: The man walks swiftly.

Walking is an action existing in the man; hence it is an
attribute of substance. Swiftness is a quality existing in the
walking; hence *swiftly* expresses an attribute of an attribute
of a substance. The reality spoken of is a "swiftly walking
man."

C. Definitives are words associated to one word.

1. A definitive is a word which, when associated to a common
name, is capable of singling out an individual or a group of
individuals from the whole class designated by the common
name. This is the essential function of the definitive. The
definitive joined to a common name is called an empirical
description.

James Harris notes that a definitive may designate individuals as:

a. Known: the man.

b. Definite: a certain man

c. Present and near: this man

d. Present and distant: that man

e. A definite multitude: a thousand men

f. An indefinite multitude: many men, some men

g. The ones of a multitude taken with distinction: each man

h. The ones of a multitude taken in order: the first man, the
second, etc.

2. Classes of definitives: the article and the pronominal

a. The article never stands alone. It may be either indefinite
or definite.

1) An indefinite article singles out an individual, but does
not designate which one; it also signifies first acquaintance.

Example: I saw a tall, red-haired, hooknosed man
downtown today.

Note. The repetition of the article is often an aid to
clarity. Example:

Ambiguous: He entertained a poet and philosopher.
(One or two?)

Unambiguous: He entertained a poet and a philosopher. (Two)

2) The definite article singles out a particular individual. It may also signify:

   a) Pre-established acquaintance. Example: There goes the tall, red-haired, hooknosed man I saw downtown yesterday.

   b) Eminence. Examples: the poet; the philosopher; the Mrs. Jamieson.

b. The pronominal has as its primary function to act as a definitive, that is, to limit a common name. Sometimes, however it stands alone and thereby performs the functions of a pronoun.

Example: (Definitive) This pencil. (Pronoun) This is a pencil.

Pronominals used as definitives may be employed to express antithesis.

Example: This hat I like, but that one I dislike.

3. A modifier of a substantive, whether it be a word, a phrase, or a clause, is either definitive or attributive (adjectival) in function. The definitive modifier is essentially associated to the subject, whereas the attributive modifier is essentially a predicate.

Examples: This apple.   This is an apple.
              Red apple.   Apple is red.

This essential and profound difference in function between the definitive and the adjective requires that they be sharply distinguished in general grammar. So great is the difference between them that the adjective is a categorematic word and the definitive is syncategorematic.

Here again we see that the point of view of general grammar differs radically from that of the special grammars. The latter, such as Latin, German, or French grammar, treat the definitive as an adjective, since it has inflectional endings like those of the adjective, and must likewise agree in number, gender, and case with the noun it modifies. The definitive is not one of the eight parts of speech distinguished in the special grammars, but in them it is classified as an adjective.

Rule for punctuation:

a. Since its function is to point out, the definitive modifier is restrictive, and it is never separated by commas from the substantive it modifies. Example: The man who is standing nearest the window is a labor leader.

    b. Since its function is to describe, the attributive modifier is non-restrictive, and if it is a clause, it should be separated by commas from the substantive it modifies. **Example**: John Lewis, who is standing nearest the window, is a labor leader.

        It is to be noted that the distinction between a definitive and an attributive modifier is functional. If a modifier describes in order to point out, it is a definitive, as in the first example above. If the individual is already designated by a proper name, the modifier, no longer needed to point out the individual, becomes attributive—descriptive, non-restrictive, merely additive, as in the second example above.

        It is important to distinguish functional and part-of-speech analyses. For instance, a definitive modifier need not contain a single definitive. Example: The girl with red hair is my cousin. *With red hair* is a definitive modifier of *girl;* but not a single word in this phrase is a definitive.

D. Connectives, words associated to many words, include: prepositions, conjunctions, and the pure copula.

    Connectives are words analogous to cement, for they hold the categorematic parts of speech together in the unity of thought expressed in the sentence.

1. Prepositions join words.

    a. A preposition unites substantives, which do not naturally coalesce. In nature accidents exist in substance, and in grammar attributives and substantives naturally coalesce; e. g., red rose. But substances do not unite with one another in nature, nor do substantives coalesce in grammar; hence the need of prepositions, the verbal cement for uniting substantives; e. g., the curtain on the window. (*On* joins *curtain* and *window.*)

        Analogy: If you add 5 apples, 3 tables, 4 chairs, and 2 dogs, what is the sum? The answer is: 5 apples, 3 tables, 4 chairs, and 2 dogs. It is true that there are 14 objects, or things, or substances, and under this most general aspect the sum may be stated as 14; but so to lump objects together is to ignore their specific nature. One can, **however,** say: Two dogs, chasing each other, knocked five apples off three tables under four chairs. The prepositions express a relation between these substances without robbing them of their specific nature.

b. Prepositions show the precise relation between substances. Example: The dog ran around the table, crept under the table, jumped over the table, lay beside the table, stood near the table.

Note. The repetition of the preposition is often a means to secure clarity. Examples: (1) The invasion of the Angles and Saxons (one invasion). (2) The invasion of the Danes and of the Normans (two invasions).

1) Relationships, especially those of place, may undergo transfer to intellectual relationships. Examples: to come under authority, to rule over minds, to act through jealousy.

2) Such relationships may also enter into compounds. Examples: overlook, understand. (Compare: look over; stand under.)

c. Prepositions are often used to express the genitive and dative relationships of nouns. Examples: the faces of the children; giving bread to the children.

d. Prepositions may lose the connective function and become adverbs; then, of course, they become categorematic words.

Adverbs derived from prepositions convey a meaning more vague, less specific, than the corresponding preposition. Examples:

He walked around the house. He walked around.

They gazed up the shaft. They gazed upward.

2. Conjunctions join sentences. The sentences joined may be either explicit or implicit.

Explicit: The guests arrived, and dinner was served.

Implicit: The army and navy prepared for war.

Explicit: The army prepared for war, and the navy prepared for war.

a. Pure conjunctions are coordinating. They join independent clauses or sentences. They may:

1) Conjoin, i. e., join both sentences and meanings. Example: *and*.

2) Disjoin, i. e., join sentences, but not meanings. Exam-

ples: *but; or; either . . . or; neither . . . nor.*

Rule for punctuation: Unless the coordinate clauses joined are very short, use a comma before the coordinating conjunction.

b. Conjunctive adverbs may be:

1) Coordinating. These conjoin independent clauses or sentences. Examples: *hence, consequently, therefore, then, nevertheless.*

Rule for punctuation: Use a semicolon or a period between clauses or sentences conjoined by a conjunctive adverb. Example: It rained; therefore we postponed the picnic.

The violation of this rule results in the very serious error, the run-together sentence or comma splice, two sentences punctuated as if they were one.

2) Subordinating. These subjoin a dependent clause to an independent clause, forming a complex sentence. Examples: *while, where, when, although, unless, if.*

Rule for punctuation: Use either a comma or no punctuation where a dependent clause is subjoined to an independent clause by an adverbial conjunction. Example: Because it rained, we postponed the picnic.

The violation of this rule results in the very serious error, the sentence fragment or half-sentence, punctuated as if it were a complete sentence.

3. The pure copula connects subject and predicate.

Because of its relation to logic, nothing else in general grammar is so necessary to understand as the nature and functions of the pure copula.

The pure copula *is* is a strictly syncategorematic word which asserts the relation between a subject and a predicate, both of which are categorematic. It is to be noted that in general grammar, as in logic, the pure copula is neither the predicate, nor a part of the predicate, but is completely distinct from the predicate. The predicate itself is equivalent in the broad sense to a subjective complement which completes the pure copula.

Every simple declarative sentence is made up of subject, pure copula, and predicate. The pure copula and the subjective complement, or predicate, are either explicit or implicit.

a. If the sentence contains an explicit copula, it will, of course, also contain an explicit subjective complement, which may be either an adjective, a verbal, or a noun. Examples:

1) The grass is green.
2) The rose is blooming.
3) The horse is an animal.

b. If the sentence contains the simple verb form, the copula and the subjective complement are implicit in the verb and may be made explicit in English by changing the simple verb form to the progressive form (see p. 59). If the verb has modifiers, or if it is either a transitive or a copulative verb, the subjective complement is a construct of which the modifiers and the direct object or other complements form parts. Examples:

1) The sun shines. The sun is shining.
2) The green leaves become yellow. The green leaves are becoming yellow.
3) The wind bends the trees. The wind is bending the trees.
4) The girl swam gracefully in the lake. The girl was swimming gracefully in the lake.
5) He gives her his college pin. He is giving her his college pin.

For instance, in the third example above, *bending the trees* is a construct, an attributive joined by the pure copula, *is*, to *wind*. The reality spoken of is a tree-bending wind.

In the progressive verb form the pure copula *is* links the attributive (a participle, which is a verbal) to the subject. Consequently, it makes clear and explicit the precise nature and functions of both the pure copula and the verb (or verbal). In the simple verb form these functions are not so clear.

Tense	Simple form	Progressive form
Pres. ind.	The bird flies.	The bird is flying.
Past	The bird flew.	The bird was flying.
Future	The bird will fly.	The bird will be flying.
Pres. perf.	The bird has flown.	The bird has been flying.
Past perf.	The bird had flown.	The bird had been flying.
Fut. perf.	The bird will have flown.	The bird will have been flying.
Pres. subj.	The bird may fly.	The bird may be flying.
Past subj.	The bird might fly.	The bird might be flying.

The progressive form makes clear the following points, important in general grammar:

1) The pure copula *is*, undergoing inflection, performs three functions: (1) it asserts; (2) it expresses mood; (3) it indicates tense.

2) The verb, which in the progressive form is reduced to a verbal, a participle, performs its one, genuine, and essential function, which is to express an attribute along with the notion of time; *flying* involves change and hence involves time.

3) The bird's flying requires time, but tense is inconsequential to the act; tense indicates merely that the speaker chooses to make the remark either during, after, or before the act. Hence tense is not an essential characteristic of a verb.

4) The pure copula *is* is strictly syncategorematic; the only reality symbolized here is the flying bird. On the other hand, there is a different meaning in the following: "The flying bird is. The flying bird was." In these two sentences *is* and *was* are verbs, meaning *exists* and *existed*; they are not copulas at all. The second sentence might imply that the bird was shot; in any case it states that the bird has ceased to be.

IV. Syntactical analysis in general grammar

    A. Any simple sentence or complex sentence may be divided into the complete subject and the complete predicate. A compound sentence can be divided into simple sentences.

        Because we are preparing to study logic, the important analysis of a simple declarative sentence is that which divides it into complete subject, pure copula, and complete predicate, as explained above.

    B. A less important but more detailed syntactical analysis is that which divides a sentence into a maximum of five functional units as follows:

      1. Simple subject.

      2. Simple predicate, including the complement or complements, if present. There are four kinds of complements: the subjective; the objective; the direct object; the indirect object. (See pages 61 f.)

      3. A modifier or an appositive of one of these. The modifier

will be either attributive or definitive.

4. A modifier of a modifier.

5. Connectives to join these parts or to join simple sentences so as to form a compound sentence.

C. The analysis which shows that each functional unit must be classified materially as either:

1. A word.

2. A phrase. This is a group of words which does not contain a subject and a predicate, which functions as either a substantive, an attributive, or a definitive, and which can be classified as either a prepositional or a verbal phrase.

a. A prepositional phrase, e. g., *on that day, into the house*

b. A verbal phrase. This will be either:

1) An infinitive phrase, e. g., *to sing, to make excuses*

2) A gerund phrase, e. g., *Making excuses* is the weakling's first thought.

3) A participial phrase, e. g., John stood before his employer *making excuses*.

3. A clause. This is a group of words which does contain a subject and a predicate and which functions as either a substantive, an attributive, or a definitive.

Analogy: Functionally, a building may be a hotel, a church, a school, a home, a factory, a jail, a garage, a barn. Materially, it may be of brick, stone, or wood.

V. The fundamental function of grammar is to establish laws for relating symbols so as to express thought.

A sentence expresses a thought, a relation of ideas, in a declaration, a question, a command, a wish, a prayer, or an exclamation.

Categorematic symbols are what is related; syncategorematic symbols are means for relating them; the relation itself is the sentence.

The rules for relating symbols govern three grammatical operations: substituting equivalent symbols, combining symbols, and separating symbols.

A. Rules for substituting equivalent symbols

1. Expansion

a. Every proper name is convertible into an empirical description; e. g., Benjamin Franklin = the man who discovered that lightning is electricity = the inventor of the lightning rod = the diplomatic representative of the Continental Congress to France during the Revolutionary War.

b. Every common name is convertible into a general description; e. g., cat = a small, furry, sharp-clawed, whiskered animal that mews.

c. A word can be expanded into a phrase, a group of words; e. g., horseshoe = a shoe for a horse; bookseller = a seller of books.

Not every compound word, however, can be thus expanded without a change of meaning. Consider: wallflower, moonshine, streetwalker, goldenrod, sheepskin, greenhorn, greenback.

d. A phrase can be expanded into a sentence or a group of sentences; e. g., This clock = This object is a clock. Cloudy sky = Sky is cloudy. The cheerful, crippled soldier = The soldier is cheerful. The soldier is crippled.

Compare in meaning: a large hot dog; a large, hot dog; a juicy hot dog; an angry, hot dog.

2. Contraction

a. Theoretically every empirical description is convertible into a proper name. Actually we have not invented proper names for every existent object.

b. Theoretically every general description is convertible into a common name. Examples:
A rushing, roaring, violent stream = torrent.
Walked with long and measured steps = strode.
Walked slowly and aimlessly = sauntered.

c. A sentence may be contracted into a phrase; e. g., The man has a red beard = the man with a red beard = the red-bearded man.

d. A phrase may be contracted into a word; e. g., Man who sells = salesman; light of day = daylight; herder of sheep = shepherd.

Contraction of some phrases creates a change in both the logical and the psychological dimensions; e. g., man fearing God, Godfearing man; man of God, godly man.

Contraction and expansion are devices determining style and its effects. Contraction should characterize language addressed to adults; expansion, that addressed to children.

B. Rules for combining symbols.

There are five means of combining symbols: form words, inflection, word order, stress, intonation.

1. Form words are syncategorematic words of operation: the pure copula, verbal auxiliaries, conjunctions, prepositions, definitives.

   Form words are the most important means of relating words in a sentence. They are indispensable to every language.

2. Inflections have the same grammatical functions as form words. Example: *Puero* expresses the dative relation by means of an inflectional ending; *to the boy* expresses the dative relation by means of form words.

3. Word order is very important in a comparatively uninflected language like English or Chinese.

   Probably the reliance of English on word order has given rise to some of its illogical idioms, such as the so-called retained object (illustrated in the third example below.) Thus:

   a. Active voice: She gave me a pencil. (*Pencil* is the direct object.)
   b. True passive (in which the direct object of the action is the subject): A pencil was given to me by her. (*Pencil* is the subject.)
   c. Pseudo-passive: I was given a pencil by her. (Is *pencil* a retained object?)

   The assumption that reliance on word order probably occasioned the development in English of the pseudo-passive with the co-called retained object is supported by the effect of more logical re-statement, as follows.

   d. True passive, with word order of pseudo-passive: To me was given a pencil by her.

   Here *pencil* appears in its true function as subject, not as object, retained or otherwise, and *I* becomes *me* to express precisely its true function of indirect object.

   Only the true passive, expressed in normal word order in the second sentence above and in abnormal word order in the fourth sentence, can be translated into a precise, logical language, such as Latin or French.

   Although it is illogical, the pseudo-passive, like the pseudo-copula, is correct, idiomatic English; it has been in use at least since the thirteenth century.

4. Stress. This means of expressing relations of words is of importance chiefly in spoken language. Interpret:

a. That that is is not that that is not
b. He was my friend
c. A tall dark man with a mustache who is he stole my purse

Compare the effect of stress within words, by accenting each of the following on the first and then on the second syllable: record, object, converse, project, compact, august, entrance.

5. Intonation. This means of expressing relation is of importance chiefly in spoken language. Interpret:

a. He's a fine fellow
b. Oh she is dead
c. Yet Brutus says he was ambitious
   And Brutus is an honorable man
d. *Macbeth.*   . . . If we should fail
   Lady Macbeth: But screw your courage to the sticking place
   And we'll not fail

No language can dispense with form words. No language can rely exclusively on word order, stress, and intonation. English relies chiefly on word order and form words, and so does Chinese; hence English and Chinese are structurally, or morphologically, similar. Latin relies mainly on inflection. English is related to Latin genealogically, because many English words are derived from Latin. Likewise, many English words are derived from Germanic, and English is therefore related to German genealogically. It is also related to German morphologically because both languages employ form words extensively. English, German, Latin, Greek, and a number of other languages are all derived from the parent Indo-European language.

C. Rules for separating: punctuation

Marks of punctuation do for written language what phrasing, stress, and some forms of intonation, such as raising the voice for a question, do for spoken language.

That oral punctuation does for reading what punctuation marks do for writing becomes evident if one tries to read pages unpunctuated. A passage read with grotesque phrasing, that is, with wrong methods of combining and separating, becomes almost nonsense.

Interpret:

1. There's a divinity that shapes our ends
   Rough hew them how we will
2. That that is is that that is not is not
3. He said that that that that that sentence contains is a definitive
4. The boy said his father was to blame

Since languages are imperfect because they are too rich in meaning, the grammatical problem is to interpret the written page. Spoken language is clarified by the speaker who punctuates it orally, who combines and separates the elements by phrasing, by stress, and by intonation. Difficulties in writing are identical with difficulties in reading. Students fail in expression, in speaking or writing, for the same reason that they fail in impression, in listening or reading: they do not understand or do not apply the rules of grammar which must guide both writer and reader, both speaker and listener.

QUESTIONS AND EXERCISES

1. Distinguish between general grammar and the special grammars.
2. From the point of view of general grammar, what is the essential distinction between words?
3. What are categorematic words? syncategorematic words? Give examples of categorematic and syncategorematic symbols in music; in mathematics.
4. Which of the four fundamental parts of speech distinguished in general grammar are categorematic? syncategorematic? Briefly describe each. Subdividing these, name nine true parts of speech. State two reasons for not including the interjection among the true parts of speech.
5. Why, in general grammar, are verbs classified with adjectives as attributives? Why are verbs not grouped with adjectives in the special grammars?
6. Discuss the importance of man's power of abstraction.
7. Classify each of the following nouns as a symbol of a natural substance, an artificial substance, or an abstraction: hardness, velvet, milk, ink, apple, truth, desk, virtue, radiator, liberty, rose, difference, grass, house, rabbit, gun, justice, snow, book.
8. Classify each noun in the following groups as a symbol of an individual, a species, or a genus: flower, plant, this rose; virtue, caring for this sick woman, charity; Assault, animal, horse; automobile, vehicle, this car; Henry V, ruler, king; habitation, San Francisco, city; dwelling, the White House, building; Senator Vandenberg, legislative body, senate.
9. Name the four grammatical characteristics of a substantive; ten grammatical functions.

10. What determines the person, number, and gender of a pronoun? the case?
11. What three functions does the relative pronoun simultaneously perform?
12. Briefly describe each of the four cases distinguished in general grammar. Name three methods of expressing these cases; illustrate each.
13. How do primary attributives differ from secondary attributives? Name three classes of primary attributives.
14. State Aristotle's definition of a verb.
15. Name the four functions of a verb. Which is the essential one?
16. Define and distinguish time and tense. Which of these is essential to a verb?
17. Why are statements of general truths, strictly speaking, tenseless? Illustrate.
18. Name and illustrate three forms of the present and the past tense of an English verb.
19. Define mood. Illustrate the four moods distinguished in general grammar. Which moods are capable of expressing truth or falsity? Which are not? Why does general grammar distinguish between the interrogative and the indicative mood? Why do English grammar and Latin grammar not make this distinction?
20. Name four kinds of complements. Illustrate each. Which of them may complete a transitive verb? an intransitive?
21. Distinguish between a copulative verb and the pure copula. Illustrate the difference between the verb *is* and the copula *is* by using each in a sentence.
22. Show that *becomes* is a true copula and a true verb.
23. Name three pseudo-copulas. Use each as a copula; as a transitive verb.
24. Name and illustrate three classes of verbals. Name two characteristics of the verbal which make it like a verb; two which make it different. In what respect are the gerund and the infinitive alike? How does the gerund differ from the participle?
25. What is the essential difference between the adjective and the verb or verbal?
26. Explain clearly by an illustration that an adverb is an attribute of an attribute of substance.
27. What is the essential function of a definitive? Show that an attributive modifier is essentially a predicate.
28. When is the modifier of a substantive definitive? attributive? What rules for punctuation follow from this distinction? Apply these rules to the following: The largest American city that is located on the Pacific Ocean grew very fast. Los Angeles which is the largest American city located on the Pacific Ocean grew very fast.
29. Show that a phrase or a clause may be a definitive modifier although it does not contain a definitive.
30. Distinguish: article, pronominal; minor functions of the indefinite and the definite article.
31. Distinguish three classes of connectives.
32. What is the function of a preposition? Use *on* and *up* as prepositions; as adverbs.
33. Show by illustration that the repetition of a preposition is often a means to secure clarity; the repetition of an article.
34. Show that conjunctions join sentences that are either explicit or implicit.

35. Name four pure conjunctions; five coordinating conjunctive adverbs; five subordinating conjunctive adverbs. State the rules for punctuating sentences in which each is used.
36. Show that every simple declarative sentence can be understood as made up of subject, pure copula, and predicate. Why is this analysis important? Restate the following sentence so as to make the copula explicit and draw vertical lines to separate it from the subject and the predicate: Johnny eats spinach.
37. Express "The bird flies" in all tenses, first in the simple verb form, then in the progressive verb form. State which of the following functions of the verb are, in the progressive form, expressed by the copula, which by the participle: tense, time, mood, assertion. State four points, important in general grammar, which this illustration clarifies.
38. Name the five fuctional units of a sentence which may be distinguished by a detailed syntactical analysis; three material units. Distinguish four kinds of phrases.
39. What is the fundamental function of grammar? Name three grammatical operations.
40. Illustrate four forms of expansion; four of contraction. Which style should characterize language addressed to adults? to children? Do these outward changes ever affect the logical dimension of language? the psychological dimension?
41. Name the five means of combining symbols. Which one is indispensable to every language? Which other one is of special importance in English? in Latin? Which two are important mainly in spoken language?
42. How is the true passive formed? the pseudo-passive? Is the latter good English idiom?
43. What is meant by saying that English is related to Latin genealogically, but not morphologically? that it is related to Germanic in both ways?
44. What is the function of punctuation? How does one punctuate orally?

CHAPTER IV

TERMS AND THEIR GRAMMATICAL EQUIVALENTS
DEFINITION AND DIVISION

I. Terms and their grammatical equivalents

A term is a concept communicated through a symbol.

Communication is dynamic; it is the conveying of an idea from one mind to another through a material medium, words or other symbols. If the listener or reader receives through language precisely the ideas put into it by the speaker or writer, these two have "come to terms"—the idea has passed successfully, clearly, from the giver to the receiver, from one end or term of the line of communication to the other.

A term differs from a concept only in this: the term is an idea in transit, hence, is dynamic, an *ens communicationis;* the concept is an idea representing reality, an *ens mentis.* A concept is a potential term; it becomes an actual term when it is communicated through a symbol.

Hence a term is the meaning, the form (see p. 15), the logical content, of words. Words are therefore the symbols, the means by which terms are conveyed from mind to mind.

Analogy: The coffee in the coffee pot can reach me only by means of a conveyor, such as a cup. An idea can get from one mind to another only by means of a conveyor, a symbol. The idea is analogous to the coffee; the symbol, to the cup.

Not every word, however, can symbolize a logical term. Only categorematic words (substantives and attributives) can do so. Although a syncategorematic word (a preposition, a conjunction, a definitive) cannot symbolize a logical term it can be grammatically a part of the complete symbol which expresses a logical term. A complete symbol, which must be either a proper name, an empirical description, a common name, or a general descrption, is, therefore, the grammatical equivalent of a logical term. Whether the complete symbol is one word or a group of words, it expresses only one logical term.

A term is the element of logic just as the word is the element of grammar and the letter is the element of spelling.

A term is always unambiguous, or univocal, because a meaning is always one: it is itself and not another. The grammatical symbol which expresses a term may, however, be ambiguous, for the same symbol is capable of expressing different terms. (See pp. 33 and 41.) The dictionary lists for every word a number of meanings. Whoever uses a word normally intends but one of its various meanings; that one meaning is the term symbolized by the word in that particular instance.

The same term, whether it signifies a particular individual or an essence, may be expressed through different symbols in the same or in different languages. Examples:

Individual	*Essence*
The red-bearded man	An equilateral rectangle
The man with a red beard	A rectangular equilateral
The man who has a red beard	A rectangle with equal sides
L'homme qui a une barbe rouge	A square
Der Mann mit einem roten Barte	Le caré
El barbirroja	Ein gleichseitiges Rechteck
Dan Dravot (in Kipling's "The Man Who Would Be King"	Un cuadrado

Complete symbols that are logically equivalent in meaning, in designation, or in both, are substitutable for one another. (See p. 71.) Such equivalency makes possible translation from one language to another; it also makes possible a variety of styles within the same language and provides means to improve style.

Words in different languages are usually equivalent in their logical dimension but often are not equivalent in their psychological dimension. That is why poetry is difficult to translate satisfactorily. Synonyms within the same language are seldom exactly the same in meaning. The least ambiguous of all symbols is a general description, especially one so perfect as to be a definition.

II. Classification of terms

    A. The fundamental distinction between terms is that which classifies them according to the kind of reality signified as either an empirical term or a general term.

        1. An empirical term designates an individual, or an aggregate of individuals. It must be symbolized by either a proper name or an empirical description; e. g., Christopher Columbus; the desk in this room. (See p. 18.)

        2. A general term, also called a universal term, signifies essence (of either a species or a genus). It must be symbolized by a common name or a general description; e. g., tree; a three-sided, rectilinear plane figure.

To be able to distinguish between an empirical term and a general term is of the utmost importance. In doing this, one cannot rely on grammatical tags; one must look through the words at the reality symbolized. Examples:

a. A bird has feathers (Bird is a general term.)

b. A bird flew past my window. (Bird is an empirical term.)

c. The dance lasted until midnight. (Dance is an empirical term.)

d. The dance is an art form. (Dance is a general term.)

B. Contradictory terms: positive and negative terms

Terms are contradictory when one is positive and the other is the corresponding negative. Examples: voter, non-voter; Christian, non-Christian; white, non-white; conscious, unconscious; complete, incomplete; varnished, unvarnished.

1. A positive term is one that expresses what is present in reality.

2. A negative term is one that expresses what is absent.

Some words grammatically negative symbolize terms logically positive. Examples: infinite (the absence of limit connotes fullness of being), unkind (meaning positively cruel or harsh), impatient (meaning positively peevish or irritable).

Some words grammatically positive symbolize terms logically negative. Examples: zero, vacuum, void, empty, minus.

3. A privative term is a kind of negative term which expresses a deprivation, the absence from a reality of a characteristic which belongs to its nature and which ought to be present. Examples: lame, blind, dead, idiot, headless. A dog may be blind; a stone cannot be blind, for sight does not belong to the nature of stone.

C. Concrete and abstract terms

1. A concrete term is one that represents realities as they actually are in the order of being. Examples: animal, fast, smooth, long, near, warm.

2. An abstract term is one that represents either substance or accident mentally abstracted from concrete reality and regarded, for the sake of emphasis, as an object of thought; it is symbolized by an abstract substantive. Examples: animality, speed, smoothness, length, nearness, warmth.

The importance of abstract terms was stressed on pages 21 f. and 54. There, too, it was noted that concrete terms are more vivid (to the senses); abstract terms are more clear (to the intellect).

D. Absolute and relative terms

1. An absolute term is one that can be understood by itself without reference to another term. Examples: man, tree, dog, field, red, hard.

2. A relative term is one of two terms, each of which must be understood with reference to the other. Examples: husband, wife; parents, child; teacher, pupil; cause, effect; friend, friend; larger, smaller; longest, shortest.

Relative terms are correlatives, and are always absolute in at least one of the categories. They have meaning in at least two and often in three or more categories; one of these is always the category relation; another is usually action or passion, for this is most often the bond by which the two terms are related to each other. For example, teacher and pupil may be thus analyzed:

Teacher is a term having meaning in the following categories:	Pupil is a term having meaning in the following categories:
Substance: man	Substance: man
Quality: knowledge and the skill to impart it	Quality: ignorance
Relation: to a pupil	Relation: to a teacher
Action: imparting knowledge ➠	Passion: receiving knowledge

Note. Receiving knowledge cannot be purely passive, although it is passive with reference to its correlative, imparting knowledge. Teaching and being taught must be cooperative. (See page 4.)

E. Collective and distributive terms

1. A collective term is one that can be applied only to a group as a group, but not to the members of the group taken singly. Examples: army, jury, crew, group, senate, family, team, flock, swarm, herd. (John may be soldier in an army, but he cannot be an army.)

The rule of grammar requiring the agreement of subject and verb or copula, and also of pronoun and antecedent, makes it necessary to distinguish two uses of a noun symbolizing a collective term:

a. The collective use, requiring that the verb or copula and the pronouns be singular. Example: The audience shows its pleasure by demanding encore after encore.

b. The distributive use, requiring that the verb or copula and the pronouns be plural, because the members of the group are thought of as acting individually rather than collectively. Example: The audience express uproarious approval by tossing their hats into the air and shouting with loud voices.

2. A distributive term is one that can be applied to individual members of a group taken singly. For example, man is applicable both to every individual man and to the species man.

F. The ten logical categories of terms constitute an important classification. They correspond exactly to the ten metaphysical categories of being, namely: substance, quantity, quality, relation, action, passion, *when, where,* posture, habiliment. (See p. 21.)

III. Differences between terms

A. According to the basis of the difference, terms may be either categorically, generically, specifically, or individually different.

1. Terms are categorically different, if they are in different categories. Example: apple, large, red, there, now, chosen. (In which category is each of these?)

2. Terms are generically different, if they belong to different genera within the same category. Examples: round, smooth, sour; stone, tree, animal.

3. Terms are specifically different, if they belong to different species within the same genus. Examples: white, red, blue, yellow, gray, black; round, square, triangular; elm, oak, maple, pine; dog, elephant, horse; walk, creep, fly.

4. Terms are individually different, if they designate individuals within the same species, for every individual is unique, is itself and not another. Examples: this man, that man, my father; the Hudson River, the Mississippi River, the Snake River.

B. According to the nature of the difference, terms are either repugnant or not. Terms are repugnant when they are incompatible, that is, when they signify realities that are mutually exclusive, that cannot coexist in the same substance at the same time and in the same respect.

1. Terms that are categorically different or generically different are not necessarily repugnant, for often they signify

realities that can coexist in the same substance. (See the examples above.)

2. The following terms are necessarily repugnant:

a. All terms that are individually different. (See the examples above.) An individual cannot be itself and another at the same time.

b. All terms that are specifically different; e. g., elm, oak, maple; dog, horse; square, circle, triangle.

c. Contradictory terms, e. g., white, non-white.

d. Contrary terms, which are pairs of terms that are either:

1) Species within the same genus, e. g., black, white (color); long, short (length).

2) Species in contrary genera, e. g., truthfulness and lying, the one a species of virtue, the other of vice.

3) Contrary genera, e. g., good and evil.

Contrary terms represent extremes of difference. Not every term has a contrary. There are, for instance, no contraries in the following genera: animal, tree, flower, vehicle, shape.

Some of the classifications of terms in this chapter are contrary terms which together constitute a genus; they are therefore specifically different and, consequently, repugnant, or incompatible. This is true of each of the following pairs: general and empirical terms; positive and negative terms; concrete and abstract terms; absolute and relative terms.

The members of each pair of contrary terms are repugnant and therefore mutually exclusive; but a given term may be simultaneously a member of more than one pair, because the pairs themselves are not mutually exclusive. Thus, a given term cannot be both general and empirical, or both positive and negative, etc. It can, however, be at one and the same time general, positive, abstract, and absolute; for example, *length* is all of these simultaneously. *My grandmother* is, at one and the same time, empirical, positive, concrete, and relative.

Of great importance is the distinction between contrary terms and contradictory terms:

1) There is no middle ground between contradictory terms. For example, everything is either white or non-

white; and everything is either a tree or a non-tree. Every pair of contradictory terms thus performs a dichotomy, that is, cuts everything in two sharply, leaving no middle ground between.

There is a middle ground between contrary terms. For example, everything need not be either white or black; it may be gray, or red, or blue.

2) Every term has its contradictory; not every term has a contrary.

3) Contrary terms represent the greatest degree of difference. Contradictory terms represent a necessarily clean-cut difference.

IV. The extension and intension of terms (Compare page 42.)

A   Every term has both extension and intension.

1. The extension of a term is its designation: the total number of objects to which the term can be applied. This is its objective, extramental reference to reality.

Examples: The extension of *friend*, for you, is the total number of persons who are your friends; the extension of *ocean* is the five oceans; the extension of *tree* is the total number of all trees.

I am using a term in its full extension when I am applying it to all the objects it designates. I need not know the number.

2. The intension of a term is its meaning, the sum of the characteristics that the term implies. This is its conceptual or logical reference. To make explicit the intension, the meaning, of a term is to define it.

Examples: The intension of *friend* is the sum of the qualities which make a friend, such as loyalty, congeniality, mutual affection, unselfish devotedness, trustworthiness, fidelity. Likewise, the intension of *ocean* or of *tree* is made explicit in its definition.

The extension and intension of terms have their roots in the two-fold reference of the phantasm which is a mental image of the objects (extensional reference) from which the intellect derives the concept (intensional reference).

B. The relation of the extension and the intension of terms

The law of this relation: As a term increases in intension, it decreases in extension; as a term increases in extension it decreases in intension. Illustration: the Tree of Porphyry. This is a progressive, essential, dichotomous division leading from the *summum genus* substance to the *infima species* man. It was devised by Porphyry (233-303 A.D.) It illustrates not only the inverse relation between the extension and the intension of terms, but also the relation between these and definition and division.

The *summum genus* is the highest and largest genus; it cannot become a species, for there is no higher genus of which it can form a species or part. The *infima species* is the lowest and smallest species; it cannot become a genus by further division into species essentially different.

A division that proceeds from the *summum genus* to the *infima species* is, therefore a complete series; it cannot be continued above or below these.

Tree of Porphyry

Substance

Material	Immaterial
	Body	
Animate	Inanimate
	Organism	
Sentient	Non-sentient
	Animal	
Rational	Non-rational
	Man	

Explanation: Every term between the *sumum genus* and the *infima species* can be either genus or species, because for intermediate terms, genus and species are relative to the point of view: a term is a genus of those below it and species of those above it. A term is the proximate genus of the term directly below it; e. g., animal is the proximate genus of man; body is the proximate genus of organism. All terms above a given term, but not immediately above it, are remote genera of that term; e. g., organism, body, and substance are remote genera of man, substance being the most remote.

Accordingly, the Tree of Porphyry illustrates the law of the inverse relation of the extension and the intension of terms: as the intension of substance is increased (by adding the attributes material, living sentient, rational) its extension is decreased. Substance, the *summum genus*, has the greatest extension and the least intension. Man, the *infima species*, has the least extension and the greatest intension, that is, the greatest number of characteristic notes: man is a rational, sentient, animate, material substance.

V. Definition

Definition makes explicit the intension or meaning of a term, the essence that it represents. A definition is symbolized by a general description, not by one word. A definition is a perfect general description.

A. There are two kinds of definition constructed from a logical point of view: a logical definition and a distinctive definition.

  1. A logical definition expresses the essence of a species in terms of its proximate genus and specific differentia.

Pattern: Species is proximate genus plus specific differentia. Example: Man is an animal possessing rationality.

    a. Species is the term to be defined; the subject of a definition is, therefore, always species.

    b. The specific differentia is that part of the essence which belongs only to a given species and which distinguishes it from every other species in the same genus. Example: Rationality is that part of his essence which makes man different from every other species of animal.

    c. Genus is that part of essence which is common to all the species that constitute the genus. Example: Animality is that part of his essence which man shares with other species of his genus, such as horse, sparrow, oyster.

The Tree of Porphyry provides data for the logical definition of man, animal, organism, and body.

A logical definition cannot be constructed for every term, because for some terms there is no proximate genus, or the specific differentia is not known. Such terms can be made clear, however, by a general description that is not a logical definition.

A logical definition cannot be constructed for the following:

(1) *A summum genus,* such as substance or any other one of the ten categories, or a predicable.

It might seem that being is the genus of substance and of the other categories, since the ten categories classify being. Being is not, however, understood in the same way of substance and of accident, nor of the different accidents; furthermore, being transcends the categories, and therefore it cannot be their genus.

(2) A transcendental concept. This is a concept that cannot

be classified, because it extends through and beyond all categories. The transcendentals are: being and its transcendental attributes, unity, truth, goodness, *res, aliquid;* some philosophers include beauty.

(3) An individual. The individual, as an individual, cannot be defined, for its essence is that which it shares with other individuals of its species. That which makes the individual unique, different from other individuals in its species, serves for designation rather than for signification.

Hence only species can be defined. When a term such as animal is defined, it must be defined as species of its genus (organism), not as genus of its species (man, horse, etc.) Thus: An animal is a sentient organism.

2. A distinctive definition is definition by property.

Pattern: Species is genus (proximate or remote, or even being) plus property. Example: Man is a being (or animal or organism) capable of mirthfulness.

Property is not the essence, nor a part of the essence, but it is a necessary concomitant of the essence and follows from it. Thus, mirthfulness is not man's essence, nor a part of his essence, but it follows from his essence, that is, from both the genus and the differentia: because man is rational, he can see that something is funny; because he is an animal, he can laugh. A man possesses a capability for mirth, whether he exercises it or not. The laugh of a hyena is not mirthful nor is that of an idiot; they are merely cachinations, noises, hideous, not mirthful.

Note. This question is very likely to occur. Is an idiot a rational animal? Yes, essentially. His rationality may show itself but slightly or not at all. This merely means, however, that some physical defect prevents his rational soul from operating through his brain and nervous system. His rationality is only potential, but it is none the less real and constitutes him a human being, with the dignity of man and all the fundamental, inalienable rights in this world and the next, that follow from that dignity.

Analogy: If Fritz Kreisler or Jascha Heifetz were to play the most exquisite Chopin nocturne on a cracked, cheap violin with some strings missing, it would sound hideous. The defective insrument would prevent the artistry of violinist and composer from becoming evident; it would not signify the non-existence of the artistry.

Examples of a concomitant:

(1) On a sunny afternoon, my shadow is a concomitant of my body.

(2) If I draw a convex line, it is concomitantly a concave line, viewed from the other side.

(3) Taste is the concomitant of an animal's eating; it is not a concomitant of a tree's nutrition.

A distinctive definition by property is usually the best definition that science can achieve. In chemistry, an element, such as hydrogen, chlorine, sodium, copper, zinc, is defined by its specific properties such as natural physical status (gas, liquid, solid), atomic weight, specific gravity, valence. In geometry, the propositions to be proved simply make explicit the properties of the triangle, the circle, the sphere, etc. It is to be noted that a species has but one specific differentia; it may have a number of specific properties.

B. Other types of definition

1. A causal definition is one that makes explicit the meaning or intension of a term by naming the cause which produced the reality which the term signifies.

A causal definition may name any one of the four causes, efficient, material formal, final. (See page 234.) Examples:

a. Pneumonia is a disease caused by the pneumococcus. (Efficient cause.)

b. Water is H_2O. (Material cause, naming the constituents; formal cause, indicating how they are related.)

A definition by matter and form is sometimes called a genetic definition. Such are all chemical formulas and chemical equations. Such also are all recipes, e. g., for fudge.) A definition by final cause is sometimes called a purposive definition.

2. A descriptive definition merely enumerates the characteristics by which the species can be recognized.

Example: An elephant is a huge, thickset, nearly hairless mammalian quadruped with a long, muscular proboscis and two long tusks.

3. Definition by example provides data for definition rather

than the definition itself. Sometimes the presentation of familiar examples will enable the mind to make from them an abstraction clearer to it than the ready-made abstraction presented in an actual definition would be. Examples:

a. An evergreen is a tree· such as the cedar, pine, spruce, hemlock.

b. A military genius is a man like Alexander the Great, Julius Caesar, Washington, Napoleon, Marshall Foch, George Patton, Jr., Douglas MacArthur.

c. The only authentic and really enlightening definition of a neighbor is that by example, Our Lord's parable of the good Samaritan (St. Luke 10:30-37).

4. Grammatical and rhetorical definition or nominal definition

Here the problem is not to make explicit the meaning of a term but to make clear which term is imposed upon a given symbol, a word or a phrase. Consequently, the problem is the clarification of language, the getting rid of ambiguity, the "coming to terms" of reader and writer, of listener and speaker, both of whom must attach the same meaning to the given symbol.

a. Definition by etymology

A word is often understood more clearly from its derivation. Examples: *Infinite* is derived from Latin *in* (not) plus *finis* (limit); *elect* is derived from Latin *e* (out) plus *lectus* (chosen).

Warning: Etymology is not a secure guide, for sometimes the present meaning does not agree with the etymological meaning. Examples: Etymologically, *hydrogen* means water-former, and *oxygen* means acid-former. But hydrogen is really the acid-former, and oxygen is the principal water-former in the sense that it constitutes nearly eight times as much of the weight of water as hydrogen does. Their names should therefore be interchanged, but this will not be done, for although oxygen is misnamed, the name had become permanently attached to the element before the error was discovered. This is only one striking instance which shows that etymology is not a safe guide to the current meaning of words, even though it is usually very helpful and illuminating. By a strange anomaly, goods transported in a car by rail are called a shipment, and goods transported in a ship are called a cargo.

b. Definition by synonyms

This pointedly illustrates the fact that grammar provides a choice of nearly equivalent symbols for the same term. Such symbols, however, usually differ somewhat either in the logical or in the psychological dimension or in both.

c. Arbitrary definition

There are certain words, very important words, about whose precise meaning there is not common agreement. The dictionary offers little practical help in defining such words.

1) Certain legal terms, like larceny, treason, vagrant, must be defined by law for the courts of each state. Such legal definitions may differ greatly. Thus treason as defined by the Constitution of the United States is a term very different from treason as defined by law under Henry VIII or Elizabeth of England or under the Czars of Russia.

2) Many commonly used terms, like liberty, patriotism, justice, religion, courtesy, culture, and literary terms, like classicism, romanticism, style, poetry, ought, for clarity, to be defined by each user of the word. A reader must be careful to discover just what meaning a writer is attaching to words so ambiguous as these; otherwise reader and writer cannot "come to terms." Debaters, in particular, must "come to terms"; otherwise they argue beside the point.

To define words of such broad and shifting meaning, one should tell what is included in the term and what is excluded, dealing especially with disputable border-line instances, not merely with those obviously included or excluded. Examples:

a) Charity is patient, is kind: charity envieth not, dealeth not perversely; is not puffed up; is not ambitious, seeketh not her own, is not provoked to anger, thinketh no evil; rejoiceth not in iniquity, but rejoiceth with the truth; beareth all things, believeth all things, hopeth all things, endureth all things. Charity never falleth away whether prophecies shall be made void or tongue shall cease, or knowledge shall be destroyed.   —St. Paul I Cor. 13:4-8

b. Literature is the best that has been thought and said in the world.—Matthew Arnold, "Literature and Science"

c) A classic is a work that gives pleasure to the passionate few who are permanently and intensely interested in literature.
—Arnold Bennett, "Why a Classic Is a Classic"

C. Rules of definition. A definition should be:

1. Convertible with the subject, the species, the term to be defined. Example: A man is a rational animal. A rational animal is a man.

   The term to be defined and its definition coincide perfectly both in intension and in extension; hence they are always convertible.

   Convertibility is the test of a definition. A statement is convertible if it is equally true with the subject and predicate interchanged. (Compare a convertible blanket and a convertible coat; they are equally finished, equally satisfactory turned either way.)

2. Positive rather than negative.

   Violation: A good man is one who does not harm his fellowmen. (It is not very enlightening merely to tell what something is not.)

3. Clear, symbolized by words that are neither obscure, vague, ambiguous, nor figurative.

   Violation: Network is anything reticulated or decussated, at equal distances with interstices between the intersections.
   —Samuel Johnson

4. Free from a word derived from the same root as the word to be defined.

   Violation: Success is succeeding in whatever you undertake.

5. Symbolized by parallel, not mixed, grammatical structure; e. g., a gerund should be used to define a gerund; an infinitive to define an infinitive.

   Violations: Pessimism is when a person looks on the dark side of everything. To cheat is defrauding or deceiving another.

VI. Logical division

   Logical division is the analysis of the extension of a term whereas definition is the analysis of its intension.

   A. Logical division distinguished from other kinds of division

   1. Logical division is the division of a genus into its constituent

species. Example: Tree may be divided into its species—oak, elm, maple, poplar, etc.

    a. The test of logical division is that the logical whole (genus) can always be predicated of each of its parts (species). Example: Tree can be predicated of each of its species. Oaks are trees. Elms are trees.

    b. Logical division never deals with the individual. It is always the division of a group (genus) into smaller groups (species), never of a species into its individual members. This last is enumeration, not division. Nor is logical division concerned with the division of an individual into its parts.

2. Physical division is the division of a single concrete whole into its physical parts. Example: An orange may be divided into halves or into sections, or into skin, juice, pulp, seeds.

    a. The physical whole cannot be predicated of each of its physical parts; e. g., the skin is not an orange; the juice is not an orange.

    b. Physical division always deals with the individual.

3. Metaphysical division is the distinction between substance and accidents or between accidents. Example: An orange (substance) is distinct from its accidents (color, size, shape, weight, taste, smoothness, coldness, etc.) and these are distinct from one another.

    a. A metaphysical division is a distinction, not a separation. It cannot be physically performed; e. g., the shape of an orange cannot be actually separated from the orange, nor can its taste, size, and color be set separately before us, apart from the orange and apart from one another.

    b. The distinctions perceived in metaphysical division are used as the bases of logical division; e. g., we may divide fruits according to accidents, such as color, shape, size, sugar content, etc. Or we may divide them according to their essential nature into oranges, apples, bananas, cherries, etc.

4. Verbal division is the distinction which the dictionary makes between the meanings that have been imposed upon a word, that is, between the terms that a given notation can symbolize.

B. Elements of logical division

    1. The logical whole to be divided: the genus

2. The basis of division, the metaphysical aspect, the point of view from which the division is made
3. The dividing members: the species, resulting from the logical division

C. Kinds of logical division
  1. According to the character of the basis of division, we distinguish:
  · a. Among natural objects
      1) Essential division, determining natural species. Example: the division of edible plants into carrots, lettuce, peas, beets, spinach, potatoes, etc.
      2) Accidental division, based on accidents that do not determine natural species. Examples: the division of edible plants according to color, shape, or nutritive value; the division of men according to color, nationality, religion, occupation, height, or weight.
        Note. The *infima species*, such as man, resulting from natural essential division, can undergo further division only on an accidental basis.
    b. Among artificial objects
      1) Essential division, based on the form imposed by man on matter; this is the division of an artificial genus into artificial species. Examples: the division of silverware into knives, forks, spoons, ladles, etc.; the division of vehicles into wagons, buggies, cars, bicycles, etc.
      2) Accidental division, based on accidents that do not determine artificial species. Example: The division of chairs according to size, color, weight, etc.
  2. According to the manner of applying the basis of division, we distinguish:
    a. Positive division of a genus into its constituent species. Examples: The division of elements into hydrogen, oxygen, nitrogen, sulphur, carbon, silver, gold, etc.; the division of color into white, red, yellow, blue, gray, black, etc. This is the type of division science aims to accomplish.
    b. Dichotomy, division by contradictory terms. Examples: the division of elements into gold and non-gold; of color into red and non-red, or white and non-white.
        In division by dichotomy, the negative term is unexplored in the sense that it may contain within itself either

a number of positive species or only one. Thus, investigation reveals that non-white contains many positive species: red, yellow, blue, green, brown, gray, black, etc.; but non-even number is a negative term which contains only one positive species, namely, odd.

D. Rules of logical division

1. A logical division must have one and only one basis.
2. The constituent species must be mutually exclusive (with no overlapping).
3. The division must be collectively exhaustive, or complete; that is, the constituent species must equal the genus.

No one species may equal the genus, for then there would be no division. This is the error present in an outline when a person attempts to divide by one subtopic. Such an attempt results in no division at all; there must be at least two species, at least two subtopics.

4. If a division is progressive (continued), each step should divide a genus into its proximate species. There should be no leaps, no gaps. Progressive division involves subdivision. Example: The Tree of Porphyry.

From a strictly logical point of view, although not from a scientific one, dichotomy is superior to positive division, because, since there is no middle ground between contradictory terms, dichotomy guarantees the realization of the aims of logical division as stated in the foregoing rules whereas positive division cannot do so with equal assurance.

The principle of contradiction, that a thing cannot both be and not be at the same time and in the same respect, is an axiom of thought, a law of reason, of greater certitude than any law of science. Dichotomy employs this principle.

Positive division is based on empirical knowledge, which often requires revision, because further investigation proves earlier conclusions to have been incomplete, inadequate, misleading. For example, the early Greek observers classified the elements as four: earth, water, fire, air. Modern chemistry distinguishes nearly one hundred elements, and shows that not one of the four so long regarded as elements is really an element; e. g., water is a compound, air is a mixture. We cannot be certain how many elements science will distinguish five hundred years from now. Because positive division relies upon investigation, not on a principle of reason, it is inferior from a logical point of view.

The Tree of Porphyry is a division by dichotomy. By no other means could we achieve a progressive, essential, exhaustive, and mutually exclusive division of all substance.

E. Co-division. This is a number of independent divisions of the same genus, each employing a different basis of division.

Co-division must be distinguished from subdivision and from a shift in the basis of division.

1. Subdivision is progressive division, resulting in a single, orderly system of division. Example: the Tree of Porphyry.

2. Co-division is the legitimate process of applying successively, and each time completely, two or more different bases of division. Example: A co-division of books could be made, applying successively, and each time completely, these four bases of division: (1) language; (2) subject; (3) size; (4) color of binding.

Each of these divisions would conform to the rules of logical division: each division would be collectively exhaustive; the dividing members would be mutually exclusive. Another example of co-division is the classification of terms on pages 79-82. Each of the six classifications is a division of all terms according to one selected basis of division into species mutually exclusive and collectively exhaustive.

3. A shift in t he basis of division is the error of applying simultaneously, but incompletely, two or more different bases of division. Example: the division of books into Latin, English, French, poetry, history, science, octavo, quarto, blue, red.

A shift in the basis of division is the prime error in division, creating confusion and disorder. It makes it impossible to achieve what logical division aims at: a division that is collectively exhaustive (complete) and mutually exclusive (with no overlapping).

F. Applications of logical division

1. To science. Some sciences, e. g., biology, which undertake primarily to describe nature (rather than to discover causal relations) achieve the systematic order essential to all science by means of division, or classification. The division may be an analysis, proceeding from the whole to the parts, or a synthesis, proceeding from the parts to the whole; in either case,

the result is ordered, systematic knowledge.

2. To writing or other expression. The skeleton outline or plan for the whole composition, which is simultaneously analytic and synthetic, is essential to orderly and logical progression of thought, especially when the composition is of considerable length. It may be either a mental or a written outline. By means of coordinate and subordinate topics, it shows the division of the whole subject, the subdivision of the parts, the relation of the parts to the whole and to each other. The blueprint or plan of an architect or an engineer illustrates the application of division to other forms of expression.

3. To reading, or impression. To abstract from a given composition the skeleton outline that guided its author in its construction is to recover from the rhetorical medium the essential logic which it symbolizes. This is to exercise true intellectual apprehension. It is by this same process that the intellect gains its concepts: it abstracts the essence from the individual objects of experience. This is what is meant by studying and understanding instead of merely perceiving or memorizing. It is the precise difference between sense apprehension and intellectual apprehension. Abstraction, analysis, insight into the relations of parts to each other and to the whole, relations of coordination and of subordination, are essential to human learning, to intellectual apprehension; they are wholly absent from animal learning, from mere sense apprehension.

QUESTIONS AND EXERCISES

1. What is a term? How does it differ from a concept? from words? Explain by analogy. When have two persons "come to terms"?
2. What is the grammatical equivalent of a logical term? Name the four grammatical symbols capable of expressing a logical term.
3. Is a term ever ambiguous? a symbol? May the same term be expressed by different symbols? Illustrate. What bearing has this on style? on translation?
4. Which of the four grammatical symbols is the least ambiguous?
5. Name the two classes of terms distinguished according to the kind of reality signified. How may each be symbolized?
6. Classify as either a general or an empirical term: the students in this class; a squirrel; the squirrels in Central Park; the books in our library; cedar; lake; the Great Lakes; green; this color; a patriot; Nathan Hale; a citizen; the citizens of Boston; three policemen; wolves; thinking; creek; creak; my watch; clocks; the employees of General Motors; galloped; an acorn; your mother.

7. Explain and give examples of: contradictory terms; a privative term; a concrete term; an abstract term; an absolute term; a relative term; a collective term; a distributive term. May the same term be in more than one of these classes at the same time?

8. Which of the six classifications of terms is based on the fundamental distinction between terms, that is, the kind of reality signified by the term?

9. When are terms categorically different? generically different? specifically different? individually different?

10. When are terms repugnant? Mention four groups of terms necessarily repugnant.

11. Distinguish three groups of contrary terms. State three differences between contrary terms and contradictory terms.

12. Classify the following pairs of terms as either categorically, generically, specifically, or individually different: chemistry, physics; prudent, deaf; Tom, Dick; letter, written; Detroit, Henry; near, fifty; bee, daisy; Mars, Venus; long, yellow; round, square; tiger, trout; successive, loud; winter, autumn; elephant, oyster; cold, sour; month, sang; rabbit, grass; Iowa, Maine; run, walk; tall, ten; brave, dark; agile, helmeted.

13. Classify the following pairs of terms as either contradictory or contrary: full, empty; visible, invisible; Christian, non-Christian; sad, joyful; sane, insane; intelligent, stupid; matter, spirit; furnished, unfurnished; rough, smooth; natural, artificial; credible, incredible; odd, even; purchaser, non-purchaser.

14. Judge whether the following words, grammatically negative, symbolize terms logically positive or logically negative: incompetent, infamous, ignorant, uncounted, impious, unsuccessful, insubordination, impolite, unaware, impenetrable, impudent, inaudible.

15. Use each of the following collective nouns, first collectively, then distributively: class, regiment, committee, crew.

16. Show by analyzing the following pairs of relative terms, as on p. 81, the bond by which the terms are correlatives: architect, building; plaintiff, defendant; crime, criminal; captain, crew.

17. What is the extension of a term? the intension? State the law of the relation between the extension and the intension of a term. Consider how the Tree of Porphyry illustrates this law. Compare the number of men that have ever existed with the number of organisms; with the number of substances.

18. Classify "my friends" in each of the six classifications of terms discussed in this chapter. State its contrary; its contradictory. Head one column *My Friends* and another column the contradictory of this term. In the first column write a complete list of the names of your friends, to show the full extension of the term. Do you discover a vital relation between the extension and the intension of a term? Must you clarify the intension of friend by defining it for yourself before you can make a complete list of your friends? Do you realize through this exercise the great difference between the contradictory and the contrary of a term?

19. Show how the extension of flower is affected by increasing its intension, adding successively the characteristics many-petaled, yellow, large, sweet-smelling; show how the extension of man is affected by adding successively the characteristics tall, blond, handsome, athletic, college-educated, French.

20. Arrange the following series of terms in a graduated order of decreasing extension:
    (1) Rodent, vertebrate, rat, animal, substance, mammal, organism
    (2) Object, dwelling, building, bungalow, house
    (3) Narrative, *Iliad*, work, composition, epic
    (4) Action, tennis, recreation, contest, game
    (5) Quality, middle C, accident, tone, sound
21. Reproduce the Tree of Porphyry. What is meant by *summum genus? infima species?* a proximate genus? a remote genus?
22. How is definition related to the intension of a term? How is it symbolized?
23. Name the two kinds of definition constructed from a logical point of view. State the pattern of each. Give an example of each.
24. Classify the following definitions as either logical or distinctive:
    (1) A square is an equilateral triangle.
    (2) A man is an animal capable of communicating his thoughts through symbols.
    (3) A circle is a curvilinear plane figure with every point of its circumference equidistant from the center.
    (4) An organism is a body capable of reproducing its kind.
    (5) A plane is space in two dimensions.
    (6) Hydrogen is an element capable of uniting with certain other elements to form acids.
    (7) A circle is a curved plane figure whose circumference is 3.1416 times its diameter.
    (8) A square is a rectangle divisible by its diagonal into two equal isosceles right triangles.
    (9) A cube is an equilateral rectangular solid.
    (10) A rectangle is a plane surface whose area is equal to the product of its two dimensions.
    (11) Man is a tool-using animal.
    (12) A rectangular solid is a figure whose volume is equal to the product of its three dimensions.
25. With reference to definition, explain: species, genus, specific differentia, property.
26. Has a species more than one specific differentia? more than one specific property? How does geometry deal with the specific properties of figures? How does qualitative analysis in chemistry depend on the specific properties of substances?
27. Consulting the Tree of Porphyry for data, state the logical definition of animal; organism; body.
28. Mention three kinds of terms for which one cannot construct a logical definition. Why not? Can these terms be made clear by other methods of definition?
29. Explain and illustrate: causal definition; descriptive definition; definition by example.
30. Show by example that definition by etymology is sometimes enlightening; sometimes misleading.
31. In an adequate dictionary, look up the etymology of each of the following words and tell whether or not it clarifies the present meaning of the word:

coquette, pecuniary, immense, enormous, gigantic, inter, geometry, disaster, eccentric, television, astrology, astronomy, gospel, quell, starve, gossip.

32. Mention two classes of words subject to arbitrary definition. Cite examples.

33. Read a good essay defining a word of arbitrary or shifting meaning. Suggestions: Arnold Bennett, "Why a Classic Is a Classic"; Katherine Fullerton Gerould, "What Then Is Culture?"; Frank Swinnerton, "On Thinking Well of Oneself"; James Truslow Adams, "The Mucker Pose"; Frederick Lewis Allen, "The Goon and His Style"; Sir Arthur Quiller-Couch, "On Jargon."

34. Point out exactly where the following definitions tell what is included in, and what is excluded from, the term defined:

(1) Hence it is that it is almost a definition of a gentleman to say he is one who never inflicts pain. This description is both refined and, as far as it goes, accurate. He is mainly occupied in merely removing the obstacles which hinder the free and unembarrassed action of those about him; and he concurs with their movements rather than takes the initiative himself. His benefits may be considered as parallel to what are called comforts or conveniences in arrangements of a personal nature: like an easy chair or a good fire, which do their part in dispelling cold and fatigue, though nature provides both means of rest and animal heat without them. The true gentleman in like manner carefully avoids whatsoever may cause a jar or jolt in the minds of those with whom he is cast;— all clashing of opinion, or collision of feeling, all restraint, or suspicion, or gloom, or resentment; his great concern being to make everyone at his ease and at home. He has his eyes on all his company; he is tender towards the bashful, gentle towards the distant, and merciful towards the absurd; he can recollect to whom he is speaking; he guards against unseasonable allusions, or topics that may irritate; he is seldom prominent in conversation, and never wearisome. He makes light of favors when he does them, and seems to be receiving when he is conferring. He never speaks of himself except when compelled, never defends himself by mere retort, he has no ears for slander or gossip, is scrupulous in imputing motives to those who interfere with him and interprets everything for the best. He is never mean or little in his disputes, never takes unfair advantage, never mistakes personalities or sharp sayings for arguments, or insinuates evil which he dare not say out. From a long-sighted prudence, he observes the maxim of the ancient sage, that we should ever conduct ourselves towards our enemy as if he were one day to be our friend. He has too much good sense to be affronted at insults, he is too well employed to remember injuries, and too indolent to bear malice. He is patient, forbearing, and resigned, on philosophical principles; he submits to pain, because it is inevitable, to bereavement, because it is irreparable, and to death, because it is his destiny. If he engages in controversy of any kind, his disciplined intellect preserves him from the blundering discourtesy of better, perhaps, but less educated minds; who, like blunt weapons, tear and hack instead of cutting clean, who mistake the point in argument, waste their strength on trifles, misconceive their adversary, and leave the question more involved than they find it. He may be right or wrong in his opinion, but he is too clear-headed to be

unjust; he is as simple as he is forcible, and as brief as he is decisive. Nowhere shall we find greater candor, consideration, indulgence; he throws himself into the minds of his opponents, he accounts for their mistakes. He knows the weakness of human reason as well as its strength, its province and its limits. If he be an unbeliever, he will be too profound and large-minded to ridicule religion or to act against it; he is too wise to be a dogmatist or fanatic in his infidelity. He respects piety and devotion; he even supports institutions as venerable, beautiful, or useful, to which he does not assent; he honors the ministers of religion, and it contents him to decline its mysteries without assailing or denouncing them. He is a friend of religious toleration, and that, not only because his philosophy has taught him to look on all forms of faith with an impartial eye, but also from the gentleness and effeminancy of feeling, which is the attendant on civilization.

Not that he may not hold a religion, too, in his own way, even when he is not a Christian. In that case his religion is one of imagination and sentiment; it is the embodiment of those ideas of the sublime, majestic, and beautiful, without which there can be no large philosophy. Sometimes he acknowledges the being of perfection. And this deduction of his reason, or creation of his fancy, he makes the occasion of such excellent thoughts, and the starting-point of so varied and systematic a teaching, that he even seems like a disciple of Christianity itself. From the very accuracy and steadiness of his logical powers, he is able to see what sentiments are consistent in those who hold any religious doctrine at all, and he appears to others to feel and to hold a whole circle of theological truths, which exist in his mind no otherwise than as a number of deductions.

Such are some of the lineaments of the ethical character, which the cultivated intellect will form, apart from religious principle. They are seen within the pale of the Church and without it, in holy men, and in profligate; they form the beau-ideal of the world; they partly assist and partly distort the development of the Catholic. They may subserve the education of a St. Francis de Sales or a Cardinal Pole, they may be the limits of the contemplation of a Shaftesbury or a Gibbon. Basil and Julian were fellow-students at the schools of Athens; and one became the Saint and Doctor of the Church, the other her scoffing relentless foe.

—Newman. *The Idea of a University*

(2) Literature, from the derivation of the word, implies writing, not speaking. . . . I insist on this, because it shows that speech, and therefore literature, which is its permanent record, is essentially a personal work. It is not some production or result, attained by the partenership of several persons, or by machinery, or by any natural process, but in its very idea it proceeds, and must proceed, from some one given individual. Two persons cannot be the authors of the sounds which strike our ear; and, as they cannot be speaking one and the same speech, neither can they be writing one and the same lecture or discourse—which must certainly belong to some one person or other, and is the expression of that one person's ideas and feelings—ideas and feelings personal to himself, though others may have parallel and similar ones—proper to himself, in the same sense as his voice, his air, his countenance, his carriage, and his actions are

personal. In other words, literature expresses, not objective truth, as it is called, but subjective; not things, but thoughts. . . .

Science, then, has to do with things, literature with thoughts; science is universal, literature is personal; science uses words merely as symbols, but literature uses language in its full compass, as including phraseology, idiom, style, composition, rhythm, eloquence, and whatever other properties are included in it.

Let us then put aside the scientific use of words when we are to speak of language and literature. Literature is the personal use or .exercise of language. That this is so is further proved from the fact that one author uses it so differently from another. Language itself in its very origination would seem to be traceable to individuals. Their peculiarities have given it its character. We are often able in fact to trace particular phrases or idioms to individuals; we know the history of their rise. Slang surely, as it is called, comes of, and breathes of the personal. The connection between the force of words in particular languages and the habits and sentiments of the nations speaking them has often been pointed out. And, while the many use language as they find it, the man of genius uses it indeed, but subjects it withal to his own purposes, and molds it according to his own peculiarities. The throng and succession of ideas, thoughts, feelings, imaginations, aspirations, which pass within him, the abstractions, the juxtapositions, the comparisons, the discriminations, the conceptions, which are so original in him, his views of external things, his judgments upon life, manners, and history, the exercises of his wit, of his humor, of his depth, of his sagacity, all these innumerable and incessant creations, the very pulsation and throbbing of his intellect, does he image forth, to all does he give utterance, in a corresponding language, which is as multiform as this inward mental action itself and analogous to it, the faithful expression of his intense personality, attending on his own inward world of thought as its very shadow; so that we might as well say that one man's shadow is another's as that the style of a really gifted mind can belong to any but himself. It follows him about as a shadow. His thought and feeling are personal, and so his language is personal.

Thought and speech are inseparable from each other. Matter and expression are parts of one; style is a thinking out into language. This is what I have been laying down, and this is literature: not *things*, not the verbal symbols of things; not on the other hand mere *words*, but thoughts expressed in language. Call to mind, gentlemen, the meaning of the Greek word which expresses this special prerogative of man over the feeble intelligence of the inferior animals. It is called Logos. What does Logos mean? It stands both for *reason* and for *speech*, and it is difficult to say which it means more properly. It means both at once. Why? Because really they cannot be divided—because they are in a true sense one. When we can separate light and illumination, life and motion, the convex and the concave of a curve, then will it be possible for thought to tread speech under foot, and to hope to do without it—then will it be conceivable that the vigorous and fertile intellect should renounce its own double, its instrument of expression, and the channel of its speculations and emotions.

—Newman,"Literature and Science"

35. Memorize Saint Paul's definition of charity; Matthew Arnold's definition of literature; Arnold Bennett's definition of a classic.
36. In a section of your notebook, copy good or interesting definitions culled from your reading. State the source of each.
37. Write an essay of 200-450 words defining one of the following words, or a similar word, telling what is included and what is excluded; it may be well to divide those to whom the term does and does not apply into groups, and to give examples: a lady, a friend, a prig, a radical, a conservative, leadership, school spirit, class spirit, sportsmanship, loyalty, courtesy, sincerity, progress, civilization, materialism, comedy, tragedy, education.
38. State five rules of definition. Which of these is the test of definition? In the light of these rules, criticize the following:
    (1) The eyes are windows of the soul.
    (2) Evolution is to be defined as a continuous change from indefinite, incoherent homogeneity to definite, coherent heterogeneity of structure and function through sucessive differentiations and integrations.
                                                         —Herbert Spencer
    (3) Humor is the oil and wine of merry meeting.—Irving.
    (4) Sleep is being unconscious.
    (5) A pen is an instrument used for writing.
    (6) Embarrassment is when your face gets red.
    (7) Humor is wit and love.—Thackeray
    (8) A fish is an animal that swims.
    (9) A socialist is to believe in socialism.
    (10) Poetry is a synthesis of hyacinths and biscuits.—Carl Sandburg.
39. How is logical division related to the extension of a term? to definition?
40. Distinguish: logical division; physical division; metaphysical division; verbal division; enumeration. Which kind of division is each of the following: (1) the division of a tree into roots, trunk, branches, leaves, sap, etc.? (2) of flower into rose, tulip, daisy, lily, violet, etc.? (3) of river into length, width, depth, temperature, speed of current, direction of flow, etc.? What is the test of logical division? Illustrate.
41. What are the elements of logical division? Illustrate.
42. Distinguish: essential division; accidental division; positive division; dichotomy. Illustrate each.
43. State the rules of logical division. Show how dichotomy guarantees the observance of these rules. Use the Tree of Porphyry as illustration.
44. State the principle of contradiction. Why is dichotomy, from a logical point of view, superior to positive division?
45. Distinguish: co-division; subdivision; a shift in the basis of division. Illustrate.
46. Criticize the following divisions. Point out examples of legitimate co-division; of an illegitimate shift in the basis of division; of selected items that could be related by subdivision.
    (1) Of terms into empirical and general.
    (2) Of terms into relative and absolute.
    (3) Of terms into positive, concrete, collective, privative, contrary, repugnant.

(4) Of dogs into large, short-haired, brown, black, terrier, collie, retriever, Newfoundland, St. Bernard.

(5) Of animals into vertebrates, insects, fishes, birds, bees, mammals, lions, savage, carnivorous, domestic, unicellular, cud-chewing.

(6) Of trees into deciduous, fruit, hickory, ash, conifer, pine, oak, cedar, walnut, elm.

(7) Of men into white, European, German, Parisian, English-speaking, poets, Communists, lawyers, politicians, criminals, athletes, husbands, church-goers.

47. Make a valid positive logical division of one of the following, continuing it by means of subdivision. State whether the division is essential or accidental: animals; micro-organisms; rectilinear plane; regular rectilinear solid; curvilinear figure; qualities; virtues; biological sciences; physical sciences; social sciences; forms of discourse; armed forces of the United States; occupations; the surface of the earth.

48. Make a series of co-divisions of one of the following, employing subdivision as far as you can: schools; forms of government; archtitecture, music; poetry; foods; chemical elements; chemical compounds.

49. In what kinds of science is division important?

50. Explain how division is an important tool in writing; in reading. Why is it absurd to have one subtopic in any part of an outline?

CHAPTER V

PROPOSITIONS AND THEIR GRAMMATICAL EXPRESSION

I. The proposition. Definition and distinctions.
   A. The proposition asserts a relation of terms. It consists of subject, copula, and predicate. The terms (the subject and the predicate) constitute the matter of the proposition; the copula which relates them constitutes its form.
   B. A proposition may or may not assert the mode of the relation of its terms. If it does, it is modal; if it does not, it is categorical, that is, asserted simply as a matter of fact.
      1. A modal proposition explicitly asserts the relation of its terms as either necessary or contingent.
         a. Necessary. The necessity may be:
            1) Metaphysical. The relation is metaphysically necessary if it could not be otherwise for the reason that it would be impossible, inconceivable, involving sheer contradiction.
               Metaphysical necessity is such that not even God can make it otherwise. God is the source of order, not of disorder and confusion. To be unable to do what is contradictory is not a limitation of His Omnipotence; it is not an imperfection, but a perfection. Thus God cannot make a square circle, nor can He make a stone so big that He could not lift it.
               The following propositions express relations metaphysically necessary:
               a) An equilateral triangle is necessarily equiangular.
               b) The effect cannot be greater than its cause.
               c) A being is necessarily itself, and not another.
               d) Things equal to the same thing are necessarily equal to each other.
            2) Physical. Physical necessity rests on the laws of nature which, however, could conceivably be otherwise. The Author of nature can, if He wills it, set aside the laws of nature. Consequently, the abrogation of the physically necessary is the very essence of a miracle: it involves no contradiction.
               The following propositions express relations only physically necessary.

    a) Fire necessarily burns. (Compare the miracle of the three young men in the fiery furnace. Daniel 3:46-50.)

    b) Water necessarily boils at 100 degrees centigrade at sea level.

    c) A man cannot walk upon the sea. (Compare St. Matthew 14:29.)

3) Moral. Moral necessity is a normative necessity referring to a free agent. Because of his free will, man can act counter to these laws; but, even so, the laws remain, either expressing natural human tendencies, as in economic laws; or expressing the demands of order in society, as in civil laws; or, most important, expressing a duty binding on conscience, as in the moral law, strictly so called.

    The following propositions express relations morally necessary in the three senses explained above.

    a) The quality of the goods being equal, men necessarily tend to buy the goods priced lowest. (This tendency can be counteracted to some extent by a contrary appeal to the free will, as, for instance, by a campaign to "Buy American.")

    b) Cars must stop when the traffic light is red.

    c) Good must be done and evil avoided.

4) Logical. For a consideration of the relations of necessity and contingency, on strictly logical grounds, see the predicables, pages 112-114.

b. Contingent. Whatever is not necessary is contingent. A relation is contingent, or possible, that does not involve either necessity or metaphysical incompatibility; it may or may not exist in the natural order. It may also be contingent on future acts or events or on our knowledge. Examples:

1) A raven may be red.

2) A lion may be tame.

3) A triangle may be isosceles.

4) This water may contain typhoid germs.

5) Your mother may be writing you a letter now.

6) Mr. Jones may win the election.

2. A categorical proposition asserts the relation of its terms as they are actually related, without expressing the mode of

their relation. If the mode is afterwards considered, it is, of course, found to be either necessary or contingent. Consequently, the copula in a categorical proposition is ambiguous in the sense that, if examined, the simple *is* means either *is necessarily* (*must be*) or *is contingently* (*may be*).

Note on grammar. The indicative mood of the copula expresses the categorical relation; the potential mood, the contingent relation.

C. A proposition is either simple or compound.

1. A simple proposition is one that asserts the relation of two terms and only two.

    a. A simple propostion is categorical if it asserts the relation as a matter of fact. Every categorical proposition is a simple proposition but not every simple proposition is categorical.

    b. A simple proposition is modal if it explicitly asserts the relation as either necessary or contingent.

2. A compound proposition is one that relates at least three terms.

    a. A hypothetical proposition asserts the dependence of one proposition on another. Example: If he does not study, he will fail. (Three terms.)

    b. A disjunctive proposition asserts that of two or more suppositions, one is true. Example: A triangle is either equilateral, isosceles, or scalene. (Four terms.)

II. Characteristics of propositions: (1) reference to reality; (2) quantity; (3) quality; (4) modality; (5) value.

Each of these characteristics divides propositions into two classes thus:

A. Reference to reality: general or empirical

This, the fundamental distinction between propositions, is determined by the reference of the subject.

1. A general proposition is one whose subject is a general term, referring to an essence, symbolized by a common name or a general description.

2. An empirical proposition is one whose subject is an empirical term, referring to an individual or an aggregate, symbolized by a proper name or an empirical description.

B. Quantity: total or partial

The quantity of a proposition is determined by the extension of the subject.

1. A proposition is total if its subject is a term used in its full extension.

   a. A general proposition does not have quantity in the concrete sense, because its subject is essence, a class nature. The subject of a general proposition is, however, used in its full extension, and is, in that sense, regarded as total,

     1) When the general proposition is asserted categorically. It may be worded in various ways. Examples:

      a) Spinach is a vegetable.

      b) A rabbit is an animal.

      c) All birds have feathers. (This is explicitly quantified by "All.")

      d) To be a square is to be a rectangle.

     2) When the general proposition is asserted as a necessary modal. Example: A square must have four equal sides.

   b. A singular empirical proposition, because its subject is one individual, is used in its full extension, and is, in that sense, regarded as total,

     1) When the singular empirical proposition is asserted categorically. Example: This man is a thief.

     2) When the singular empirical proposition is asserted as a necessary modal proposition. Example: John is necessarily mortal.

   c. Quantity, in the strict sense, is proper only to plural empirical propositions. A plural empirical proposition is total when the subject is a total aggregate of individuals. Examples:

     1) All the members of this class are American citizens.

     2) No chair in this room is a rocker.

     3) These men are carpenters.

     4) Twelve horses were entered in the race.

2. A proposition is partial if its subject is a term used in only part of its extension.

   a. In plural empirical propositions the partial extension of the subject is expressed by a limiting word such as "some" or an equivalent. Examples:

     1) Some men are handsome.

     2) Some roses are not red.

      3) All violets are not purple. ("All are not" idiomatically means "Some are not.")

      4) Not every day is rainy. (This means: Some days are not rainy).

   b. When a general proposition or a singular empirical proposition is contingent in modality, the subject is used in only a part of its extension (as is proved by the test of conversion). Examples:

      1) A contingent general proposition: A rectangle may not be a square.

      2) A contingent singular proposition: John may not be a lawyer.

C. Quality: Affirmative or negative

   The quality of a proposition is determined by the copula.

  1. A proposition is affirmative if it asserts the inclusion of the subject (all of it or a part of it) in the predicate.

  2. A proposition is negative if it asserts the exclusion of the predicate (always all of it) from the subject.

D. Modality: necessary or contingent

   The modality of a proposition is determined by the copula. Necessary and contingent relations have been explained and illustrated above. (See page 104.)

E. Value: true or false

  1. The truth or falsity of an empirical proposition can be known only from investigation, from experience, from an appeal to the facts. In this sense it is synthetic, a putting together of facts.

     Example: Every farm in Hancock County, Ohio, is equipped with electric lighting.

     To discover the truth or falsity of this proposition, one must either visit every farm in Hancock County or by other means get authentic information about every one of them on this point.

  2. The truth or falsity of a general proposition can be known from an analysis of the terms without an investigation of all the facts. In this sense it is analytic. Because it depends upon intellectual insight into a class nature or essence, our knowledge of its truth or falsity has greater certainty than that of an empirical proposition which depends on the investigation of individual instances.

Example: A blind man cannot umpire a football game.

To discover the truth or falsity of this proposition, it is not necessary to find all the blind men and try them at umpiring. Intellectual insight reveals the incompatibility of the terms, once they are understood.

A proposition must be either true or false. Whatever is capable of being true or false must be a proposition or more than one, for this characteristic (truth or falsity) is a property of propositions.

A proposition is true if the relation it asserts is really as asserted; otherwise it is false. For example, a proposition which asserts a possibility is true if the relation is really possible, even though it is not actual: A raven may be red. It is, however, false to assert as a matter of fact: Some ravens are red.

Note. We may distinguish three kinds of truth:

(1) Metaphysical truth is the conformity of a thing to the idea of it in the mind of God primarily and in the minds of men secondarily. Every being has metaphysical truth.

(2) Logical truth is the conformity of thought to reality; its opposite is falsity.

(3) Moral truth is the conformity of expression to thought; its opposite is a lie.

III. Propositional forms: A E I O forms

Every proposition can be classified as A, E, I, or O. These forms differ both in quality and in either quantity or modality. Hence we have either quantitative or modal A E I O forms. In the following formulas S symbolizes the subject and P the predicate.

Quantitative A E I O forms. (The propositions are categorical.)

A Tot. affirm.	SaP	All S is P.	All lions are animals.
E Tot. neg.	SeP	No S is P.	No lions are horses.
I Part affirm.	SiP	Some S is P.	Some lions are tame.
O Part. neg.	SoP	Some S is not P.	Some lions are not tame.

Modal A E I O forms. (The propositions are explicitly modal.)

A Nec. affirm.	SaP	S must be P.	A lion must be an animal.
E Nec. neg.	SeP	S cannot be P.	A lion cannot be a horse.
I Cont. affirm.	SiP	S may be P.	A lion may be tame.
O Cont. neg.	SoP	S may not be P.	A lion may not be tame.

The indefiniteness characteristic of I and O propositions may be expressed either by the indefinite *some* or by the contingent *may*. The quantity of a proposition is determined by its subject, and hence by the matter, not by the form. The modality and the quality of a proposition are determined by the copula. Since the copula is the form of a proposition, the modal forms, determined altogether by the copula, more properly express propositional forms. Yet the quantitative forms are usually more convenient and are more frequently used, for we are inclined to use categorical propositions more often than modal ones.

IV. The distribution of terms. Distribution is a characteristic of terms used in a proposition, not of a term standing alone.

A term is distributed if it is used in its full extension. It is undistributed if it is used in less than its full extension.

A. The formal rules of distribution: The quantity (or modality) of a proposition determines the distribution of its subject. The quality of a proposition determines the distribution of its predicate. Thus:

1. A total (or necessary) proposition distributes its subject.
2. A partial (or contingent) proposition has its subject undistributed.
3. A negative proposition distributes its predicate (because it excludes all of it from the subject).
4. An affirmative proposition has its predicate undistributed (because the predicate is normally a term wider in extension than the subject).

The predicate of an affirmative proposition is, however, distributed whenever the proposition is a definition, by virtue of the following reasoning: (1) a definition is always an A proposition (necessary affirmative) and therefore its subject is distributed through the form; (2) the predicate, being the definition of the subject (whether by genus and differentia or by property), has not only the same intension but the same extension as the subject, namely, full extension (see p. 91), and is therefore distributed (through the matter, the terms, although not through the form, the copula). The very fact that a definition is convertible proves that the predicate has the same extension as the subject, and therefore, since the subject is distributed, so is the predicate. Conversion is the test of distribution.

B. Application of these rules to the A E I O forms (*d* means distributed; *u* means undistributed).

d u
1. SaP Because it is total (or necessary) an A proposition distributes its subject; because it is affirmative, its predicate
   is undistributed.

d d
2. SeP Because it is total (or necessary) an E proposition distributes its subject; because it is negative, it distributes
   its predicate.

u u
3. SiP Because it is partial (or contingent) an I proposition has
   its subject undistributed; because it is affirmative, its
   predicate is undistributed.

u d
4. SoP Because it is partial (or contingent) an O proposition
   has its subject undistributed; because it is negative, it
   distributes its predicate.

Note. Knowing the distribution of terms is as indispensable
to success in the study of logic as knowing the basic axioms is
in the study of geometry. If you become bewildered, or seem
to get lost in a fog, go back to this point, grasp it clearly, and
then work your way through to the light.

C. The relation and the distribution of terms in A E I O forms
   may be graphically represented by Euler's circles. Two terms,
   S and P, can be related in four ways:

A

A

S and P

1. Total inclusion of S in P. S is distributed. If P ex-
   ceeds S in extension, as it usually does, P is undistributed.

   If P exactly coincides with S in extension, as
   when one dime is placed on another, P is distributed through the matter, not through the form;
   this occurs only when P is the definition or the
   propery of S.

E

I

O

2. Total exclusion of P from S. Both are distributed.

3. Inclusion of part of S in part of P. Neither is distributed.

4. Exclusion of all of P from part of S. Therefore
   S is undistributed; P is distributed.

V. The predicables. These represent the ultimate classification of the
   relations a predicate may be affirmed to have to a subject, just as

the categories represent the ultimate classification of being-as-it-is (the metaphysical categories) and of being-as-it-is-known (the logical categories).

The classification of predicates in the predicables in logic is analogous to the syntactical analysis of the sentence in grammar, just as the classification of terms in the categories in logic is analogous to the part-of-speech analysis in grammar.

A. The predicables are: species, genus, differentia, definition, property, and accident.

Although in the treatment of definition (see pp. 86-87) all these have been explained except accident, for convenience they are repeated here.

1. Species as a predicate expresses that which the individual members of a class have in common. When a species is the predicate of a categorical proposition, the subject is always an individual or an aggregate. *Infima* species, as a predicate, expresses the whole essence or intension of its subject, an individual member (or members) of the *species*. Examples: Socrates is a man. These animals are horses.

2. Genus is that part of the essence which is common to all its constituent species. Examples: Man is an animal. A square is a rectangle.

3. The differentia is that part of the essence which belongs only to a given species and which distinguishes it from every other species in the same genus. Examples: Man is rational. A square is equilateral.

4. Definition is constituted of the genus plus the differentia; it makes explicit the essence of the species which stands as its subject, and therefore it coincides perfectly with the subject in both intension and extension. Examples: Man is a rational animal. A square is an equilateral rectangle.

5. Property is not the essence nor a part of the essence but it flows from the essence and is present wherever the essence is present, for it is a necessary concomitant of the essence. Therefore it perfectly coincides with the subject in extension, but not in intension. Examples: Man is mirthful. A square is divisible by its diagonal into two equal isosceles right triangles.

6. Accident is a predicate contingently related to the subject whereas all the other predicables are related necessarily to

the subject. The contingency may be either explicit or implicit. Examples: Man may be black. A square may be large. The grass is green.

The predicable accident must be carefully distinguished from the predicamental accident (any of the nine categories of accident). The predicables and the categories (or *praedicamenta*) are co-divisions of terms, each using a different principle of division, one depending altogether on the relations of terms, the other classifying terms independently.

The predicates of the following propositions are classified in each of these two ways:

Proposition	Predicable	Category
Man is rational.	Differentia	Accident (quality)
Man is mirthful.	Property	Accident (quality)
Man is animal.	Genus	Substance
John is a man.	Species	Substance
John is a lawyer.	Accident	Substance (construct)
John is tall.	Accident	Accident (quantity)
Snow is white.	Accident	Accident (quality)

An inseparable accident, which is a contingent predicate, must not be confused with property, which is a necessary predicate. For example, a raven is always black, but blackness is not therefore a necessary predicate of raven. The contingent general proposition *A raven may be red* is therefore true as a possibility.

For years whiteness was considered an inseparable accident of swans, for no swans except white ones were known until black swans were discovered in Australia. Nevertheless, even before the discovery, white was correctly regarded as a contingent, not a necessary, predicate of swan.

B. The number of the predicables

There are five predicables which classify the predicates of a general (or universal) affirmative proposition, and a sixth, which appears only in an empirical affirmative proposition.

1. In his exposition of the predicables wherein he shows that they analyze modality as either necessary or contingent, Aristotle distinguishes five. His analysis is applicable only to general affirmative propositions. Let SaP symbolize a general affirmative proposition. Then P is either convertible with S or it is not. If it is convertible, P is either the definition (signifying the essence) or a property. If it is not convertible, P

is either one of the elements of the definition (genus or differentia) or it is not; if it is not one of the elements of the
definition, it is an accident. (*Topics*, 1.8).

Aristotle also says emphatically in another place (*Catego-
gories*, 2,5) that all predication is primarily and essentially
of first substance, that is, of an individual, the object of our
experience, expressed by a singular empirical term as subject. A general or universal term can stand as subject only
because it can itself be predicated of singulars, that is, of
individuals. Hence Aristotle includes a sixth predicable, species, which states the class nature of an individual and can
therefore be predicated normally only of individuals. In its
extensional relation to its subject, as revealed by the test of
conversion, species resembles genus in not being convertible,
for its extension is greater than that of the subject. Example:
Socrates is a man.

The extensional relationships of the six predicables to the
subject can be graphically represented by Euler's circles.

a. Coincidence		1) definition
S and P	○	2) property
b. Total inclusion	⊚ P	3) genus
" "		4) differentia
" "	s-Ⓟ	5) species
c. Partial inclusion	ⓈⓅ	6) accident

2. Porphyry and the Scholastics listed five predicables, including species, but omitting definition. It is true that species and
   definition are identical in both extension and intension, and
   that in the order of being, on which Porphyry's classification
   is based, species, like definition, signifies the whole essence;
   moreover, the Scholastics exemplify the predicable species
   by a predicate which is definition. Yet species, as commonly
   understood, when used as a predicate cannot be identified
   with the predicable definition, since species is the subject, the
   one possible subject, of the predicable definition (see p. 86);
   and species can be the predicate normally only of a singular
   empirical subject. Species as a predicate has more in common
   with genus than with definition because in both of these relations the subject is totally included in a wider predicate, as
   Euler's circles indicate.

C. In their narrow signification, the six predicables do not represent an exhaustive analysis of predication, not even of necessary predication, for

1. A predicate is affirmed necessarily of a subject if it is a property or the differentia of a remote genus of the subject; but it cannot be classified as either a property or the differentia of *that* subject.

Example: Man necessarily has weight (is ponderable).

Weight is a property of body, and body is a remote genus of man; but weight is not, in the narrow sense, a property of man, for it is not a term convertible with man. Yet it is predicated necessarily of man. In terms of Aristotle's analysis, a property or the differentia of a remote genus of the subject would be a part of the definition, in the broad sense that it is included in its intension, but not in the narrow sense of being the differentia of *that* subject, or a property of *that* subject, as differentia and property are defined. (Property, as defined, is, of course, not a part of definition in the narrow sense, because it is not a part of the essence, although it flows from the essence.) The same is true of the Scholastic interpretation of species as a predicable.

2. Because the individual is a member of a species, one can predicate necessarily of an individual not only species, but other necessary predicates which he has by virtue of his species.

Examples: John is necessarily a man, an animal, a rational animal, capable of mirth.

Animal is genus of man, but not of John. Rational animal is the definition of man, but not of John, for an individual cannot be defined. Mirthfulness is a property of man, but not of John, for it is not convertible with John.

The predicables are, moreover, a classification of the predicates in affirmative propositions only, for the predicate in a negative proposition, always wholly excluded from the subject, obviously cannot be related to the subject as its species, genus, differentia, definition, property, or accident. Yet the predicate may be necessarily excluded from the subject. Some of the most important propositions in philosophy are necessary negative propositions. Examples: Contradictory judgments cannot both be true. A square is necessarily not a circle.

Predicates can, of course, also be classified in the categories or *praedicamenta*. When the predicate is in the same category as the subject, it states the species or the genus of the subject with greater or less determinateness. Examples: John is a man, an animal, an organism, a body, a substance. A square is a figure, a shape, a quality. Prudence is a habit, a virtue, a good, a quality.

The categories are direct metaphysical universals, called terms of first intention because they classify our concepts of being or reality. The predicables are reflex logical universals, called terms of second intention because they are wholly mental in that they classify the relations which the mind perceives between our concepts of reality.

VI. Sentences and propositions

  A. Grammatical symbols required to express propositions

    1. A proposition must be symbolized by a declarative sentence. A non-declarative sentence (a command or prayer or wish, a question, or an exclamation) cannot symbolize a proposition, for it is neither true nor false; it expresses volition, not cognition, and has therefore no status in logic, although it has thoroughly sound status in grammar.

    Because every simple declarative sentence is made up either explicitly or implicitly of subject, copula, and subjective complement (see p. 68), is can symbolize perfectly the logical proposition made up of subject, copula, and predicate. Consequently, every declarative sentence symbolizes a proposition or a number of propositions, whether the copula and subjective complement are explicit or not.

    a. A general proposition must be symbolized by a sentence whose subject is a common name or a general description.

      If the common name or the general description does not symbolize an essence that is possible, it does not express a term, for one cannot have a concept of an impossible essence.

      Violation of rule: A square circle is a curvilinear figure. This sentence does not symbolize a proposition, because it does not express a relation of two terms; it has but one term. It lacks a logical subject, for square circle expresses no meaning whatever, although square and circle understood separately are words that have meaning. This sentence is neither true or false, for only a proposition is true or false.

b. An empirical categorical proposition must be symbolized by a sentence whose subject is a proper name or an empirical description.

If the proper name or the empirical description does not symbolize an individual or an aggregate existent at present or in the past, in fact or in fiction, it does not express a term, because one cannot experience what is non-existent.

Violation of rule: The grandchildren of Shirley Temple are blondes. Because it does not express a relation of two terms, this sentence does not symbolize a proposition; therefore it is neither true nor false.

The following two empirical modal propositions, however, are true as possibilities: Shirley Temple may have grandchildren and they may be blondes.

2. The same proposition can be expressed by different but equivalent grammatical symbols in the same or in different languages. Examples:

a. The first man elected as executive head of the United States is noted for his skill as a military leader.

b. The first President of the United States is famed as a great general.

c. Le premier président des Stats-Unis est renommé comme un grand général.

d. Der erste Präsident der Vereinigten Staaten ist als ein grosser General berühmt.

e. El primer presidente de los Estados Unidos es renombrado como un gran general.

A sentence which symbolizes a proposition may be ambiguous. A proposition cannot be ambiguous because the meaning, the judgment, which the mind intends to express must be one, that is, univocal. When the listener or reader obtains from and through language the identical proposition intended by the speaker or writer, he understands; they have "come to terms."

The purpose of translation is to express in the symbols of other languages the propositions embodied in the symbols of a given language. Unless the propositional content of a scientific treatise obtainable in four different languages were univocal and common to all of them, there would be four treatises, not one. These books differ in language, that is, in the symbols used to embody one and the same logical content.

When a given composition is compared with its translation in another language, we recognize that there is something the same (the form, the logical content) and something different (the matter, the grammatical symbols). If the composition is a poem, the something different includes not only the difference of symbols but differences in the psychological dimension of language, its sensuous and emotional qualities, such as sound, rhythm, tone, associated ideas and feelings, all having their roots in the particular language. To embody in different symbols only the logical content of a poem is to translate only a part of the complex whole that is the poem. Consequently, poetry is in its total effects practically untranslatable.

Differences of style in expressing a given logical content in the same language are occasioned by a difference of choice between symbols logically, but not psychologically, equivalent — between words, phrases, and clauses that vary in rhythm, structure, and emotional connotation. To improve style through revision is to substitute better equivalent symbols for those first chosen. The master art of rhetoric guides one in this choice.

B. Propositional content of various types of declarative sentences

  1. A simple declarative sentence may symbolize:

    a. One simple proposition. Example: That chair may be uncomfortable.

    b. Two or more simple propositions. Example: This tall, handsome boy is exceptionally intelligent.

      This sentence symbolizes four propositions:

      1) This boy is tall.

      2) This boy is handsome.

      3) This boy is intelligent.

      4) His intelligence is exceptional.

    c. A disjunctive proposition. Examples:

      1) A rectangle is either a square or an oblong.

      2) Either Mary or John or James will be valedictorian.

      Here it should be noticed that a simple sentence may have a compound subject or a compound predicate.

  2. A complex declarative sentence may symbolize:

a. One simple proposition. Example: The yellow cat which was prowling around our garage yesterday was run over.

The clause is definitive in function, for it points out a particular cat.

b. Two or more simple propositions. Example: Tall, gaunt Abraham Lincoln, who was the first Republican to become President of the United States and who issued the Emancipation Proclamation, was assassinated. (Five propositions.)

The clauses are attributive in function for they state attributes of an individual already clearly designated by a proper name.

Grammatical modification except by definitives is implicit logical predication. Hence, if the modifier is not definitive in function, that is, if it is not necessary to the designation of the subject, it is an implicit predicate and in relation to the subject it symbolizes another proposition; if it is definitive in function, it constitutes but one term with the subject and does not symbolize another proposition. Example:

1) That tall man with brown eyes, brown hair, and a small mustache, standing near the microphone, is a Frenchman. (This symbolizes but one proposition, for the modifiers are definitive.)

2) Charles De Gaulle, who is a tall Frenchman with brown eyes, brown hair, and a small mustache, was standing near the microphone. (This symbolizes seven propositions, for the modifiers are attributive in function.)

c. A hypothetical proposition. Example: If it does not rain this afternoon, we shall go to the woods.

d. A syllogism. Example: Eighteen is an even number, because it is divisible by two. This sentence symbolizes three propositions in a syllogistic relation (to be explained in Chapter VII):

Eighteen is a number divisible by two.

Every number divisible by two is an even number.

Therefore eighteen is an even number.

3. A compound declarative sentence may symbolize:

a. Two or more simple propositions. Example: Wages are high, but so are prices.

b. A disjunctive proposition. Example: Either the train is late or we have missed it.

4. Less than a sentence may sometimes symbolize a simple proposition. Example: Fire!

This is equivalent to, and more idiomatic than, "Fire has broken out." To cry "Fire!" is to give an alarm that is either true or false. This proves that under such circumstances the word is understood as a proposition.

"Fire!" meaning "Shoot!" is a command, and does not symbolize a proposition.

5. A declarative sentence which is grammatically complete but which violates the rules governing common names and general descriptions or proper names and empirical descriptions (see pp. 20, 116) symbolizes no proposition, for it symbolizes fewer than two logical terms.

QUESTIONS AND EXERCISES

1. What is a proposition? What constitutes its matter? its form?
2. When is a relation of terms metaphysically necessary? physically necessary? morally necessary? Illustrate each. Which of these necessities can God not change? Which can He alone change? Which can man sometimes change?
3. When is a relation of terms contingent? Illustrate. What mood of the copula expresses contingency? matter of fact?
4. When is a proposition modal? categorical? simple? compound? Name and illustrate two kinds of compound propositions. Is a categorical proposition always simple? Is a simple proposition always categorical?
5. Name five characteristics of a proposition. What is the fundamental distinction between propositions?
6. What is an empirical proposition? a general proposition? Illustrate each.
7. Into which two classes does each of the following characteristics divide propositions: reference to reality? quantity? quality? modality? value?
8. In what sense is an empirical proposition synthetic? In what sense is a general proposition analytic? Of which of these can the truth or falsity be known with greater certainty?
9. Why is truth or falsity present whenever a proposition is present? Are truth and falsity limited to matters of fact? Tell why one of these propositions is true and the other false: A horse may be blue. Some horses are blue. Distinguish three kinds of truth: compare Francis Bacon's essay "Of Truth."
10. State the formula for A E I O forms if the propositions are categorical; if they are modal. Illustrate each.
11. Classify each of the following propositions as: A, E; I, or O; general or empirical; categorical or modal; true or false. Diagram the relations of each by means of Euler's circles, writing the terms of each proposition in the circles.

(1) All the Senators of the United States are more than twenty-five years old.

(2) Some trees on this campus are not evergreens.

(3) Your father is perhaps signing a check now.

(4) Every lake is not salty.

(5) A crow may be yellow.

(6) Some crows are yellow.

(7) Every flame must give light.

(8) To be a square is to be a parallelogram.

(9) No deaf man can act as judge in a radio audition.

(10) Two of John Smith's five daughters have red hair.

(11) All the houses in that block are not bungalows.

(12) Robert Millikan is a great physicist.

(13) Having life necessarily implies being an organism.

(14) The area of Texas, inclusive of water, is 265,896 square miles.

(15) Men are capable of cooking their food.

12. When is a term said to be distributed? undistributed? What determines the distribution of the subject of a proposition? Which kinds of propositions have the subject distributed? undistributed? What determines the distribution of the predicate? Which kinds of propositions have the predicate distributed? undistributed?

13. State the distribution of each term in the following: SaP; SeP; SiP; SoP; SaP when P is known to be the definition or the property of S.

14. By means of Euler's circles, show graphically the relation and distribution of terms in the following propositions. In each circle write the term it represents, and mark each proposition A, E, I, or O:

(1) All roses are flowers.

(2) No roses are lilies.

(3) Some roses are red.

(4) Some roses are not red.

15. To which grammatical analysis is the classification of terms in the predicables analogous? the classification of terms in the categories?

16. Name the six predicables. Explain and illustrate each. Which of these are convertible with the subject? Which are not? Which are necessary predicates? Which is not?

17. Distinguish between the predicable accident and the nine accidents of the categories. Illustrate. Which are terms of first intention? of second intention? Why are they so called?

18. Distinguish: separable accident, inseparable accident, property, differentia.

19. State Aristotle's analysis of the five predicables applicable to general affirmative propositions; his argument for species as a predicate. Why is not species, as commonly understood, identical as a predicate with definition?

20. By means of Euler's circles show graphically the three extensional relationships of the six predicables.

21. State two proofs that the six predicables in their strict, narrow meaning, do not represent an exhaustive analysis of the predicates that can be affirmed of a subject.

22. Which kind of sentence can symbolize a proposition? Which kinds cannot? Why?
23. Can a proposition be ambiguous? a sentence? Explain.
24. If you have spoken a simple judgment in three languages, how many propositions have you stated? What bearing has this on the translation of a chronicle? of a poem? on style?
25. How many propositions may a single declarative sentence symbolize? a complex declarative sentence? a compound declarative sentence?
26. Show that grammatical modification, except by definitives, is implicit logical predication.
27. Make explicit the full propositional import of the following sentences. Then classify each of your propositions as: A, E, I, or O; general or empirical; necessary or contingent; simple, hypothetical, or disjunctive. Punctuate the sentences correctly.
    (1) This large red juicy apple grew on my grandfather's farm in Michigan.
    (2) The present King of Switzerland is not tall.
    (3) You must either be there when the concert begins or expect to be excluded.
    (4) Unless he studies harder he will fail and his ambitious parents will be keenly disappointed.
    (5) Thomas Morton the valedictorian of his class whose home is in sunny California and who took an extremely difficult course in organic chemistry sailed for China yesterday.
    (6) Some triangular squares are circular.
    (7) Hurricane!
    (8) Her quiet timid slender twin is either more talented or more studious than she.
    (9) Neither overripe nor green bananas are tasty or healthful.
    (10) The three men who escaped from that prison last August have been caught.
    (11) Two formal dances and an operetta are scheduled for February which promises to be moderately cold and snowy this year.
    (12) This black and yellow bird which I have been observing for a week sings three songs daily.

CHAPTER VI

Relations of Simple Propositions

From the time of Aristotle it has been recognized that both logic and rhetoric, as arts of composition, have in common invention and disposition. Invention is the art of finding material for reasoning or discourse, and disposition is the art of properly relating or ordering the material.

In logic, disposition includes definition, division, the framing of propositions, and relating them. In rhetoric, disposition is the proper ordering of the parts of a composition, its introduction, body, and conclusion, according to the principles of unity, coherence, and emphasis.

Cicero simplified Aristotle's treatment of invention, and distinguished sixteen logical topics, collectively exhaustive, by which any subject may be amplified through analysis: definition, division (of a whole, either logical or physical, into its parts), genus, species, adjuncts (of a subject, including all the categories of accident: quantity, quality, relation, action, passion, *when, where,* posture, and habiliment), contraries, contradictories, similarity, comparison (greater, equal, less), cause, effect, antecedent, consequent, notation (the name), and conjugates (names derived from the same root, as *just, justice, justly*). A seventeenth topic, testimony, is external to the subject of inquiry, and includes all recourse to authority, such as laws, contracts, witnesses, proverbs, apothegms, oaths, pledges, prophecies, revelation.

Note. The relation of subject to adjuncts is broader than that of a substance to the accidents which inhere in it, because one accident, while itself inhering in a substance, may become the subject in which another accident inheres as its adjunct; e. g., The man is walking slowly. Here man is the subject in which the adjunct walking inheres, while walking is at the same time the subject in which the adjunct slow inheres.

The logical topics of invention are general. The rhetorical topics are particularized by time, place, persons, and circumstances. They include such questions as what was done, who did it, when, where, how, was it possible, necessary, credible, honest, prudent, just, profitable, difficult, easy, pleasant?

At the present day, the development of a paragraph from the topic sentence by means of definition, division, adjuncts (details), comparison, contrast, cause, effect, etc. (seldom consciously undertaken by the student) is the only vestige of the systematic analysis of a subject by means of the topics of invention which for centuries was taken for granted as the habitual first step in composition, to provide subject matter. The student who finds little to say on a subject would do well to adopt this method. It is, moreover, helpful to notice in one's reading the topics from which the subject matter is derived.

The relations of propositions are four: conjunction, opposition, eduction, and the syllogism.

I. Conjunction

    Conjunction is the mere joining of two or more propositions.

    A. The conjunction may be either explicit or implicit. Examples:

        1. Explicit: The telephone rang and John answered it. (Two propositions.)

        2. Implicit: The large, sunlit lake is tranquil. (Three propositions.)

    B. The conjunction may be either a bare conjunction or a material conjunction. Bare conjunction violates the unity required by rhetoric for the sentence, the paragraph, and the whole composition, whereas material conjunction is the very basis of that unity.

        1. A bare conjunction joins propositions unrelated in thought. Example: The cherry trees are in bloom, and many veterans are enrolled in colleges and universities.

        2. A material conjunction joins propositions that have a real or a logical relation, such as that of parts to a whole, of place, time, cause, effect, comparison, contrast, or any of the other topics mentioned above. The following illustrate a few of these.

            a. A temporal relation, expressed by *while, before, after, then, etc.* Examples:

                1) The child slept after the nurse had given him the medicine.

                2) The visitors had left before the telegram was delivered.

            b. A causal relation, expressed by *because, for, since, consequently, etc.* Examples:

                1) She carried an umbrella because the dark clouds threatened rain.

                2) The father died; consequently the mother supports the family.

c. An excellent example of development by effects, along with cause, is Dante's description of the gates of hell:

> Through me the way is to the city of woe;
> Through me the way unto eternal pain;
> Through me the way unto the lost below.
> Justice commoved my high Creator, when
> Made me Divine Omnipotence, combined
> With Primal Love and Wisdom Sovereign.
> Before me nothing was of any kind
> Except eterne, and I eterne abide:
> Leave, ye that enter in, all hope behind!
>
> —*Inferno*, III, 1

d. The paragraph from Aristotle's *Rhetoric* (on p. 187) is an outstanding illustration of development by division.

C. Rules governing value in the conjunction of propositions

In Chapter V it was stated that every proposition must be either true or false, whether it is asserted categorically as a matter of fact, or modally as a necessity or a possibility. Whatever is probable must, of course, be possible. Sometimes, however, for practical purposes it is desirable to distinguish three values: true, probable, and false. The rules of conjunction deal with these three values.

Rule 1. A conjunction of propositions is true only when every proposition conjoined is true. Conversely, if each of the propositions conjoined is true, their conjunction is true.

Rule 2. A conjunction of propositions is false, if any one of the propositions conjoined is false. Conversely, if one proposition is false, the conjunction is false.

Rule 3. A conjunction of propositions is probable, if at least one of the propositions conjoined is merely probable, and none is false. Conversely, if one proposition is probable, and none is false, the conjunction is merely probable.

Applying these rules, we find that when only two propositions are conjoined, there are nine possible values for their conjunction; if more propositions are conjoined, the number of possible values increases accordingly.

These rules are summarized in the following table where X and Y symbolize two propositions conjoined; 1 symbolizes truth, 0 falsity, and .n probability.

Rule	Prop. X	Prop. Y	Props. X and Y
1	1	1	1
2	0	1	0
2	1	0	0
2	0	.n	0
2	.n	0	0
2	0	0	0
3	1	.n	.n
3	.n	1	.n
3	.n	.n	.n x .n*

*When two or more propositions are merely probable, their conjunction becomes less probable. Example: If a mutilated corpse has a triangular scar on the left shin, it may or may not be the body of a certain missing man, for a number of persons are likely to have that mark; but if it also has webbed toes and an x-shaped scar on the left shoulder from an operation, and if the missing man had these marks, it becomes less probable that the corpse is that of any person other than this missing man, for it is very improbable that these three peculiar marks should be conjoined in any other one person.

D. Practical applications of conjunction

1. In a true-false test, the rules of conjunction must be applied. A statement is to be marked true only when every part of it is true, it is to be marked false when any part of it is false.

2. In estimating the chances of a candidate to win both nomination and election, and in estimating the probability of guilt of a person accused of a crime, one may apply the principles of the conjunction of probabilities.

3. Often one needs to distinguish clearly which part of a conjunction he accepts and which part he rejects. Many young people will agree with Perdita that true love persists through affliction.

> *Camillo.* Prosperity's the very bond of love,
> Whose fresh complexion and whose heart together
> Affliction alters.
> *Perdita.*   One of these is true,
> I think affliction may subdue the cheek,
> But not take in the mind.

> —Shakespeare, *The Winter's Tale,* 4.4.584

When King Cymbeline declares him a banished traitor, **Belarius** replies:

> Indeed a banished man;
> I know not how a traitor.
> —Shakespeare, *Cymbeline,* 5.5.319

4. Misunderstandings, even breaking up of friendships, may result from ignoring the rules of conjunction. Example: In a group, someone remarks that Jane is a beautiful, brilliant, honest girl. Jane's friend says she doesn't agree. (She doesn't think Jane is brilliant.) A busybody later tells Jane that her friend said she wasn't honest.

5. In discussing politics, religion, and similar subjects with others, one should remember that the human mind is made for truth and instinctively seeks truth; that it often embraces error along with truth because it fails to distinguish the error that is mixed with the truth; that seldom does the mind embrace what is all error and no truth, and never does it embrace error except under the misapprehension that it is truth. Consequently, it is well in discussion to advert to truths held in common and to point out the errors that are mixed with the truth. A person naturally resents having his convictions attacked as all wrong; he will be much more receptive to the ideas of one who first takes account of what truth he does hold before proceeding to point out errors.

II. Opposition of propositions

A. Propositions are in opposition when they have the same matter, that is, the same subject and the same predicate, but differ in form, that is, in quality, in quantity or modality, or in two of these.

The four relations of opposition exist between the A E I O forms of any given proposition. These forms may be either quantitative or modal. Examples:

Quantitative forms (categorical)

A	All S is P.	All lions are animals.
E	No S is P.	No lions are animals.
I	Some S is P.	Some lions are animals.
O	Some S is not P.	Some lions are not animals.

Modal forms

A	S must be P.	A lion must be an animal.
E	S cannot be P.	A lion cannot be an animal.
I	S may be P.	A lion may be an animal.
O	S may not be P.	A lion may not be an animal.

B. The four relations of opposition and the rules governing them

1. Contradictories: A and O; E and I. Two propositions are opposed as contradictories if they differ both in quality and in either quantity or modality.

There is no middle ground between contradictory propositions (just as there is no middle ground between contradictory terms, e. g., white and non-white). Contradictory propositions represent a clean-cut difference.

Rule 1. Of contradictory propositions, one must be true and the other must be false.

2. Contraries: A and E. Two propositions are opposed as contraries if they differ in quality and if both are either total in quantity or necessary in modality.

There is a middle ground between contrary propositions (just as there is a middle ground between contrary terms, e. g., white and black). Contrary propositions represent the greatest degree of difference.

Rule 2. Of contrary propositions, both cannot be true, but both may be false. Hence, if one is known to be true, the other must be false; but if one is known to be false, the value of the other is unknown.

The fallacy which most frequently occurs in opposition is to assume that of contraries, if one is false the other is true (instead of unknown).

Note. The truth or falsity of a proposition involved in a formal relation is said to be unknown if its value cannot be known from the form alone but is determined by the matter, that is, if it must be learned from a knowledge of its terms.

Analogy: Standard measures may be regarded as empty forms. Examples: Two pints equal one quart. Four quarts equal one gallon. The truth or falsity of these statements can be known from the forms alone without a knowledge of what these measures contain.

These forms may, however, contain various kinds of matter, such as milk, water, mercury, wine, nitric acid, maple syrup. About these one may make various statements. Examples: A quart is healthful. A gallon is sickening. A pint is poisonous. A half-pint is not intoxicating. The truth or falsity of these statements cannot be known from the forms alone, but is determined by the matter, that is, by the content of these forms. Examples: A pint of milk is not poisonous. A pint of nitric acid is poisonous.

3. Sub-contraries: I and O. Two propositions are opposed as sub-contraries if they differ in quality and if both are either partial in quantity or contingent in modality.

Rule 3. Of sub-contrary propositions, both cannot be false, but both may be true. Hence, if one is known to be false, the other must be true; but if one is known to be true, the value of the other is unknown.

4. Subalterns: A and I; E and O. A proposition is subaltern to another if it has the same quality but differs from it either in being partial instead of total or in being contingent instead of necessary.

Strictly speaking, subalterns are not opposed, for they do not differ in quality. Traditionally, this relation has, however, been treated with opposition, for it is present among the A E I O forms of a given proposition.

The normal relation of subject and predicate in an I proposition was stated on page 111 as that of partial inclusion of the subject in the predicate; and that of an O proposition as the exclusion of part of S from P. Both I and O propositions were represented by overlapping Euler's circles; I and O differ in the parts of the circles shaded, indicating the different parts of the subject being talked about.

In the opposition of propositions, however, I and O propositions are to be understood as including also the following (the parts talked about are shaded):

 If it is true that All S is P, it must be true that some of that S is P. Example: All lions are animals. Some lions are animals. (Both are true.)

 If it is true that No S is P, it must be true that some of that S is not P. Example: No lions are elephants. Some lions are not elephants. (Both are true.)

Rule 4. Of subalterns, if the total (or necessary) proposition is true, the partial (or contingent) must be true; but if the former is known to be false, the value of the latter is unknown. Conversely, if the partial (or contingent) proposition is false, the total (or necessary) must be false; but if

the former is known to be true, the value of the latter is unknown.

In categorical forms, the opposition of singular empirical propositions is restricted to contradiction, and this relation is achieved through a difference of quality alone. Example: John is tall. John is not tall.

In modal forms, the opposition of singular empirical propositions includes all four relations. Example:

A John must be courteous.

E John cannot be courteous.

I John may be courteous.

O John may not be courteous.

C. The four relations of opposition are graphically represented by the square of opposition. The lines represent the four relations as numbered:

1. Contradictories: A and O; E and I.
2. Contraries: A and E.
3. Sub-contraries: I and O.
4. Subalterns: A and I; E and O.

Application of the rules of opposition:

To use a familiar analogy, on this square of opposition, the lines between contradictories, AO and EI, represent the only "two-way streets"; for if A is true, O is false, and if O is false, A is true; or if A is false, O is true, and if O is true, A is false; the same holds for the relations of E and I. But all the other lines represent only "one-way streets": AE, IO, AI, EO; thus, if A is true, E is false, but if E is given as false, the value of A is unknown.

When one form is given as either true or false, one can arrive at the value of the other three forms by applying only two of the rules of opposition, namely, that of contradictories and that of contraries. Thus:

Given, A is true; then: O is false, for of contradictories, one must be true and the other must be false (*Rule 1*); E is false, for of contraries both cannot be true(*Rule 2*); I is true (*Rule 1*), for it is the contradictory of E, which we have just shown must be false. (We can, of course, also know that I is true by applying *Rule 4*.)

Given, A is false; then: O is true (*Rule 1*); E is unknown, for of contraries both may be false; I is also unknown, for it is the contradictory of E, and if the truth or falsity of one were known, that of the other could be known from it. (Also according to *Rule 4*, if A is false, I is unknown; that is, it may be either true or false, depending on the terms related.)

In both the following sets of propositions, A is false; but in the one set E is false and I is true, whereas in the other set E is true and I is false. The possibility of having such contrasting results demonstrates that when A is false, the truth or falsity of E and I is determined by the matter, not by the form, for different matter involved in the same formal relation yields different results.

0	A	All roses are red.		0	A	All squares are circles.
0	E	No roses are red.		1	E	No squares are circles.
1	I	Some roses are red.		0	I	Some squares are circles.
1	O	Some roses are not red.		1	O	Some squares are not circles.

Following is a summary of all the other relations involved in the square of opposition:

Given, E is true; then: I is false (*Rule 1*); A is false (*Rule 2*); O is true (*Rules 1* and *4*).

Given, E is false; then: I is true (*Rule 1*); A and O are unknown (*Rules 2, 1,* and *4*).

Given, I is true; then: E is false (*Rule 1*); A and O are unknown (*Rules 2, 1, 3,* and *4*).

Given, I is false; then: E is true (*Rule 1*); A is false (*Rules 2* and *4*); O is true (*Rules 1* and *4*).

Given, O is true; then: A is false (*Rule 1*); E and I are unknown (*Rules 2, 1, 3,* and *4*).

Given, O is false; then: A is true (*Rule* 1); E is false (*Rules 2* and *4*); I is true (*Rules 1* and *3*).

Sometimes a sentence which seems to symbolize but one proposition actually symbolizes a conjunction of two or more propositions. Such a conjunction must be resolved into its constituent simple propositions before it can be expressed in A E I O forms. Example:

Conjunction: All the crew save one were drowned.
Simplification: One of the crew was not drowned.
            The rest of the crew were drowned.

D. The nature of a formal relation

Since opposition is the first formal relation we have studied, and since logic is concerned chiefly with formal relations, it

will be profitable to consider here the essential difference between a formal relation, such as opposition, and a material
relation, such as conjunction.

1. Unlike a conjunction of propositions, which is either true or
   false or probable, a formal relation of propositions, such as
   opposition, is neither true nor false nor probable; it is either
   formally correct or formally incorrect.

2. The basic distinction between a material and a formal relation of propositions is this: The truth or falsity of a conjunction of propositions depends upon the truth or falsity
   of each of the propositions conjoined, and the value of each
   must be ascertained independently by reference to the facts;
   but the truth or falsity of propositions formally related is
   interdependent, and if the value of one proposition is known,
   the value of the others can be ascertained therefrom by ap-
   lying the rules of the formal relation, without a knowledge
   of the terms related or any knowledge of the facts, that is,
   without any material knowledge at all. Thus:
   a. The formal correctness of the opposition of the contradic-
      tory propositions A and O does not determine whether A
      is true or false or whether O is true or false.
   b. But it does determine that if A is true, O must be false,
      and if A is false, O must be true; likewise that if O is
      true, A must be false, and if O is false, A must be true.

3. A material relation holds between any propositions, regardless of their forms, whereas a formal relation holds only
   between propositions having certain forms.

4. A formal relation is really a relation of propositional forms,
   a formula. It holds regardless of what matter, what terms,
   are substituted for the symbols of the formula.

   Analogy: A relation of propositional forms, such as opposition, is analogous to an algebraic formula. The relations
   are correct, regardless of what matter, what numbers are
   substituted for the symbols of the formula.

   Examples: $(x+y)^2 = x^2 + 2xy + y^2$
   $$C = 2\pi R$$

In contrast, a material relation of propositions, such as conjunction, is analogous to an arithmetical equation; the truth
or falsity of every such equation must be checked independently with the facts and is determined altogether by the mat-

ter, not at all by a form, for such an equation is not a formula.

Examples: $3 \times 8 = 2 \times 12$
$$6 \times 3 = 9 \times 2$$

5. A propositional formula, such as that of opposition, eduction, or the syllogism, operates as a rule of assertion thus: If a given proposition having a certain form has a given value, then another proposition related to it by a correct formula must have the value required by the formula.

E. Practical application of opposition:

In *Current History* (March, 1928) are two articles which together constitute a debate entitled "The Pope and the Presidency." The first, entitled "The Case for the Opposition to a Catholic President," is by the Reverend Charles Hillman Fountain, a minister of the Baptist Church. It is answered by Monsignor John A. Ryan, D. D., of the Catholic University of America, in his article entitled "The Catholic Reply to the Opposition." Mr. Fountain charges that since the Catholic Church has anathematized the doctrine of the separation of Church and State, Alfred E. Smith could not possibly be at one and the same time a good President of the United States and a good Catholic, for he maintains that as a good Catholic Mr. Smith would be obliged to work for the union of Church and State in this country. In reply, Father Ryan points out that in anathematizing the doctrine of the separation of Church and State, the Catholic Church has simply declared false a general proposition. The opposition of propositions may be stated as follows:

A Church and State ought always to be separated.
   (Declared false.)
E Church and State ought never to be separated.
I Church and State ought sometimes to be separated.
O Church and State ought sometimes not to be separated.

Applying the rules of opposition, we find that if A is false, O must be true; E and I are unknown; that is, their truth or falsity depends on an investigation of the facts. The point is, writes Father Ryan, that in condemning A as false, the Catholic Church did not, implicitly or otherwise, pronounce E to be true. Therefore neither Alfred E. Smith nor any other Catholic need hold that Church and State ought never to be separated. The fact is that in a country like the United States where there is no unanimity of religious belief, it is right that Church and State be separated, for religious beliefs should not and cannot be forced upon the consciences of men, nor should citizens be required to support financially a religious establishment in opposition to their honest convictions. An investigation of the facts reveals that in this set of propositions E is false and I is true.

If anyone should hold that the Church errs in declaring A false, and if, accordingly, he holds that A is true in principle, he is guilty of the effrontery of pronouncing false in principle the theocracy that God Himself established over the Jews, for the books of Leviticus and Deuteronomy, to say nothing of God's personal rule through the Judges and His reluctance to grant the Jews a king when they insisted on having one, clearly demonstrate that God established union between Church and State among His Chosen People.

III. Eduction

Eduction is the formal process of making explicit all that is implicit in a given proposition. Hence it is not an advance in knowledge. In this it differs radically from deduction, of which the syllogism is the form, for through the syllogism the mind advances to new knowledge. Through eduction, we turn a proposition, as it were, inside out and upside down until we have explored all its content.

Analogy: A lump of pie dough contains no more molecules after it has been rolled out thin than before; but more of them are on the surface and therefore more are visible.

In the following bit of doggerel, an anonymous parodist has expressed a very simple idea with an explicit thoroughness analogous to that of eduction.

HIAWATHA'S MITTENS

He killed the noble Mudjokivis.
Of the skin he made him mittens,
Made them with the fur side inside,
Made them with the skin side outside.
He, to keep the warm side inside,
Put the inside skin side outside;
He, to get the cold side outside,
Put the warm side fur side inside.
That's why he put the fur side inside,
Why he put the skin side outside,
Why he turned them inside outside.

Eduction is a formal process which never involves a change of value. Provided that the eductions are correctly made, if the original proposition is true, the eductions must be true; if the original proposition is false, the eductions must be false.

Eduction employs two processes, obversion and conversion. By applying these two processes alternately, seven eductive forms (their names appear below where they are derived) may be obtained from a general or a total proposition, fewer from a partial or a contingent one.

A. Obversion

1. Rules for obverting a proposition:
   a. Change the quality (determined by the copula).
   b. Substitute for the predicate its contradictory (P′).

2. Warning, to avoid illicit obversion:
   Do not confuse a contradictory modifier of a term with the full contradictory term. Contradictory terms are always dichotomous; they divide all being, not merely a genus. For example, the contradictory of starchy food is not non-starchy food; it is non-starchy-food. Pencils and door knobs and stars are non-starchy-food; they are not non-starchy food, for they are not food at all.

3. Obversion of A E I O forms. Each of these can be obverted.
   SaP is obverted to SeP′. Example: All voters are citizens. No voters are non-citizens. (P′ symbolizes non-P.)
   SeP is obverted to SaP′. Example: No Mohammedans are Christians. All Mohammedans are non-Christians.
   SiP is obverted to SoP′. Example: Some chairs are comfortable. Some chairs are not uncomfortable.
   SoP is obverted to SiP′. Example: Some pupils are not attentive. Some pupils are inattentive.

Drill: Obvert A to E; E to A; I to O; O to I.

4. Principle: If S is included in P, it is certainly excluded from non-P.
   Obversion is an application of the Law of Excluded Middle: Between contradictories there is no middle ground.

5. Practical applications of obversion
   The rhetorical figure named litotes, used extensively in Old English literature and still used widely in modern English and in other literatures, is an application of obversion. It has an important effect on tone. It may be used:

a. To tone down what might appear to be the egotism of a person speaking of his own deeds:
Original: I was successful in that undertaking. (SaP)
Obverse: I was not unsuccessful in that undertaking. (SeP′)

b. To remark more mildly to a person, for instance, upon her friend's vanity:
Original: She is aware of her charms. (SaP)
Obverse: She is not unaware of her charms. (SeP′)

c. As Alexander Pope has well expressed it, to

> Damn with faint praise, assent with civil leer
> And without sneering teach the rest to sneer.
> Willing to wound, and yet afraid to strike,
> Just hint a fault and hesitate dislike.
> —Prologue to the *Satires*

Original: He has acted nobly in these difficult circumstances. (SaP)
Obverse: He has not acted ignobly in these difficult circumstances (SeP′)
Original: I found his book interesting. (SaP)
Obverse: I found his book not uninteresting. (SeP′)

Note: A tragic result of illicit inference (resembling obversion) was recorded in *Time* (March 4, 1946, p. 25). The order "Arrival of combat ships is not to be reported" (to increase security) was misinterpreted to mean also "Non-arrival of combat ships is not to be reported." Accordingly, the acting port director at Tacloban failed to investigate the non-arrival of the *Indianapolis*. The few survivors weltered in the sea for three days before it even occurred to anyone that the ship might be in trouble.

Consider the effect of using litotes in the following examples:

1) *Gloucester.* [*of Edgar*] Let him fly far,
Not in this land shall he remain uncaught.
Shakespeare, *King Lear*, 2.1.58

2) Adam observed, and with his eye the chase
Pursuing, not unmoved to Eve thus spake.
—Milton, *Paradise Lost*, **XI**, 191

3) One of the heavenly host, and by his gait
None of the meanest.   —*Ibid.*, 230

4) Be that as may, my oracles from hence
   Shall be unveiled, far as to lay them bare
   May be not unbefitting thy rude sense.
                          —Dante, "Purgatorio," Canto 33

5) As to courage, the world knows that I don't lack it.
                          —Molíere, *The Misanthrope*, III, i

6) I remained upon the field not wholly discomfited.
                          —Boswell, *The Life of Johnson*

7) My life has been not altogether uneventful.
                          —Winston Churchill

Many writers, particularly those of the Renaissance, have achieved interesting effects by the use of negative and privative terms:

(1) He is unqualitied with very shame.
(2) My death's sad tale may yet undeaf his ear.
(3) A royal king . . . By you unhappied and disfigured clean.
(4) Let me unkiss the oath 'twixt me and thee.
(5) In his meed he's unfellowed.
(6) Lest her beauty . . . unprovide my mind again.
(7) Unshout the noise that banished Marcius.
(8) I have no hope That he's undrowned.
(9) The dateless limit of thy dear exile.
   The hopeless word of 'never to return.'
(10) Tremble, thou wretch, That hast within thee undivulged crimes
    Unwhipped of justice.
                          —Shakespeare

(11) Then who created thee lamenting learn
    When who can uncreate thee thou shalt know.
(12) And of their wonted vigor left them drained,
    Exhausted, spiritless, afflicted, fallen.
                          —Milton

(13) I here unsay all that I have said.—Molíere.
(14) Who can thus . . . having observed, observe again from the same unaffected, unbiased, unbribable, unaffrighted innocence—must always be formidable.—Emerson.
(15) I seemed every night to descend . . . into the chasms and sunless abyss . . . from which it seemed hopeless that I could ever reascend.
                          —De Qunicey

B. Conversion
   1. Rules for converting a proposition:
      a. Reverse the position of the subject and the predicate.
      b. If it is necessary to do so in order to avoid an illicit process, change the quantity (or the modality), and thereby convert by limitation or *per accidens*.
      c. Do not change the quality (determined by the copula).
   2. Warning, to avoid an illicit process in converting:

No term may be distributed in the converse that was undistributed in the proposition from which it was derived.

An illicit process is an attempt to get more out of a proposition than there is in it by using in its full extension a term which in the original proposition was used in only a part of its extension.

Illicit conversion is among the most prolific sources of error to which the mind of man is prone. The fallacies occasioned by it are discussed in Chapter IX.

3. Conversion of A E I O forms. Not every proposition can be converted.

   a. SaP is regularly converted by limitation (that is, by loss of total quantity or of necessary modality) to PiS, in order to avoid an illicit process. Example: All lions are animals. Some animals are lions. PaS cannot ordinarily be correctly derived from SaP, for to attempt this involves an illicit process of P. Thus:

   d   u   In this original proposition, P is undistributed (u),
   S a/P   for it is the predicate of an affirmative proposition.
          /   In this illicit converse, P is distributed (d), for it
   d'   u   has become the subject of a total (or a necessary)
   P a S   proposition. The line drawn from u to d indicates the illicit process.

   b. SaP is correctly converted to PaS, when P is known to be either the definition or the property of S, for then P is distributed through the matter, not through the form (see p. 110). It is the test of definition and of property that these predicates be convertible with the subject (see pp. 91, 111, 112). Examples:

   Definition: Man is a rational animal. A rational animal is a man.

   Property: Man is mirthful. A mirthful being is a man.

   c. SeP is converted simply to PeS, for since an E proposition distributes both S and P, an illicit process cannot occur when the terms are transposed in converting the proposition. Example: No lions are elephants. No elephants are lions.

   d. SiP is converted simply to PiS, for since an I proposition distributes neither S nor P, an illicit process cannot occur when the terms are transposed in converting the proposition. Example: Some roses are red. Some red things are roses.

e. SoP cannot be converted at all, for

  1) To convert it simply would involve an illicit process of S. Thus:

  u d In the original proposition, S is undistributed, for
  S o P it is the subject of a partial (or a contingent) proposition.

  u d In this illicit converse, S is distributed, for it has
  P o S become the predicate of a negative proposition.

  2) It cannot be converted by limitation (as in the case of SaP), for SoP is already partial in quantity (or contingent in modality).

  3) Since conversion never involves a change in quality, there is no possible way validly to convert O.

  It is a fact that often SoP remains true when converted to PoS, but the process is, nevertheless, always formally invalid.

  Example: Some roses are not red. Some red things are not roses.

  Here *roses* is distributed in the converse and is undistributed in the original proposition. Therefore the conversion involves an illicit process of S. That both these propositions are materially true is merely an accident of the matter. Their truth cannot be guaranteed through the formal process; hence the process itself is always invalid, regardless of whether the proposition derived from a true SoP is materially true or false.

  In the following examples the converse proposition is both materially false and formally invalid.

  Categorical: Some animals are not lions. Some lions are not animals.

  Modal: An animal may not be a lion. A lion may not be an animal.

Drill: Convert A to I; E to E; I to I; O not at all.

C. The eductive forms

  1. Seven eductive forms can be derived from SaP and from SeP, and three from SiP and from SoP, by alternately and successively applying the two eductive processes, obversion and conversion; whenever, because of having had to convert

SaP by limitation to SiP, one arrives at SoP to be converted, one can go no further but must return to the original proposition, applying to it the process alternate to that first applied. In these eductions all implications of a given proposition are made explicit.

a. Eductions of SaP

		Process	
Original proposition	SaP	*Process*	All voters are citizens.
Obverse	SeP'	Obversion	No voters are non-citizens.
Partial contrapositive	P'eS	Conversion	No non-citizens are voters.
Full contrapositive	P'aS'	Obversion	All non-citizens are non-voters.
Full inverse	S'iP'	Conversion	Some non-voters are non-citizens.
Partial inverse	S'oP	Obversion	Some non-voters are not citizens.
Converse (of original)	PiS	Conversion	Some citizens are voters.
Obverted converse	PoS'	Obversion	Some citizens are not non-voters.

Consider carefully the exact meaning of each of the propositions above, noting just which persons are being talked about, and which statements you fit into, and which you do not. Euler's circles may prove helpful by graphically showing the content of each of the propositions. This series may remind you of "Hiawatha's Mittens" but it seriously performs the function of expressing all the possible relations between citizens, voters, and the contradictory of each of these terms.

b. Eductions of SeP

		Process	
Original proposition	SeP	*Process*	No Mohammedans are Christians.
Obverse	SaP'	o	All Mohammedans are non-Christians.
Partial contrapositive	P'iS	c	Some non-Christians are Mohammedans.
Full contrapositive	P'oS'	o	Some non-Christians are not non-Mohammedans.
Converse (of original)	PeS	c	No Christians are Mohammedans.
Obverted converse	PaS'	o	All Christians are non-Mohammedans.
Partial inverse	S'iP	c	Some non-Mohammedans are Christians.
Full inverse	S'iP'	o	Some non-Mohammedans are not non-Christians.

c. Eductions of SiP

		Process	
Original proposition	SiP		Some chairs are comfortable.
Obverse	SoP'	o	Some chairs are not uncomfort-able.
Converse (of original)	PiS	c	Some comfortable things are chairs.
Obverted converse	PoS'	o	Some comfortable things are not non-chairs.

d. Eductions of SoP

		Process	
Original proposition	SoP		Some pupils are not attentive.
Obverse	SiP'	o	Some pupils are inattentive.
Partial contrapositive	P'iS	c	Some inattentive beings are pupils.
Full contrapositive	P'oS'	o	Some inattentive beings are not non-pupils.

2. Eductions of SaP when P is known through the matter (for it cannot be known through the form) to be either the definition or a property of S.

Then SaP is throughout the series correctly convertible to PaS (see p. 91); in this case the seven eductions can be derived by one continuous process of alternate conversion and obversion (it does not matter which process is applied first) and if the eduction is carried one step further, the original proposition is again obtained. Example:

		Process	
Original proposition	SaP		All men are rational animals.
Converse	PaS	c	All rational animals are men.
Obverted converse	PeS'	o	No rational animals are non-men.
Partial inverse	S'eP	c	No non-men are rational animals.
Full inverse	S'aP'	o	All non-men are non-rational-animals.
Full contrapositive	P'aS'	c	All non-rational-animals are non-men.
Partial contrapositive	P'eS	o	No non-rational-animals are men.
Obverse (of original)	SeP'	c	No men are non-rational-animals.
Original	SaP	o	All men are rational animals.

D. Supplementary eductions
   1. By added determinants (attributive modifiers)
      a. Formula: S is P; therefore Sa is Pa.
      b. Principle: An added determinant decreases the extension of a term and increases its intension. (See pages 84 f.)

This process of eduction is valid if the added determinant affects S and P to the same degree and in the same respect. The eduction is invalid,

1) If it does not modify them to the same degree. Examples:

   a) Original: Kings are men.
      Invalid: A majority of kings is a majority of men.

   b) Original: An ant is an animal.
      Invalid: A large ant is a large animal.
      Valid: A small ant is a small animal.

2) If it does not modify the terms in the same respect. Examples:
   Original: A contralto is a woman.
   Invalid: A low contralto is a low woman.
   Valid: A blonde contralto is a blonde woman.

2. By omitted determinants

   a. Formula: S is Pa; therefore S is P.

   b. Principle: A subject that is included in a more determined (less extended) predicate is necessarily included in that predicate when it is less determined (more extended). This principle is especially evident when the two predicates are related to the subject as species and genus, or as proximate and remote genera. Examples:

   1) Socrates is a rational animal; therefore Socrates is an animal.

   2) A rattlesnake is a poisonous reptile; therefore a rattlesnake is a reptile.

   Mere grammatical likeness (of words) must not be mistaken for true logical likeness (of terms). The following example may seem to disprove the principle stated above, but the difficulty is only verbal.
   Original: The pauper is a pretended prince.
   Invalid: The pauper is a prince.

   Only verbally do these sentences appear to exemplify the formula S is Pa; therefore S is P. *Pretended prince* does not express the logical term *prince* plus a determinant decreasing its extension; but it expresses an altogether different term which is equivalent to *imposter*, a term which is incompatible with prince and excluded from it, certainly not included in it.

3. By converse relation

   a. Formula: S r1 P; therefore P r2 S. (Here r1 and r2 symbolize copulas with correlative modifiers, not simple copulas.)

   b. Principle: Because relative terms necessarily imply their correlatives, the subject and predicate of a proposition with a relative copula may be transposed if for the relative copula is substituted its correlative.

      1) Action and passion are correlatives. Hence the change in a sentence from the active to the passive verb-form symbolizes eduction by converse relation. Examples:

         a) Original: Aristotle taught (or was the teacher of) Alexander the Great.
Valid inference: Alexander the Great was taught by (or was the pupil of) Aristotle.

         b) Original: Mary saw the sand dunes.
Valid inference: The sand dunes were seen by Mary.

      2) Genus and species are also correlatives which permit this form of conversion.
Original: Lily is a species of flower.
Valid inference: Flower is genus of lily.

      3) Similarly, from propositions stating quantitative relations we may draw inferences by converse relation. Example:
Original: A is greater than B.
Valid inference: B is less than A.

IV. The syllogism

This is the most important of the four relations of propositions, for it is the characteristic form of reasoning. According to the kind of propositions syllogistically related we distinguish four types of syllogism: the simple (usually categorical) syllogism; the hypothetical syllogism; the disjunctive syllogism; the dilemma. These types of syllogism will be studied in succeeding chapters.

V. Summary of the relations of propositions

There are four relations: conjunction, opposition, eduction, the syllogism. Conjunction is a material relation; the others are formal relations. A formal relation is a process of either mediate or immediate inference.

   1. Immediate inference involves only two propositions; it proceeds directly from one to the other without the mediating

function of a third term or of a third proposition. There are three processes of immediate inference: opposition, obversion, and conversion. Eduction is a common name given to the two processes of obversion and conversion.

2. Mediate inference involves three terms in three propositions. Two terms, S and P, are related to each other by virtue of the relation of each to a third term M, which is the medium for relating them.

Analogy: Two rods can be related to each other in length by virtue of the relation of each to a yardstick, which serves as a medium between them.

QUESTIONS AND EXERCISES

1. What is invention? disposition? What does disposition include, in logic? in rhetoric?
2. Name the sixteen logical topics of invention internal to a subject, which Cicero distinguished. What does testimony include?
3. How do the logical topics of invention differ from the rhetorical? Name ten rhetorical topics. Explain how the topics of invention are used in developing paragraphs. What practical use in composition and in reading can you make of the topics of invention?
4. Give an example of the conjunction of two propositions that is explicit; implicit; bare; material. Mention seven relations of material conjunction.
5. Explain the bearing conjunction has on the unity required by rhetoric in the sentence, the paragraph, and the whole composition.
6. Write an original topic sentence. Illustrate five different methods of developing it by composing (and labeling) two sentences for each. Try to have these eleven sentences form one unified coherent paragraph.
7. State the rules of conjunction. Write the table illustrating them.
8. Mention four practical applications of the rules of conjunction.
9. When are propositions in opposition? Illustrate with quantitative categorical A E I O forms; with modal A E I O forms.
10. Which propositional forms are contradictories? contraries? sub-contraries? subalterns? State the rules governing each of these relations.
11. What is meant by saying that the truth or falsity of a proposition involved in a formal relation is formally unknown? Clarify your explanation by an analogy.
12. Which two rules of opposition are most important? Disregard of which one is a frequent occasion of fallacy in argument?
13. Represent the square of opposition; label all its relations. Given, A is true, state the value of each of the three other forms; given, A is false, do the same. Do the same with respect to E; I; O.
14. Is the truth or falsity of propositions materially related independent or interdependent? of propositions formally related? State three other differences between a material and a formal relation. Which relation is like an algebraic formula? Which is like an arithmetical equation?
15. Explain how an argument advanced in the presidential campaign of 1928

illustrates a fallacy which violates the rule for the opposition of contraries.

16. What is the purpose of eduction? Name the two processes of eduction. If the original proposition is false, will eductions correctly derived ever be true?

17. State the rules for obverting. Memorize the drill.

18. State the principle underlying obversion. Can every proposition be obverted? Cite an instance of illicit obversion.

19. Obvert: Sep, SoP; SaP; SiP; PiS'; SaP'; S'eP; PoS; P'eS'; SiP'.

20. Obvert, writing in left margin of your paper the formula of both the original and its obverse:
    (1) Everyone respects men who are honest.
    (2) No college graduate is an uneducated person.
    (3) Many of the workmen are incompetent.
    (4) Only the brave deserve the fair. (See p. 131.)
    (5) All that glitters is not gold. (See p. 108.)
    (6) Dancing is enjoyable.
    (7) The future looks promising.
    (8) All who venture cannot win.
    (9) Swimming is a skill which everyone does not possess.
    (10) Some chairs are not occupied.

21. What is litotes? State three practical uses of this form of obversion. Note examples in your reading.

22. Each of the following examples of litotes may be regarded as the obverse of an original proposition which you may recover by obverting again. In some instances the contrary of the predicate may be substituted instead of the contradictory, for the sake of a better style. Compare the two forms in literary effect.
    (1) Composing their travailed spirits with the . . . harmonies of music . . . would not be unexpedient after meat.—Milton, "Of Education."
    (2) Thus was the first day even and morn:
        Nor passed uncelebrated, nor unsung
        By the celestial choirs.—Milton, *Paradise Lost*, VII, 252.
    (3) If you do that, you do not do a little.—Molière, *The Misanthrope*, I, i.
    (4) I think that a friend who is zealous, and of my quality, too, is certainly not to be rejected.—*Ibid.*, I, ii
    (5) You have that regard for people which by no means is agreeable to me.
        —*Ibid.*, II, iii
    (6) Your prudery and your violent zeal were not by any means cited as a good model.—*Ibid.*, III, v

23. State the rules for converting. Memorize the drill. Can every proposition be converted? What is an illicit process?

24. Convert: SiP; P'eS; PaS; S'eP; PiS'; SaP; P'eS'; SaP; PeS'.

25. Convert, writing in left margin of your paper the formula of both the original and its converse:
    (1) Hydrogen is inflammable.
    (2) Planets are not stars.
    (3) Milk may be sour.
    (4) The whole is equal to the sum of its parts.
    (5) Man is an animal capable of cooking his food.
    (6) A plow is a capital good.

(7) All odd numbers are numbers not evenly divisible by two.

(8) Some berries are poisonous.

(9) John caught the ball.

(10) Chicago is west of New York.

26. Derive and name all the eductive forms of SaP; SeP; SiP; SoP; SaP, when P is known to be either the definition or a property of S.

27. State the formula, the principle, and an example of eduction by: added determinants; omitted determinants; converse relation. Name three bases of eduction by converse relation. State the relation between the following propositions:

(1) To live, for a rational creature, is to know and to love.

(2) To live most perfectly is to know most intimately and to love most intensely the Supreme Object of knowledge and love.

—Edward Leen, *Why the Cross?*

(3) Power corrupts, and absolute power corrupts absolutely.—Lord Acton.

28. Name the four relations of propositions. Which are formal relations? material?

29. How does mediate differ from immediate inference? Which processes of inference are immediate? mediate?

30. Can we proceed logically from the proposition "All good students deserve praise" to "All who deserve praise are good students"? Explain.

31. The simplest proposition which must be established to disprove another is its contradictory. Apply this principle to the following:

(1) All men prefer blondes.

(2) No D student was accepted.

(3) Not all ivy is poisonous.

(4) Helen is the best tennis player in America.

(5) No man but a barbarian would have done this. (See p. 131.)

32. In the following, state the logical process by which each proposition is derived from the one that precedes it, and point out precisely where an error is introduced:

Granted that it is true that____All beautiful women are mortal,

Then _____No beautiful women are immortal,

And _____No immortal beings are beautiful women.

Hence it is false that _____Some immortal beings are beautiful women.

And that _____Some immortal beings are not unbeautiful women.

But if this is false, it must be

    true that _____All immortal beings are unbeautiful women.

33. By what logical process do we pass from each of the following propositions to the succeeding one? At the left of each proposition, write the formula: at the right, name the process.

a. All metals are elements.

b. No metals are non-elements.

c. No non-elements are metals.

d. All non-elements are non-metals.

e. All metals are elements.

f. Some elements are metals.

g. Some metals are elements.—Jevons

CHAPTER VII

The Simple Syllogism

I. The syllogism

  A. Definition: The syllogism is the act of reasoning by which the mind perceives that from the relation of two propositions (called premises) having one term in common there necessarily emerges a new, third proposition (called the conclusion) in which the common term, called the middle term (M), does not appear. Example:

    A bat is a mammal.
    No bird is a mammal.
  ∴ A bat is not a bird.

Since all bats are included in mammals and all mammals are excluded from birds, all bats must be excluded from birds. It is by virtue of the relation of each of the terms bat and bird to the mediating term mammal, common to both premises, that their relation to each other is understood and expressed in the conclusion as one of total exclusion from each other.

A premise is a proposition so related to another proposition by means of a common term that from their conjunction a new proposition, the conclusion, necessarily follows.

The syllogism is a formal relation of three terms in three propositions. Each term occurs twice: the middle term, in each premise; each of the other terms, in one premise and in the conclusion.

Every premise is a proposition; but not every proposition is a premise. A proposition becomes a premise by being joined to another proposition which has one term in common with it; the rules governing the valid conjunction of premises are stated below. The conclusion, a new truth, is implicit in the conjunction of the premises; it is not implicit in either one of them alone. Hence the syllogism results in an advance in knowledge achieved by the conjunction of the premises.

Analogy: Every husband is a man, but not every man is a husband. A man becomes a husband by being joined to a wife through a common bond of mutual love. The child, a new being, owes its existence to both parents, not to one alone.

The syllogism is the very formula of reasoning. It is a relation of propositional forms. The syllogism itself is neither true nor false; it is correct or incorrect. In a correct syllogism the truth or falsity of its propositions is interdependent and can be ascertained from the formula. An incorrect syllogism is one whose conclusion does not follow from its premises.

B. Matter and form of the syllogism

1. The matter of the syllogism consists of its three propositions relating its three terms (minor, major, middle).

To analyze a syllogism, we must begin with the conclusion:

a. S, the minor term of a syllogism, is the subject of the conclusion. P, the major term, is the predicate of the conclusion.

The conclusion is always symbolized S — P (with a, e, i, or o inserted in the space left blank).

b. The minor premise is that one which contains the minor term S and the middle term M. M is the term present in both premises but not in the conclusion.

c. The major premise is that one which contains the major term P and the middle term M.

2. The form of the syllogism is the logical necessity with which the conclusion follows from the premises by virtue of their correct relation, which is achieved by a combination of figure and mood (explained below).

C. The principle on which syllogistic reasoning is based (*Dictum de omni et nullo*):

Whatever is affirmed of a logical whole must be affirmed of the parts of that whole; whatever is denied of a logical whole must be denied of the parts of that whole.

This means that if P is affirmed of M, it must be affirmed of S, which is a part of M; if P is denied of M, it must be denied of S, which is a part of M (or, less frequently, if P is affirmed of M and M is denied of S, P must be denied of S).

Another way of stating the relation is this: If S is included in M, and M is included in P, S must be included in P; if S is included in M, and M is excluded from P, or if S is excluded from M, and M is included in P, S must be excluded from P. These relations can be made clearer by means of Euler's circles.

Hence the function of the middle term, the logical whole, is, as it were, to draw the meaning out of the major term and transmit it to the minor. It is a mediating term, which having served in the premises as a means of comparison, is dropped from the conclusion.

D. General rules of the syllogism and formal fallacies resulting from their violation

Rule 1. A syllogism must contain three and only three terms. Fallacy resulting from violating this rule: Four terms.

Rule 2. A syllogism must contain three and only three propositions. Fallacy: Four propositions.

Rule 3. The middle term must be distributed in at least one of the premises (because it must serve as the logical whole on which the principle of syllogistic reasoning is based). Fallacy: Undistributed middle term.

Rule 4. No term may be distributed in the conclusion which was undistributed in its own premise. Fallacy: Illicit process of of the major term or of the minor term.

> *Note.* A term that is distributed in its premise may, however, be undistributed in the conclusion, for it is not an illicit process to take out of something less than there is in it.

> There cannot be an illicit process of the middle term, for the two premises are independent; one premise is not derived from the other, as the conclusion is derived from the two premises.

Rule 5. From two negative premises no conclusion can be drawn. (One cannot infer a relation between two given terms unless at least one of them is related to a common, third term; this is the very principle on which syllogistic reasoning is based.) Fallacy: Two negative premises.

Rule 6. If one premise is negative, the conclusion must be negative. Conversely, in order to prove a negative conclusion, one premise must be negative. (If one term is included in the middle term, and the other is excluded from it, the two terms in the conclusion must accordingly be excluded from each other.)

Rule 7. From two partial or singular (or contingent) premises, no conclusion can be drawn. (This is a corollary of *Rules 3, 5,* and *6.*) Fallacy: Two partial (or contingent) premises.

Rule 8. If one premise is partial, the conclusion must be partial. (This is a corollary of *Rules 3* and *4.*)

Rule 9. If one or both premises are contingent, the conclu-conclusion must be contingent. In order to prove a necessary conclusion, both premises must be necessary in modality.

Rule 10. If one or both premises are empirical, the conclusion must be empirical. In order to prove a general conclusion, both premises must be general propositions.

Note. The ordinary man expresses the logic of the above rules in these homely axioms:

> You can't get blood out of a turnip. (This is related to *Rule 4*. To try to get out of something what is not in it or more than what is in it is to attempt an illicit process.)

> A chain is as strong as its weakest link. (This is related to *Rules 6, 8, 9* and *10*.)

Two of the general rules of the syllogism are concerned with its matter (*1* and *2*); two with distribution, the most important consideration (*3* and *4*); two with quality (*5* and *6*); two with quantity (*7* and *8*); two with modality (*7* and *9*); one with the reference to reality, to essence or to the individual (*10*).

E. Mood

The A, E, I, or O forms of its three component propositions constitute the mood of a syllogism.

The mood is designated by these letters placed in a definite, conventional order. We shall adopt this order: the minor premise, the major premise, the conclusion.

Because there are four propositional forms, A, E, I, and O, there are sixteen possible combinations of premises, namely: AA, AE, AI, AO; EA, EE, EI, EO; IA, IE, II, IO; OA, OE, OI, OO.

Rule 5, forbidding two negative premises, requires the elimination of four of these combinations. *Rule 7*, forbidding two partial (or contingent) premises requires the elimination of three more (OO is eliminated on both counts). We shall discover later that an eighth combination, EI, must be eliminated because, although it violates none of the general rules, it conforms to none of the special rules (stated on pages 170-172).

There remain eight valid combinations of premises. We can determine whether the conclusion derived from each of these combinations will be A, E, I, or O by applying *Rules 6* and *8*. Thus: AAA, AEE, AII, AOO; EAE, EIO; IAI, IEO; OAO. Sometimes, to avoid a fallacy, the conclusion is partial (or contingent); thus: AAI, AEO, EAO.

F. Figure

The figure of a syllogism is determined by the position of the middle term, in the premises. Figure and mood together constitute the form of a syllogism, that is, the logical necessity by which the conclusion must follow from the premises.

There are four possible positions for the middle term and consequently there are four figures:

Figure I	Figure II	Figure III	Figure IV
S — M	S — M	M — S	M — S
M — P	P — M	M — P	P — M
S — P	S — P	S — P	S — P

It is of no consequence whether the major premise is placed first or second; the figure and the rules of the figure remain the same. The first figure is that in which the middle term is the predicate of the minor premise and the subject of the major; the second figure is that in which the middle term is the predicate of both premises; the third, that in which it is the subject of both; the fourth, that in which it is the subject of the minor premise and the predicate of the major.

G. To determine the validity of a syllogism, merely test it by the general rules, particularly those of distribution.

Proceed as follows, and observe the examples below:

1. Find the conclusion, and write S over its subject, P over its predicate.

2. Write S and P over the same terms where they appear in the premises.

3. Write M over the term which appears in both premises but not in the conclusion.

4. At the side of each of the three propositions write its formula. The three together constitute the form of the syllogism, showing its mood and figure. At the right of the formula, name the figure and mood.

5. Mark the distribution of terms in accordance with the form of each proposition (but if one proposition is a definition, either by genus and differentia or by property, write *def.* over its predicate to indicate that it is distributed through its matter). Notice (1) whether the middle term is distributed in at least one premise, (2) whether either P or S is distributed in the conclusion, but undistributed in its premise. Draw a line, as in the examples below, to indicate any error in distribution. (Always do this in your exercises, although in the later examples below, the line is not drawn.)

6. Test the formula further to see whether there are (1) two

negative premises, (2) two partial (or contingent) premises, (3) four terms, (4) four propositions.

7. If no fallacy is discovered, write *Valid* at the right; if one is discovered, write *Invalid*, and name the fallacy; if there are two or more fallacies, name each. Examples:

<pre>
              S   M   u   d
(1) Some salesmen are not polite.   S o M Figure II
        P   M   d   u
    All true gentlemen are polite.   P a M Mood O A O
        S   P   u   d
  ∴.Some salesmen are not true gentle- S o P Valid
      men.

        M   P   d   u
(2) All oblongs are rectangles.   M a P Figure I
        S   M   d   d Mood E A E
    No squares are oblongs.   S e M Invalid: Illicit proc-
        S   P   d   d   ess of the major
  ∴.No squares are rectangles.   S e P   term

        M   S   d def. Figure III
(3) All men are capable of mirth.   M a S Mood A A A
        M   P   d   u Valid: Illicit process
    All men are mortal.   M a P   of the minor term
        S   P   d   u is avoided through
  ∴.All mirthful beings are mortal.   S a P   definition

        P   M   d   d
(4) No basketball team is a football   P e M Figure IV
      team.
        M   S   u   d Mood O E O
    Some football teams are not good   M o S Invalid: Two nega-
      losers.   tive premises
        S   P   u   d
  ∴. Some good losers are not basket- S o P
      ball teams.
</pre>

II. The enthymeme

A. An enthymeme is a syllogism logically abridged by the omission of one proposition, either the major premise, the minor premise, or the conclusion. It contains three terms and can be expanded into a full syllogism.

An enthymeme is to be distinguished from a syllogism logically complete but grammatically abridged. Example: Climbing the Alps is an undertaking dangerous but fascinating. Therefore some fascinating undertakings are dangerous.

In this logically complete syllogism the minor premise is only grammatically abridged, and the rules of grammar suffice for the expansion which must be made before its validity can be determined. Only one expansion can or need be made, for, if the sentence is analyzed or diagramed, it is perfectly clear that *Climbing the Alps* is the subject of the minor premise (as well as of the major) and that *a fascinating undertaking* is its predicate. The formula of the syllogism is MaP, MaS, SiP; it is in Figure III, Mood A A I, and it is valid.

In an enthymeme, the omitted proposition is logically abridged, because there is no rule of grammar or of logic to determine the position of its terms in the expansion which must be made before the validity of the enthymeme can be determined. Example: An oak is a plant, because it is a tree.

B. Rules for determining the validity of an enthymeme

   1. Find the conclusion. Clues: (1) *because, for* or *since* introduces a premise (a cause, of which the conclusion is the effect,) and therefore the other proposition is the conclusion; (2) *therefore, consequently,* or *accordingly* introduces the conclusion; (3) *and* or *but* connects two premises and indicates that the proposition omitted is the conclusion.

   2. Write S above the subject of the conclusion and P above its predicate. One of these terms will appear with M in the other proposition given (if the enthymeme is of the usual type with the conclusion and one premise stated). Mark both terms in the premise given. Substitute for pronouns the nouns for which they stand.

   3. Since there is no rule of logic or of grammar to determine the position of the terms in the missing proposition, that proposition may be stated in either of two ways. Hence there are two expansions possible, in two different figures.

   4. *Principles*: (1) If an enthymeme is valid and true in one expansion, it is a valid and true enthymeme, regardless of whether it is valid and true in the other expansion. (2) If an enthymeme is found to be invalid or to have a false premise in the first expansion, it is necessary to expand it in the alternate figure in order to be certain whether it is a valid and true enthymeme or not; but if it is found valid and true in the first expansion, it need not be expanded both ways. Examples:

(1) An oak is a plant, because it is a tree.

Expansion a.

```
       S        M     d    u
  An oak is a tree.   S a M   Figure I
       M        P     d    u
  A tree is a plant.  M a P   Mood A A A
       S        P     d    u
∴ An oak is a plant.  S a P   Valid
```

Since this enthymeme thus expanded into a full syllogism is valid and the premises are true, it need not be
expanded in the alternate figure. But if it is, it is found
to be invalid in Figure II, and it also has one premise
false. It must be clearly understood, however, that an
enthymeme is a good, sound argument, if it is valid and
and true in *one* of its possible expansions. It cannot be
pronounced an erroneous argument unless it has an error
in *both* expansions.

Expansion b.

S	M	d	u	Figure II
An oak is a tree.	S a M			Mood A A A
P	M	d	u	Invalid: Undistrib-
All plants are trees.	P a M			uted middle term.
S	P	d	u	Major premise
An oak is a plant.	S a P			false.

(2) These shoes will not hurt your feet, because they are
not too short. (The major premise is omitted.)

Expansion a.

S	M	d	d	
These shoes are not too short.	S e M			Figure I
M	P	d	u	Mood E A E
Shoes that are too short hurt the feet.	M a P			
S	P	d	d	Invalid: Illicit proc-
∴ These shoes will not hurt your feet.	S e P			ess of the major term

Expansion b.

S	M	d	d	Figure II
These shoes are not too short.	S e M			
P	M	d	u	Mood E A E
Shoes that hurt the feet are too short.	P a M			
S	P	d	d	
These shoes will not hurt your feet.	S e P			Formally valid

Although expansion *b* is formally valid, the major premise is false. It is true that shoes that are too short hurt
the feet, but it is not true that all shoes that hurt the
feet are too short, for they may hurt the feet because
they are too narrow, or for other reasons. An A proposition is not correctly convertible to A unless it is a
definition, and this A proposition is not a definition. This
enthymeme is an erroneous argument because there is
an error in both expansions.

(3) Blessed are the clean of heart, for they shall see God.

The conclusion is stated in an abnormal word order, with the predicate (a participle or adjective) first, for emphasis. The natural expansion is as follows:

			d	u	
S		M			
The clean of heart shall see God.			S a M		Figure I
M		P	d	u	
Those who shall see God are blessed.			M a P		Mood A A A
S		P	d	u	
∴ The clean of heart are blessed.			S a P		Valid

Since this enthymeme is valid in this expansion, it is not necessary to expand it in the second figure.

(4) That is too good to be true.

In this sentence there are three terms and two propositions. (For the sake of saving space, the terms and the distribution are not marked in some of the expansions that follow.) Expansion:

That is too good.	S a M Figure I
Whatever is too good cannot be true.	M a P Mood A A A
∴ That cannot be true.	S a P Formally valid

Although this syllogism is formally valid, both premises are false. Nothing can be literally and absolutely too good; if, however, *too good* be taken to mean very good, the minor premise can be accepted as true. But only a confirmed cynic could admit the major premise as true, for the greatest of all goods, the Beatific Vision, is true. Nonetheless, this enthymeme is repeated glibly by many who would deny the implicit major premise if they adverted to it explicitly.

(5) You are a thief, and a thief ought to be behind bars.

In this enthymeme, the omitted proposition is the conclusion. Expansion:

You are a thief.	S a M Figure I
A thief ought to be behind bars.	M a P Mood A A A
∴ You ought to be behind bars.	S a P Valid

(6) All that glitters is not gold, for diamonds are not gold.

In this enthymeme, the omitted proposition is the minor premise. Expansion:

			d	u	
M	S				
Diamonds glitter.			M a S		Figure III
M		P	d	d	
Diamonds are not gold.			M e P		Mood A E O
S		P	u	d	
∴ All that glitters is not gold.			S o P		Valid

(7) A reward is an incentive to effort, for people desire to win it.

This enthymeme illustrates the fact that the grammatical expression frequently obscures logical relations. Restatement is necessary to clarify them. Be particularly careful where there is a direct object. This usually requires conversion to the passive voice. By this means the direct object can be extricated from other terms with which it is mixed and can be placed as an unconfused term on one side of the copula. Unless you can discern logical relations as they are actually expressed in daily life, your study of logic is not really practical. Seldom do people adhere to strict logical forms of expression. Expansion:

A reward is something people desire to win.	S a M	Figure I
What people desire to win is an incentive to effort.	M a P	Mood A A A
∴ A reward is an incentive to effort.	S a P	Valid

(8) No man will take counsel. Every man will take money. Therefore money is better than counsel.

This facetious argument of Jonathan Swift, in which at least the first proposition is false, is really an enthymeme. It contains a materially modified copula instead of a simple copula. The reasoning is not precisely syllogistic, but rests on a substitution of terms. In this particular example, it is necessary to convert two of the propositions given, in order to form the minor premise. Expansion:

What every man will take is better than what no man will take.	M a P	Figure I
Money is what every man will take and counsel is what no man will take.	S a M	Mood A A A
∴ Money is better than counsel.	S a P	Valid

(9) Dear Dad: I must have ten dollars, because I want a new hat.

This sentence requires expansion into two syllogisms. Expansion:

A new hat is something I want.	S a M	Figure I
Whatever I want I must have.	M a P	Mood A A A
∴ A new hat is something I must have.	S a P	Valid
Ten dollars is needed for a new hat.	S a M	Figure I
What is needed for a new hat is something I must have.	M a P	Mood A A A
∴ Ten dollars is something I must have.	S a P	Valid

These two syllogisms are formally valid. If the suppressed major premise of the first syllogism were made explicit, however, its truth as a principle might be questioned by father, and the. desired ten dollars might not be forthcoming. It may be noted that if the reason stated were "I need a new hat," the major premise would become acceptable.

(10) A whale is not a fish, for it has not scales and gills, and it nourishes its young with milk.

This is a double enthymeme; the same conclusion is reached from two different sets of premises. Expansion:

A whale has not scales and gills.	S e M	Figure II
A fish has scales and gills.	P a M	Mood E A E
∴ A whale is not a fish.	S e P	Valid

Note. If this syllogism is constructed in Figure I by stating the major premise MaP, an illicit process of the major term would not be present, for having both scales and gills is a property of fish; therefore both terms are distributed, the one through the form, the other through the matter.

A whale nourishes its young with milk.	S a M	Figure II
A fish does not nourish its young with milk.	P e M	Mood A E E
∴ A whale is not a fish.	S e P	Valid

(11) The following is a quintuple enthymeme, because one and the same conclusion is drawn from five different sets of premises.

While the paragraph clearly illustrates this logical structure, it also illustrates the rhetorical principle of variety: in diction, in sentence structure and sentence length, in rhythm, in introducing a Biblical allusion and some emphatic repetition, in first naming together those who hold the third and fourth reasons, then giving the reasons they hold, and finally in substituting the contrary, the abstract, and the negative in stating them.

There is a chorus of voices . . . raised in favor of the doctrine . . . that everybody must be educated. The politicians tell us, "You must educate the masses because they are going to be masters." The clergy join in the cry for education, for they affirm that the people are drifting away from church and chapel into the broadest infidelity. The manufacturers and the capitalists swell the chorus lustily. They declare that ignorance makes bad workmen; that England will soon be unable to turn out cotton goods, or steam engines, cheaper than other people;

and then, Ichabod! Ichabod! the glory will be departed from us. And a few voices are lifted up in favor of the doctrine that the masses should be educated because they are men and women with unlimited capacities of being, doing, and suffering, and that it is as true now, as ever it was, that the people perish for lack of knowledge.

—Thomas H. Huxley, *A Liberal Education*

It is obvious that Huxley considers the last reason the best.

C. The enthymeme has been given careful consideration because of its great practical importance.

   1. In the enthymeme one proposition, most often the major premise, is merely implied, not explicit; and therefore it is more likely to be carelessly assumed as true, without examination, and thereby to become a source of error and fallacious reasoning.

   2. The enthymeme is the form of reasoning which we constantly employ in our thinking, conversation, and writing, and that which we should notice in our reading and listening. Logic is really practical when it is thus habitually used as a tool in daily life.

   3. The enthymeme is used extensively in exposition and in debate. Whenever the three, four, or any number of reasons for an event in history are given, they constitute a multiple enthymeme—triple, quadruple, etc. The formal brief for a debate is a series of interlinked enthymemes: each main point states a conclusion, and the subheads, introduced by *for*, are the reasons which support it. When the main points have been established and are summarized, the reasoning moves forward to the final conclusion, as in the epicheirema, discussed below.

III. The sorites

A sorites is a chain of enthymemes or abridged syllogisms, in which the conclusion of one syllogism becomes a premise of the next; one premise of every syllogism but the first and the conclusion of all but the last are unexpressed, that is, merely implicit.

There are two types of sorites: (1) that in which the conclusion of one syllogism becomes the major premise of the next; (2) that in which it becomes the minor premise of the next.

Although it is possible to construct valid sorites in each of the four figures and to combine syllogisms of different figures in one sorites, we shall consider only the two traditional types in Figure I, the Aristotelian sorites and the Goclenian sorites, both of formally unlimited length. They are the only forms likely to be actually used in our reasoning.

The relationships within these two kinds of sorites and the difference between them can be graphically represented by Euler's circles.

The formal unity of each of these sorites is emphasized by regarding it as a syllogism in Figure I with many middle terms, thus:

Aristotelian sorites

Socrates is a man.	$S \quad a\, M^1$
A man is an animal.	$M^1 a\, M^2$
An animal is an organism.	$M^2 a\, M^3$
An organism is a body.	$M^3 a\, M^4$
A body is a substance.	$M^4 a\, M^5$
Therefore Socrates is a substance.	$S \quad a\, P$

Goclenian sorites

A body is a substance.	$M^1 a\, P$
An organism is a body.	$M^2 a\, M^1$
An animal is an organism.	$M^3 a\, M^2$
A man is an animal.	$M^4 a\, M^3$
Socrates is a man.	$S \quad a\, M^4$
Therefore Socrates is a substance.	$S \quad a\, P$

A sorites of six propositions is expanded to one of twelve propositions (four syllogisms) by making explicit the suppressed premises and conclusions of each of the syllogisms.

Aristotelian sorites expanded

Socrates is a man.	$S \quad a\, M^1$
Man is an animal.	$M^1 a\, M^2$
∴Socrates is an animal	$S \quad a\, M^2$

Socrates is an animal.	$S \quad a\, M^2$
An animal is an organism.	$M^2 a\, M^3$
∴Socrates is an organism.	$S \quad a\, M^3$

Socrates is an organism.	$S \quad a\, M^3$
An organism is a body.	$M^3 a\, M^4$
∴Socrates is a body.	$S \quad a\, M^4$

Socrates is a body.	S	a	M^4
A body is a substance.	M^4	a	P
∴Socrates is a substance.	S		a P

Goclenian sorites expanded

A body is a substance.	M^1	a	P
An organism is a body.	M^2	a	M^1
∴An organism is a substance.	M^2	a	P

An organism is a substance.	M^2	a	P
An animal is an organism.	M^3	a	M^2
∴An animal is a substance.	M^3	a	P

An animal is a substance.	M^3	a	P
A man is an animal.	M^4	a	M^3
∴A man is a substance.	M^4	a	P

A man is a substance.	M^4	a	P
Socrates is a man.	S		a M^4
∴Socrates is a substance.	S		a P

A. In the Aristotelian sorites, the first proposition is the minor premise of its syllogism and all the rest are major premises, except the last, which is a conclusion; and the omitted conclusion in each syllogism becomes the minor premise of the following syllogism.

Rule a. Only one premise, the last, may be negative. (Otherwise there will be an illicit process of the major term.)

Rule b. Only one premise, the first (the minor), may be partial, contingent, or singular. (Figure I requires that the minor premise be affirmative; it may be partial or contingent.)

B. In the Goclenian sorites, the first proposition is the major premise of its syllogism and all the rest are minor premises, except the last which is a conclusion, and the omitted conclusion in each syllogism becomes the major premise of the following syllogism.

Rule a. Only one premise, the first, may be negative. (Otherwise there will be an illicit process of the major term.)

Rule b. Only one premise, the last (the minor), may be partial, contingent, or singular. (The other propositions are major premises and must be total or necessary in Figure I.)

The Aristotelian sorites is more important than the Goclenian, for it represents a more natural movement of the mind and is more often used.

IV. The epicheirema

An epicheirema, like a sorites, is an abridged polysyllogism; but unlike a sorites, it is of formally limited length, and the movement of thought is partly backward and partly forward.

A. An epicheirema is an abridged polysyllogism combining any figures, at least one of whose premises is an enthymeme. If both premises are enthymemes, the epicheirema is double; if only one, it is single.

1. Example of a single epicheirema:

Beefsteak (that is eaten) is not stored in the body, because it is protein.

Food that is not stored in the body is not fattening.

∴.Beefsteak is not fattening.

In dealing with negatives, it is very important to remember that the negative may be placed either in the copula or in the term; but it is never permissible to place the negative in the copula in one premise and in the middle term in the other, for this would create four terms: M, M′, S, and P. To make clear that a *term* is negative, it is often necessary to insert a word after the copula. If the enthymeme which is the minor premise in this epicheirema stood alone, the implied major premise "Protein is not stored in the body" would normally be treated as an E proposition. But since the middle term in the major premise of the epicheirema is negative, it is not only permissible but necessary to treat this as an A proposition, as in the following expansion:

Beefsteak is protein.   S a M   Figure I
Protein is food that is not stored
in the body.   M a P   Mood A A A
∴.Beefsteak is food that is not
stored in the body.   S a P   Valid

Beefsteak is food that is not
stored in the body.   S a M   Figure I
Food that is not stored in the
body is not fattening.   M e P   Mood A E E
∴.Beefsteak is not fattening.   S e P   Valid

Note. Beefsteak is not pure protein, and over 50% of protein is converted in the body to carbohydrates; but beefsteak is nonetheless among the least fattening of nourishing foods.

2. Example of a double epicheirema:

These stones are not diamonds, for they do not cut glass. The stolen gems are undoubtedly diamonds, for they were pronounced such by the world's greatest diamond experts.
∴ These stones are not the stolen gems.

Expanding the two enthymemes, we have in this epicheirema three complete syllogisms (the maximum number), the conclusions of the first two furnishing the premises of the third. (To save space, the distribution of terms is not marked here.)

(1) These stones do not cut glass. S e M Figure II
     Diamonds do cut glass.   P a M Mood E A E
∴ These stones are not diamonds. S e P Valid

(2) The stolen gems were pronounced diamonds by the world's greatest diamond experts.   S a M Figure I
     Stones pronounced diamonds by the world's greatest diamond experts are undoubtedly diamonds.   M a P Mood A A A
∴ The stolen gems are undoubtedly diamonds.   S a P Valid

(3) These stones are not diamonds. S e M Figure II
     The stolen gems are undoubtedly diamonds. P a M Mood E A E
∴ These stones are not the stolen gems. S e P Valid

The double epicheirema is the five-part form of argument which Cicero particularly admired and used in his orations. The five parts are: (1) the major premise; (2) the proof of the major; (3) the minor premise; (4) the proof of the minor; (5) the conclusion. In its rhetorical dress, this form of argument was elaborately illustrated and thereby considerably amplified.

A multiple enthymeme differs from an epicheirema in having only one conclusion but stating many reasons that support it. (See page 157.) A single epicheirema has two conclusions, and a double epicheirema has three, for the conclusions of its two enthymemes become premises which lead to a third conclusion.

B. Transformation of a sorites into an epicheirema—a comparison of structure

   1. A sorites not exceeding five propositions may be transformed into a double epicheirema. Example:

S   M²   S   M¹

Socrates is an animal, because he is a man.

M²   P   M²   M³

An animal is a body, because it is an organism.

S   P

∴ Socrates is a body.

The structure of this epicheirema, when expanded, is as follows:

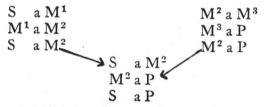

The conclusion of the first syllogism becomes the minor premise of the last.

The conclusion of the second syllogism becomes the major premise of the last.

Compare this with the structure of the sorites on page 159.

   2. An epicheirema may likewise be transformed into a sorites.

V. Analogical inference or argument from example

This is a form of inference based on a similitude. The conclusion from an analogical inference can be only probable. If it is proved to be certain, the argument ceases to be analogical.

Analogy has been used extensively throughout this book. It is common in poetry and in both literary and scientific prose. Examples of analogies commonly used are the ship of state, the body politic, etc.

Analogy is a mode of inference which has pointed the way to many of the discoveries of science. For example, Benjamin Franklin noted the similarity between sparks from an electrical machine and streaks of lightning and hazarded the guess, a tentative conclusion from the analogy, that lightning is electricity. He reasoned thus:

S1		P	Formula

Sparks from an electrical machine are electrical
  discharges, S^1 is P, for

S1   M

for they are characterized by rapid motion and   it is M.
  conductivity.

S2   S1

Lightning resembles these sparks in rapid mo- S^2 resembles S^1 in

M

tion and conductivity.   M.

S2   P

∴ Lightning is probably an electrical discharge.   ∴ S^2 is probably P.

In 1749, Franklin flew his kite and found that lightning was conductible. The lightning rod was a practical result of this experiment; it conducts the electrical discharge to the ground where it does no harm.

The worth of an analogical inference depends upon the importance of the resemblances rather than upon the number of resemblances. The validity of the argument requires that the point of resemblance M be probably a property resulting from the nature P and be not the differentia of S^1. As Aristotle has remarked, the argument from example is an inference, not from the logical whole to its parts (deduction), but from part to part when both fall under a common genus (M) but one of the two (S^1) is better known to us than the other (S^2).

VI. Mediated opposition

A. Mediated opposition is the opposition between two propositions which together contain three terms, one term being common to both. Example:

The witness is lying.

The witness is telling the truth.

Mediated opposition probably occurs more frequently in disputes than immediate opposition does. Immediate opposition would oppose to the first proposition, in the example given above, its contradictory: The witness is not lying.

Mediated opposition combines the rules of opposition with the rules of the syllogism. Since two propositions mediately opposed have three terms, they can be formed into a syllogism, which, combined with immediate opposition, clearly expresses the relations of all the propositions involved.

Let X symbolize the minor premise, Y the major premise, and Z the conclusion of a syllogism. Let X' symbolize the contradictory of X, and Z', of Z. Illustration:

X The witness is lying.	X′ The witness is not lying.
Y Whoever lies does not tell the truth.	
Z The witness is not telling the truth.	Z′ The witness is telling the truth.

B. Rules determining the validity of mediated opposition

1. The syllogism involved in relating the propositions mediately opposed must be formally correct.
2. The third proposition (Y) which serves to establish mediated opposition between two others must be materially true.
   Fallacy resulting from violation of these rules: illicit, illusory, or merely seeming mediated opposition.

C. The relations of mediated opposition

These can be understood by applying the rules of mediated opposition to the illustration above.

1. Provided that Y is materially true, X and Z′ are correctly opposed as genuine mediated contraries, and both cannot be true. (Compare the rule for immediate contraries, p. 128.)
2. Provided that Y is materially true, Z and X′ are correctly opposed as mediated sub-contraries, and both cannot be false. (Compare p. 129.)

Mediated opposition is frequently a source of fallacy, because the disputants usually do not know formal rules for determining its validity, nor do they consciously advert to and examine the third proposition (Y) to which each of their contentions is related and by virtue of which they are mediately opposed (just as in any enthymeme the omitted premise which is not consciously adverted to is often the source of fallacy).

The following illustration shows how fundamental to genuine mediated opposition is the rule that Y must be materially true:

X John was in New York last Monday.	X′ John was not in New York last Monday.
Y A man who was in New York last Monday could not have been in Chicago last Monday.	
Z John was not in Chicago last Monday.	Z′ John was in Chicago last Monday.

If John were accused of a crime committed in New York last Monday, would this argument establish an alibi, pro-

vided that Z' could be proved? We have here a correct syllogism; but in order that X and Z' be correctly opposed as
mediated contraries, it is necessary also that Y be materially
true. Y would have been materially true a hundred years ago
but not now; hence now X and Z' are not correctly opposed
as genuine mediated contraries, but merely seem to be such,
and both may be true.

The source of many fallacies in the daily use of mediated
opposition is the false, hidden assumption that the terms not
common to the propositions mediately opposed are terms mutually exclusive. For example, one person says, "Henry has
a degree in law." The other replies, "That isn't true; he has
a degree in philosophy." Neither disputant adverts to the
full, explicit argument which is as follows:

X Henry has a degree in law.	X' Henry has not a degree in law.
Y Whoever has a degree in law cannot have a degree in philosophy.	
Z Henry has not a degree in philosophy.	Z' Henry has a degree of philosophy.

We see at once that although the syllogism is correct, Y is
not materially true. Therefore X and Z' may both be true,
and X' and Z may both be false. As a matter of fact, this
Henry has a degree in law and also a degree in philosophy.
Each disputant happened to know only about the one degree,
not the other. In this, as in many arguments in daily life,
there is not genuine opposition, for both disputants are right.
A realization of this and a knowledge of the. rules of mediated opposition would forestall much needless and futile
contention. This applies to many arguments about the spelling or the pronunciation of words, for the dictionary shows
many instances where two or more ways are correct.

VII. Utility or worth of the syllogism

The various forms and combinations of the syllogism discussed
in this chapter are useful only if the syllogism itself is a means
whereby the mind advances in knowledge. John Stuart Mill and
other logicians of the Empiricist School have attacked the syllogism, contending:

1. That the conclusion is contained in the major premise, and
   has to be known before the major premise can be stated.

2. That it therefore begs the question in thus assuming the very proposition to be proved.

3. That it is therefore not an advance in knowledge.

Refutation:

1. It may be true of a syllogism whose major premise is a mere enumerative empirical proposition that the conclusion has to be known before the major premise can be stated. Example:

Every farm in Hancock County, Ohio, is equipped with electric lighting.

John Smith's farm is a farm in Hancock County, Ohio.

∴ John Smith's farm is equipped with electric lighting.

But it is never true of a syllogism whose major premise is a general proposition, for the truth of a general proposition is known, not from counting instances and adding them together, but from an analysis of the concept which stands as subject; its truth is not dependent on investigation of the individual facts, for it is understood in intension, not in extension (see pages 108 f.) Example:

A blind man cannot umpire a football game.

Tom Jones is a blind man.

∴ Tom Jones cannot umpire a football game,

2. The syllogism is not a begging of the question, because the conclusion, that is, the proposition to be proved, is not implicit in the major premise, nor in the minor premise, but in the conjunction of the two premises (see page 147).

3. The syllogism is an advance in knowledge, because its conclusion is a truth distinct from that of each of the premises and apparent only through their conjunction.

It is a common experience that a person may have knowledge of only one of the premises, and that as soon as he discovers the second, he recognizes the truth of the conclusion which instantly emerges in a spontaneous act of syllogistic reasoning. For example, you may have known that "A bird is not a mammal." But you may not have known that "A bat is a mammal." The conclusion that "A bat is not a bird" was, then, not only a distinctly new piece of knowledge to you, but the contradictory of what you had probably believed, namely, that "A bat is a bird," which you must now regard as false.

It may be further contended against Mill that even the

conclusion from two empirical premises sometimes represents an advance in knowledge, arising from the conjunction of the premises. This is the very means used to create suspense and interest in many stories and parts of stories. For example, in Hawthorne's *The House of the Seven Gables*, the reader knows that the Maule family has been hostile to the Pyncheon family, for Matthew Maule had cursed Colonel Pyncheon and his descendants because Colonel Pyncheon had persecuted him. The reader also knows that Holgrave is in-interested in Phoebe Pyncheon. But it comes as a surprise, as an advance in knowledge, therefore, to discover at the end of the story that Holgrave is a Maule. The situation may be stated thus:

> The Maules have no love for the Pyncheons.
> Holgrave is a Maule.
> Therefore Holgrave will not love a Pyncheon.

Since, however, living human beings, although rational, are not ruled altogether by cold logic, especially that of a dead ancestor's curse, but by emotion and independent judgment as well, the lovers disregarded the major premise and ended the family feud.

Another example is in Dickens' *A Tale of Two Cities*. Dr. Manette knows that Charles Darnay, a young man whom he likes and admires, wishes to marry Lucie Manette, his daughter. He also knows that the Evremonde family has grievously injured him. But when he learns Charles Darnay's true family name, these separate previously known propositions suddenly conjoin in the following disturbing sorites made up of two syllogisms.

> My daughter loves Charles Darnay.
> Charles Darnay is an Evremonde.
> The Evremondes have grievously injured me.
> Therefore my daughter loves one of a family which has
>   grievously injured me.

Dr. Manette finally consents to let Charles Darnay become his son-in-law, but so great is the emotional shock of the new knowledge arising from the conjunction of the premises that Dr. Manette for awhile loses the use of his reason, recently recovered with slowness and difficulty.

Examples could be multiplied indefinitely both from literature and from life—cases of mistaken identity, of proving an alibi in court, and the like.

VIII. The syllogism as a formula or rule of inference

A correct syllogism, like every other relation of propositional forms, is a formula or rule of inference requiring that a given assertion must be made if certain other assertions are made. Provided that the syllogism is correct, it operates as a rule of inference in the following manner:

1. If both premises are true, the conclusion must be true.
2. If the conclusion is false, at least one of the premises must be false.

   The premises together constitute a conjunction of propositions. Hence when one is false, the conjunction is false (see page 125).

   These first two rules are the most important. The others are implied in them.

3. If one or both of the premises are false, the value of the conclusion is unknown. Examples:

a.		b.	
0	All squares are circles.	0	All squares are circles.
1	No circle is a triangle.	1	No circle is a rectangle.
1	No square is a triangle.	0	No square is a rectangle.

   Since in both these examples one of the premises is false, and since in the one the conclusion is true whereas in the other the conclusion is false, it is evident that if the premises are false, the value of the conclusion is unknown through the form, although it may be learned from the matter.

4. If the conclusion is true, the value of the premises is unknown.
5. If one or both of the premises are probable, the conclusion can be only probable; it cannot be categorically true or false.
6. If the conclusion is probable, the value of the premises is unknown; for in Example a illustrating Rule 3 the conclusion is true and the premises are false, whereas in every sound syllogism the conclusion is true and the premises are true. Hence, when the conclusion is true the value of the premises cannot be known through the form but must be learned from the matter.

IX. The special rules of the four figures of the syllogism

As has been stated earlier in this chapter, a knowledge of the general rules of the syllogism, particularly those of distribution, suffices to determine the validity of any syllogism.

It is, however, a good logical exercise to apply the general rules to each figure abstractly in order to determine the special rules for each. You are now prepared to engage in this exercise with ease, profit, and enjoyment, because you have meanwhile become thoroughly and concretely familiar with the general rules by applying them to particular syllogisms in the exercises at the end of this chapter.

It is easiest to understand the rules for Figure II, and we shall therefore begin with that.

A. Special rules of Figure II

S — M   Since the middle term, which must be distributed at
P —M   least once, is predicate in both premises, and since only
S — P   a negative proposition formally distributes its predi-
cate, the first rule is apparent at once:

Rule a. One premise must be negative, in order to distribute M (in accordance with general *Rule 3*).

A second special rule follows from this. Since the conclusion will be negative (*Rule 6*), the major term P will be distributed there and must accordingly be distributed also in its own premise (*Rule 4*); but there it stands as subject, and since only a total or a necessary proposition distributes its subject, the second special rule is:

Rule b. The major premise must be total or necessary, in order to avoid an illicit process of the major term.

Applying these special rules to the nine combinations of premises permitted by the general rules (see p. 150), we find that the valid moods in Figure II, with minor premise first, are: AEE, EAE, IEO, OAO.

B. Special rules of Figure I

S — M   In considering the position of the terms, we do not
M — P   see at once, as we did in Figure II, what special rule
S — P   is necessary, because the reasoning is indirect, by dis-
proof of the contradictory of the special rule.

Rule a. The minor premise must be affirmative.

Proof: The necessity of this rule becomes clear only in considering what would follow if the minor premise were negative: the conclusion would then be negative (*Rule 6*), and consequently the major term P would be distributed there and would have to be distributed in its own premise (*Rule 4*), where it occupies the position of predicate; the major premise would then have to be negative, since only a negative proposition distributes the predicate. But we have assumed that the minor is negative, and from two negative premises no conclusion can be drawn. Therefore, in order to avoid, on the one hand, an illicit process of the major term, or, on the other hand, the formal fallacy of two negative premises, it is obvious that the minor premise must be affirmative. The second special rule follows from this:

Rule b. The major premise must be total or necessary, in order to avoid an undistributed middle term.

Proof: Since in Figure I the minor premise must be affirmative, the middle term M, as its predicate, cannot be distributed there by the form (although, if it is a definition, it will be distributed by the matter); in this figure, therefore, M can be distributed formally (*Rule 3*) only as subject of the major premise, which, consequently, must be total or necessary, because only these distribute the subject.

Applying these special rules, we find that the valid moods of this figure are: AAA, AEE, IAI, IEO.

C. Special rules of Figure III

M — S   Since in this figure, as in Figure I, the major term is
M — P   predicate in the major premise, the same special rule
S — P   follows, for the same reasons, which need not be repeated here.

Rule a. The minor premise must be affirmative.

Rule b. This follows from the first rule. Since the minor premise must be affirmative, the minor term S, its predicate, is formally undistributed there and must likewise be undistributed in the conclusion (*Rule 4*), where it stands as subject. But only partial or contingent propositions have the subject undistributed; therefore the conclusion must be partial or contingent.

Valid moods: AAI, AII, IAI, AEO, AOO, IEO.

D. Special rules of Figure IV

Aristotle and logicians of the Renaissance discussed only three figures of the syllogism. The fourth figure is, however, a possibility, and it has for a long time been treated in logic.

It is not a very satisfying figure, and it is unstable in the sense that its rules are a series of if's, two of which (without the *if*) have been discussed in relation to other figures.

Rule a. If the major premise is affirmative, the minor must be total or necessary.

Rule b. If the minor is affirmative, the conclusion must be partial or contingent.

Rule c. If the conclusion is negative, the major premise must be total or necessary.

Proof of *Rule a*: If the major premise is affirmative, the middle term M, its predicate, is formally undistributed in the major premise and must be distributed in the minor (*Rule 3*); but there it occupies the position of subject, and since only a total proposition distributes the subject, the minor premise must be total or necessary.

Proof of *Rule b*: The same as that of *Rule b* of Figure III.

Proof of *Rule c*: The same as that of *Rule b* of Figure II.

Valid moods: AAI, EAE, AII, AEO, IEO.

X. Comparison of the four figures of the syllogism

A. Figure I is called the perfect figure, because it alone can yield a total or a necessary general affirmative proposition as conclusion. Such conclusions are the goal of science, of philosophy, and of all general knowledge, for negative and partial or contingent propositions usually express limitations of knowledge rather than the perfection of knowledge. The perfect mood of the perfect figure is therefore Mood AAA in Figure I.

Figure I is also called the perfect figure because in it alone is the middle term really in the natural, middle position; in it alone is the natural synthesis of the terms given in the premises themselves; for it represents the spontaneous, natural movement of thought in the process of reasoning. In it the *Dictum*, the fundamental principle of syllogistic reasoning, has immediate and obvious application, for as the major term is affirmed (or denied) of the middle term, the logical whole, so is it affirmed (or denied) of the minor term, the logical part.

Note. In this book the minor premise has regularly been placed first, because (1) it is thereby more clearly evident that the middle term is in the middle (S — M, M — P, ∴ S — P); (2) it corresponds more closely to our experience, for we usually become interested first in a particular object, then place it mentally in a class, perhaps after careful examination (This is a toadstool, not a mushroom), join to it what we know of that class (Toadstools are poisonous), and draw a conclusion therefrom (This is poisonous, and I must not eat it)—the second conclusion making this, by the implied premise (Whatever is poisonous I must not eat) two syllogisms; (3) this is the natural movement of thought, as is evident from the fact that we find the Aristotelian sorites, which places the minor premise first, much more comfortable than the Goclenian sorites, which places the major premise first.

It is, of course, true that certain arguments seem more satisfactory with the major premise first, others with the minor premise first. So far as validity or formal correctness goes, it makes no difference which is placed first, and both alternatives are illustrated in the examples and exercises in this book.

B. Figure II, except when one premise is a definition, can yield only negative conclusions. It is therefore particularly adapted to disproof.

C. Figure III is the weakest figure because, except when one premise is a definition, it can yield only a conclusion that is partial or singular or contingent. It is adapted to proving exceptions.

D. Figure IV, whose premises are the converse of Figure I, is so unnatural in the movement of its thought that it gives the mind the least satisfaction and the least sense of conviction, whereas the first figure gives it the most in both of these respects.

XI. Reduction of syllogisms

This is an ingenious exercise of but little practical importance.

Reduction is the process by which a syllogism in one of the imperfect figures (II, III, or IV) is expressed as a syllogism of the first figure, which is called the perfect figure.

The purpose of reduction is to demonstrate the validity of an imperfect figure as a formal process of reasoning by showing that an argument carried on according to the rules of an imperfect figure is valid in the perfect figure.

The assumptions of reduction are two:

1. That the premises of the imperfect figure are true as given.
2. That the first or perfect figure is formally valid.

The mnemonic lines are a clever medieval device, enumerating the nineteen valid moods of the four figures and indicating the methods for reducing the moods of the imperfect figures to the corresponding moods of the perfect figure. They are:

Barbara, Celarent, Darii, Ferio*que prioris,*
Cesare, Camestres, Festino, Baroco, *secundae.*
Tertia Darapti, Disamis, Datisi, Felapton
Bocardo, Ferison *habet. Quarta insuper addit*
Bramantip, Camenes, Dimaris, Fesapo, Fresison.

Key to the mnemonic lines. The vowels indicate the mood in this traditional order: major premise, minor premise, conclusion.

B, C, D, F signify to what corresponding mood of the first figure the moods of the other figures are to be reduced.

s (*simpliciter*) signifies that the proposition indicated by the preceding vowel is to be converted simply.

p (*per accidens*) signifies that the proposition indicated by the preceding vowel must be converted by limitation (A to I; and in one case, I to A, namely, Bramantip to Barbara.)

m (*muta*) signifies that the premises are to be transposed.

c (*per contradictoriam propositionem*) signifies that the reduction is to be indirect, by disproving a contradictory conclusion in a syllogism of the first figure.

r, b, l, n, t, d have no significance.

Illustrations of reduction:

1. Camestres to Celarent (a. to b.)   *Camestres* decoded means:

a. All circles are curvilinear.	P a M	*m* — Transpose the premises.
No square is curvilinear.	S e M	*s* — Convert simply.
∴ No square is a circle.	S e P	*s* — Convert simply.
b. No curvilinear figure is a square.	M e P	
All circles are curvilinear.	S a M	
∴ No circle is a square.	S e P	

2. Bocardo to Barbara (a. to b.)   *Bocardo* decoded means:

a. Some lions are not tame.	M o P	*c* — Show that the conclusion of
All lions are animals.	M a S	a corresponding syllogism in
∴ Some animals are not tame.	S o P	Fig. I contradicts a premise

given as true in Fig. III. The method is: Form Barbara, using as premises the A of Bocardo and the contradictory of its conclusion; draw the con-

b. All animals are tame.	M a P
All lions are animals.	S a M
All lions are tame.	S a P

clusion implicit in these premises.

This conclusion in Barbara, since it is the contradictory of the O premise of Bocardo, which was given as true, must be false. But Barbara is accepted as a correct process of reasoning. The error therefore must be in the matter, since it is not in the form; for if the conclusion of a correct syllogism is false, at least one of the premises must be false. But the minor premise of Barbara, borrowed from Bocardo, is given as true; therefore the major premise of Barbara must be false. Since this major premise is the contradictory of the conclusion of Bocardo, that conclusion must be true.

Thus is the third figure proved to be a valid process of reasoning.   Q. E. D.

Thomas Fuller (1608-61) in "The General Artist" thus conceives the use of logic:

Logic is the armory of reason, furnished with all offensive and defensive weapons. There are syllogisms, long swords; enthymemes, short daggers; dilemmas, two-edged swords that cut on both sides; sorites, chain-shot. And for the defensive, distinctions, which are shields; retortions, which are targets with a pike in the midst of them, both to defend and oppose.

QUESTIONS

Note to the Student. You will learn the answers to these questions most readily by doing the exercises on the pages following.
1. What is a syllogism? Give an example. What constitutes its matter? its form?
2. How do you discover the minor term of a syllogism? the major term? the middle term? How is each of these symbolized? How often does each term occur? Where?
3. What is a premise? Explain by analogy. How do you discover which premise is the minor? the major?
4. State the principle upon which syllogistic reasoning is based. Which term represents the logical whole?
5. State the general rules of the syllogism as to: terms; propositions; distribution (2); quality (2); quantity (2); modality (2); reference to reality. Name the six formal fallacies that result from violation of these rules.
6. How does the ordinary man express the logic of the rules of distribution? of the rules governing the conclusion, when one premise is either negative or partial or contingent or empirical?
7. Can there be an illicit process of the middle term? Why or why not? May a term that is distributed in its own premise be undistributed in the conclusion? *vice versa?*
8. What constitutes the mood of a syllogism? How is the mood of a given syllogism designated?
9. Write formally all the possible combinations of premises; strike out those that violate the general rules; to those that remain add the letter which, according to the general rules, should represent the conclusion derived from each pair of premises. How many moods conform to the general rules? How many valid combinations of premises are there?

10. What determines the figure of a syllogism? Symbolize and number the four figures.
11. What is an enthymeme? How does it differ radically, with regard to the problem of expansion into a full syllogism, from a syllogism only grammatically abridged?
12. Explain by what clues you can discover the conclusion in an enthymeme. Why is it necessary first to find the conclusion of an enthymeme, or of any syllogism, before its validity can be determined?
13. State the principles for determining whether or not an enthymeme is a good, sound argument.
14. State two reasons why the enthymeme is of great practical importance.
15. What is a sorites? State the differences between the Aristotelian and the Goclenian sorites. Which is more often used? State the rules of each. Symbolize the formula of each in the unexpanded sorites.
16. What is an epicheirema? When is it double? single? How does it differ from a double enthymeme? from a sorites?
17. Is there any formal limit to the length of a sorites? an epicheirema? Can a sorites be transformed into an epicheirema? Can an epicheirema be transformed into a sorites?
18. What is analogical inference? What is its importance? State the formula. Illustrate. Does analogical inference yield conclusions that are certain? Upon what do its worth and validity depend?
19. What is mediated opposition? State the rules of mediated opposition. What propositions constitute mediated contraries? mediated subcontraries? Illustrate the practical use of mediated opposition.
20. State John Stuart Mill's arguments maintaining that the syllogism cannot be a means to advance in knowledge. Do we admit any part of his argument as true? Illustrate. Is even this part sometimes not true? Illustrate.
21. If the premises of a correct syllogism are true, what do we know about the conclusion? If the conclusion is false, what do we know about the premises? State the other rules of the syllogism as a formula of inference.
22. State and prove the special rules of Figure II; Figure I; Figure III; Figure IV. Why must the major premise be total in Figure II? in Figure I? Explain why and how the special rules determining the validity of a syllogism can be set aside or modified if one of the premises is a definition.
23. Whenever the major term is predicate in its premise, what special rule follows? Whenever the minor term is predicate in an affirmative premise, what special rule follows?
24. By means of the special rules of each figure, determine the valid moods of that figure.
25. State two reasons why Figure I is called the perfect figure. Name the perfect mood of the perfect figure.
26. State three reasons why, in this book, the minor premise has regularly been placed first.
27. What is the reduction of syllogisms? its purpose? What are its assumptions? Explain in detail how the mnemonic lines act as a guide to reduction. Reduce two or three syllogisms, chosen from this chapter, either in the text or in the exercises.

Examine the following arguments. Expand those that are abridged. Concerning each determine: (1) the type (simple syllogism, enthymeme, sorites, epicheirema, analogical inference, or mediated opposition); (2) figure; (3) mood; (4) validity; if invalid, name (4) the fallacy. Write out your analysis exactly as prescribed and illustrated on pp. 151-154. Consider also whether the propositions are true or false.

1. All college graduates have a superior education. This man has a superior education. Therefore this man is a college graduate.
2. Some novels are historical. All novels are fiction. Therefore some fiction is historical.
3. Some roses are not red. No lilies are roses. Therefore some lilies are not red.
4. A football player is an athlete. Some college students are football players. Therefore some athletes are college students.
5. Some flowers are not violets. All violets are plants. Therefore some flowers are not plants.
6. Coral is used in jewelry. Coral is an animal skeleton. Therefore some animal skeletons are used in jewelry.
7. Lettuce is a vegetable. Asparagus is a vegetable. Therefore asparagus is lettuce.
8. All men are intelligent. All men are finite. Therefore all intelligent beings are finite.
9. A bird is not an insect. The mosquito is not a bird. Therefore mosquitoes are not insects.
10. No man is perfect. Some men are criminals. Therefore some criminals are not perfect.
11. Fishes have scales. Scales are used for weighing things. Therefore fishes are used for weighing things.
12. A dog is faithful. A friend is faithful. Therefore a dog is a friend.
13. A novel is not a biography and a biography is not fiction. Therefore a novel is not fiction.
14. These used cars are selling at a bargain. Some of these used care are Cadillacs. Therefore some Cadillacs are selling at a bargain.
15. Some men are villains and some have whiskers. Therefore some villains have whiskers.
16. He is tired because he has worked hard all day.
17. These five lawyers, graduates of Harvard Law School, are unusually successful. Therefore whoever is a graduate of Harvard Law School will be unusually successful.
18. John is an uncle because he has a nephew.
19. Both this man and the kidnaper misspell *money* "munny." Therefore this man is the kidnaper.
20. The government of Great Britain is a democracy, for it is responsive to the popular will.
21. You are a traitor and no traitor ought to live.
22. The study of Old English is difficult but valuable. Therefore some valuable studies are difficult.
23. Capital punishment should be the penalty for murder, because it is the strongest deterrent.

24. Neither an elm nor an oak is an evergreen. Therefore an oak is not an elm.
25. Some foods that contain Vitamin B_1 are not spinach, for milk contains Vitamin B_1.
26. A horse is a mammal. A mammal is a vertebrate. A vertebrate is an animal. An animal has sense knowledge. Therefore a horse has sense knowledge.
27. *Prince Hal.* Do I owe you a thousand pound? *Falstaff.* A thousand pound, Hal? A million! Thy love is worth a million; thou owest me thy love.
          —Shakespeare, *1 Henry IV*, 3.3.153.
28. He has had a liberal education, for he is, as completely as a man can be, in harmony with Nature.—T. H. Huxley, "A Liberal Education."
29. Eggs darken silver, for they contain sulphur. Eggs darken these spoons. Therefore some silver is in these spoons.
30. Some politicians are grafters. All grafters are dishonest. All dishonest persons are a social menace. Persons who are a social menace should be punished by law. Therefore some politicians should be punished by law.
31. This chemical substance must be a base, for it turns red litmus blue and phenolphthalein red.
32. The present is the only thing of which a man can be deprived, for that is the only thing which he has, and a man cannot lose a thing that he has not.
          —Marcus Aurelius, *Meditations.*
33. He would not take the crown. Therefore 'tis certain he was not ambitious.
          —Shakespeare, *Julius Caesar*, 3.2.118.
34. Bread contains starch, for iodine turns it blue. Foods that contain starch should be eaten sparingly by those who wish to get thin, for they are fattening. Therefore bread should be eaten sparingly by those who wish to get thin.
35. A balloon filled with helium will rise, for it is lighter than air. This balloon does not rise. Therefore this balloon is not filled with helium.
36. "Those flowers are artificial." "That isn't true; they are natural."
37. The girls of today are the world's future mothers. The world's future mothers determine the character of the home. Whatever determines the character of the home has a tremendous influence on the leaders of tomorrow. Therefore the girls of today have a tremendous influence on the leaders of tomorrow.
38. Nathan Hale was a patriot, for he died in the service of his country. A traitor is not a patriot, for he is one who gives aid to the enemies of his country. Therefore Nathan Hale was not a traitor.
39. "She is taking a course in French." "That isn't true; I know for a fact that she is taking a course in German."
40. The good cannot be too much honored, nor the bad too coarsely used; for the corruption of the best becomes the worst.—Dryden, Preface to the *Fables.*
41. Having a roommate in college is a hindrance to efficient work, for it occasions much waste of time in idle conversation. Every hindrance to efficient work should be avoided, for it robs parents of the full fruits of the sacrifice they make to give their sons or daughters the opportunity of a college education. Therefore having a roommate in college should be avoided.
42. Light rays are energy rays, for they produce an image of an obstructing body on a photographic film. Rays emitted from uranium resemble light rays in producing an image of an obstructing body on a photographic film. Therefore

rays emitted from uranium are probably energy rays.
—Henri Becquerel, 1896.

43. A square is not a circle, for it has not every point on its perimeter equidistant from the center. A square is a parallelogram, for both pairs of its opposite sides are parallel. Therefore a circle is not a parallelogram.

44. *Olivia.* Y' are servant to the Count Orsino, youth. *Cesario.* And he is yours, and his must needs be yours. Your servant's servant is your servant, madam.
—Shakespeare, *Twelfth Night*, 3.1.111.

45. Cheating in school is a lie in act, because it is submitting as the product of one's own intellectual effort that of another's.

46. The specific purpose for which a college exists is the development of the intellectual virtues. The development of the intellectual virtues demands intellectual honesty. Whatever demands intellectual honesty is incompatible with cheating. Therefore the specific purpose for which a college exists is incompatible with cheating.

47. My first thoughts are certainly not better by a hair's breadth than anybody's first thoughts; and anybody's first thoughts had best be kept in the background.—Lessing, *Hamburg Dramaturgy*.

48. *Flavius.* Have you forgot me, sir? *Timon.* I have forgot all men. Then, if thou grant'st th'art a man, I have forgot thee.
—Shakespeare, *Timon of Athens*, 4.3.479.

49. She did not win the prize because winning the prize required hard work.

50. Not all animals that have tusks are elephants, for walruses have tusks.

51. Walter Reed is a benefactor of mankind, because he discovered the means to combat yellow fever. A benefactor of mankind is an inspiration to others, for they desire to imitate him. Therefore Walter Reed is an inspiration to others.

52. This novel retarded Mrs. Smith's recovery from a nervous breakdown, because it is gruesome and therefore depressing.

53. We are harmed when we lose any part of God's favor. We lose God's favor when we lose any goods of the mind, when we either rejoice at having bodily and worldly goods, or make sorrow of the lacking of the same. We are not harmed when God continues his favor, when we decay not in strength of mind, when we be not overcome either with gladness of the body's and world's prosperity or with bewailing their adversity. Thus you see, neither in the goods of the body, nor in the goods of the world can you take or escape harm. It is only the virute of your mind wherein you must search whether you be safe or harmed.
—Thomas Lupset, "Exhortation to Young Men."

54. A lie is intrinsically evil, for it is the perversion of a natural faculty. Whatever is intrinsically evil can never be justified, for it cannot become good through any extrinsic circumstance whatsoever. Therefore a lie can never be justified.

55. This man is a socialist, for he believes in government ownership of capital goods.

56. These soldiers are not likely to contract smallpox, for they have been vaccinated.

57. History both reconstructs the past and is cultural. Therefore whatever reconstructs the past is cultural.

58. That we cannot bear. Better to die, For death is gentler far than tyranny.
—Aeschylus, *Agamemmon,* lines 1450-51.

59. Death certainly, and life, honor and dishonor, pain and pleasure, all these things equally happen to good men and bad, being things which make us neither better nor worse. Therefore they are neither good nor evil.
—Marcus Aurelius, *Meditations.*

60. Each man holds that to be the highest good which he prefers before all others. The highest good is defined as happiness. Therefore each man esteems that estate happy which he prefers before all others.
—Boethius, *Consolation of Philosophy.*

61. "The report is true." "No, the report is false!"

62. If peace depends upon redistribution of raw materials, and if Stalin holds such redistribution to be "impossible" under capitalism, it follows that he thinks there will be no peace as long as there is capitalism.
—*Time,* July 21, 1947, p. 24.

63. A parallelogram is quadrilateral. A rectangle is a parallelogram. A square is a rectangle. Some equiangular figures are squares. Therefore some equiangular figures are quadrilateral.

64. Seriousness is gravity. Gravity is a law of nature. Therefore seriousness is a law of nature.

65. "C-e-l-t is pronounced *kelt.*" "That isn't true; it is pronounced *selt.*"

66. It must be yours To joy, it likewise must be yours to grieve, For you are born a mortal.—Euripides, *Iphigenia at Aulis,* lines 26-28.

67. Happiness is a virtuous activity of the soul. Therefore neither a brute animal nor a very young child is truly happy.—Aristotle, *Ethics.*

68. The earth is larger than the moon. Jupiter is larger than the earth. The sun is larger than Jupiter. Arcturus is larger than the sun. Therefore Arcturus is larger than the moon.

69. I, honest, let no thief partake my breast. For this, without a friend, the world, I quit.—Juvenal, Satire III, line 77.

70. Loving in truth, and fain in verse my love to show.
That she, dear she, might take some pleasure of my pain,
Pleasure might cause her read, reading might make her know,
Knowledge might pity win, and pity grace obtain.

—Sidney, Sonnet 1

71. This sonata, discovered recently, must be Beethoven's composition, for the style is his.

72. "You write here that the poem has no r-i-m-e; the correct spelling is r-h-y-m-e." "You are mistaken; r-i-m-e is correct."

73. Hunger was the first that ever opened a cook-shop, cooks the first that ever made sauce, sauce being liquorish, licks up good meat; good meat preserves life; hunger therefore preserves life.—Dekker, *Old Fortunatus,* II, ii.

74. Doing well the acts of this life is doing our duty. Dying is doing one of the acts of this life. Therefore dying well is doing our duty.
—Marcus Aurelius, *Meditations.*

75. *Macbeth* [*speaking of Duncan*] He's here in double trust:
First as I am his kinsman and his subject,
Strong both against the deed; then as his host

Who should against his murderer shut the door,
Not bear the knife myself.—Shakespeare.

76. Since the liberal arts are the arts of thinking and since men think by means of symbols, and since the chief symbols men think with are words and numbers, the liberal arts can be most economically acquired through the medium of languages and mathematics.—Scott Buchanan.

77. Spoiled young people are disliked because they are selfish. Persons who are disliked become unhappy, for their natural desire for esteem is frustrated. Therefore spoiled young people become unhappy.

78. A kidnaper ought to be punished severely, for others need to be deterred from a similar crime.

79. Paris has no sound courage. Therefore I deem that he will gather bitter fruit.—Homer, *Iliad*, VI, 342.

80. He was executed for treason.

81. This man is seriously ill. Some who are seriously ill need an operation. Therefore this man needs an operation.

82. Some scientific hypotheses are false. Evolution is a scientific hypothesis. Therefore evolution is a false hypothesis.

83. This book cannot be interesting, for it is not a novel.

84. Carrots are vegetables. Carrots are nourishing. Therefore all vegetables are nourishing.

85. Some wars are justified. No wars are pleasant. Therefore some justifiable activities are not pleasant.

86. A fishing rod is a capital good, for it is a product of past industry used in present or future production.

87. A square is a rectangle, for each of its angles measures 90 degrees. A circle is not a rectangle, for it is not divisible by a diagonal into two equal right triangles. Therefore a circle is not a square.

88. Select from your reading passages illustrating syllogistic reasoning and analyze their logical content.

89. Choose from your own section a partner for debate. Agree on a subject and on two to four issues that divide the subject. One of you choose to argue for, the other against, each issue. State the question. Then each of you prepare a brief, subdividing the main issues; introduce each topic and subtopic by *for*. Clip the two briefs, affirmative and negative, together when submitting them.

CHAPTER VIII

RELATIONS OF HYPOTHETICAL AND DISJUNCTIVE PROPOSITIONS

I. Hypothetical propositions
  A. Definition. A hypothetical proposition is one that asserts the dependence of one proposition on another. Example: If a man drinks poison, he will die. (It is usually an *if*-proposition; *unless* meaning *if not, provided that,* and sometimes *when* may also express this relation.)

  The proposition which depends on the other is called the consequent; the proposition on which it depends is called the antecedent. The dependence itself is the nexus.

  The hypothetical proposition expresses a relation of propositions, whereas the simple proposition expresses a relation of terms. The hypothetical proposition expresses a conditional relation of dependence, and hence of limitation, whereas the simple categorical proposition expresses without limitation a relation between a subject and a predicate.

  Because a hypothetical proposition expresses a dependence primarily in the logical order, the antecedent is more correctly called the reason, rather than the cause, of the consequent. A reason is a relation in the logical order whereas a cause is, strictly speaking, a relation in the metaphysical order. Thus, the existence of the world is a reason for believing in the existence of God, but it is not a cause of His existence; on the contrary, it is an effect of His existence.

  B. Types of hypothetical propositions. There are two:
    1. The type having three terms, one term being common to both antecedent and consequent. Formula: If S is M, it is P. Example: If you study, you will learn.
    2. The type having four terms, no term being common to both antecedent and consequent. Formula: If B is C, D is E. Example: If he comes, I will go.
  C. Reduction. The hypothetical proposition can be reduced to a categorical proposition and *vice versa,* but usually this involves a change of import, or a distortion of meaning. Distortion occurs especially in reducing the second type. Were there no difference whatever except in form, there would be no real justification for regarding the categorical and the hypothetical propositions as logically distinct types, but only as verbally

distinct. The genuine hypothetical proposition is one in which the dependence between antecedent and consequent cannot be adequately expressed in categorical form or in which such dependence persists even in the categorical form.

Formula for reduction to categorical form:

1. The first type: If S is M, it is P becomes SM is P.
2. The second type: If B is C, D is E becomes BC is DE.

Examples of reduction:

Hypothetical propositions

a. If a man drinks poison he will die.
b. If a man is virtuous he will be rewarded.
c. If he attended the freshman class meeting last week he is an American citizen.
d. If you do not return the book to the library on time, you will be fined.
e. If a boy goes wrong, his mother will grieve.

Categorical propositions:

a. Whoever drinks poison will die.
b. A virtuous man will be rewarded.
c. All who attended the freshman class meeting last week are American citizens.
d. Your failure to return the book to the library on time is the cause of your being fined.
e. A boy's going wrong is a cause of his mother's grieving.

It will be noted that all these examples, except the last, represent the first type: SM is P. The first two suffer little distortion; the last two suffer much, and in them especially the dependence between antecedent and consequent persists, and is felt even in the categorical form, for causality is the relation expressed in both forms.

Just as clearly the categorical nature of the third persists and is felt when it is expressed in hypothetical form, because its antecedent is not the reason of the consequent, nor does the one depend on the other. This is an empirical proposition, to which the categorical form is natural.

The compound nature of all these propositions (especially categorical Example b) becomes obvious if we recall that grammatical modification is implicit logical predication; therefore each of these examples is a conjunction of propositions, not one simple proposition. It is not bare conjunction, however, but one expressing a relation of dependence. Therefore, although the hypothetical proposition is compound, and can be reduced to its component simple propositions or to one simple proposition with compound terms, it represents a species of judgment, a particular kind of relationship between propositions and not merely between terms, and so merits treatment as a distinct logical form.

D. Some special characteristics of hypothetical propositions

1. Truth or falsity. The hypothetical proposition does not assert either one of its component simple propositions as true or false; it asserts only that one depends on the other, that there is a nexus between them. Hence a hypothetical proposition is true when the nexus holds in the real order and false when it does not. Example:

If a man drinks poison, he will die. (True.)

If a man drinks water, he will die. (False.)

2. Quality. The hypothetical proposition is always affirmative in the sense that it always affirms the nexus, that is, the connection of its component simple propositions; these, however, taken separately may be both affirmative, or both negative, or one may be affirmative and the other negative. Example:

If you stop eating, you will die.

If you do not eat, you will die.

If you do not eat, you will not live.

If you stop eating, you will not live.

The proposition which denies a hypothetical proposition denies the nexus, yet such a proposition is not really a hypothetical proposition, for it does not assert the dependence of one proposition on another, but denies such dependence. Example:

If a man drinks water, he will die.

If a man drinks water, he will not die.

Taken in relation to the first proposition, which is false, the second, its denial (contradictory), is true; but, taken by itself, the second proposition is not true, for by drinking water a man cannot keep from dying. Nevertheless, in relation to a given proposition, such denials provide the change of quality needful to the opposition and eduction of hypothetical propositions.

II. Disjunctive propositions

A. Definition. A disjunctive proposition is one which asserts that of two or more suppositions, one is true. (It is an *either . . . or* proposition.)

B. Types. There are three types represented by the following formulas. The first is the most important type.

  1. S is P or Q or R. Examples:

    a. A triangle is either equilateral or isosceles or scalene.

    b. A rectangle is either a square or an oblong.

    This type of disjunctive proposition is usually a summary of the results of a logical division of a genus into its constituent species and conforms to the same rules; for the alternatives are (1) collectively exhaustive; (2) mutually exclusive; (3) species resulting from division according to a single basis.

  2. S or T or U is P. Example:

  Either John or Helen or Henry will win the scholarship.

  3. B is C or D is E. Examples:

    Either this man committed suicide or someone murdered him.

    Either the captain failed to give the order or the soldier failed to obey it.

C. Reduction. A disjunctive proposition having but two alternatives can be expressed in a hypothetical proposition which denies one alternative and affirms the other. Examples:

  If this man did not commit suicide, someone murdered him.

  If a rectangle is a square, it is not an oblong. (If S is M, it is not P.)

The reduction may be carried further by reducing the hypothetical proposition to a simple proposition (SM — P). Example:

  A rectangle that is a square is not an oblong. (SMeP)

  A non-square rectangle is an oblong. (SM'aP)

If the disjunctive proposition has more than two alternatives, it may, it is true, be expressed in a hypothetical proposition, but in that case the consequent will be disjunctive. Example: If a triangle is not equilateral, it is either isosceles or scalene.

D. Some special characteristics of disjunctive propositions

  1. Truth or falsity. A disjunctive proposition is strictly true if it enumerates all the possibilities, that is, if the alternatives are mutually exclusive and collectively exhaustive. Otherwise, speaking strictly, it is false.

a. The strict purpose, then, of the disjunctive proposition of every type is so to limit the choice of alternatives that if one is true, any other must be false. Only under this condition does it serve as a true instrument of reasoning toward truth. It is this limitation of choice that makes the disjunctive proposition distinct from the hypothetical and the categorical. It is itself a conjunction of simple propositions joined by *or*, but not a bare conjunction, for the series of alternatives is fixed; to add to, or subtract from, the alternatives would falsify the series.

b. In ordinary discourse, the disjunctive proposition is often used loosely without the strict disjunctive purpose; yet this purpose is often present in the context even when it is absent from the proposition itself. Example: The package is in either the living room or the dining room.

This proposition does not seem to exhaust the possibilities, but it does so implicitly if the context in the mind of the speaker is this: Since I had the package when I entered the house, and now, having left the house, I do not have it, and since I was in only the two rooms mentioned, the package must be in either the one room or the other.

c. To deny a disjunctive proposition one may either:
1) Deny the possibilities as well as the choice.
Original: A student is either a laborer or a gentleman.
Denial: A student is neither a laborer nor a gentleman.
2) Deny that the alternatives are mutually exclusive.
Denial: A student is both a laborer and a gentleman.
3) Deny that the alternatives are collectively exhaustive.
Denial: A student is *not* either a laborer or a gentleman.
The last is the most effective method of denying this example, for a student may be a girl; the original proposition is false, however, on all three counts.

2. Quality. The disjunctive proposition is always affirmative, in the sense that it affirms a series of possibilities. The proposition which denies a disjunctive proposition is not really a disjunctive proposition, as may be seen in the first and third examples above, for it does not assert that of two or more suppositions one is true; rather it is the negation of such an assertion.

In relation to a given disjunctive proposition, however, such denials provide the change of quality needful to the opposition and eduction of the disjunctive proposition.

The hypothetical and the disjunctive proposition are effective in drama or story.

Shakespeare often used the hypothetical proposition to state an important problem.

Hamlet. [*of Claudius*] If his occulted guilt
Do not itself unkennel in one speech,
It is a damnèd ghost that we have seen.

—Hamlet, 3.2.85

Carlisle. [*of Bolingbroke*] And if you crown him, let me prophesy,
The blood of English shall manure the ground
And future ages groan for this foul act.

—Richard II, 4.1.136

Ford. If I suspect without cause . . . let me be your jest.

—The Merry Wives of Windsor, 3.3.159

The disjunctive proposition is particularly fitted to express choices upon which character or action depends.

Antony. These strong Egyptians fetters I must break
Or lose myself in dotage.

—Antony and Cleopatra, 1.2.120

Prince Hal. The land is burning; Percy stands on high;
And either they or we must lower lie.

—1 Henry IV, 3.3.226

Bastard. Straight let us seek, or straight we shall be sought.
The Dauphin rages at our very heels.

—King John, 5.7.79

The following paragraph illustrates the use of continued disjunction or subdivision in closely knit reasoning. The final sentence gathers together the parts disclosed by division.

Every action of every person either is or is not due to that person himself. Of those not due to himself some are due to chance, the others to necessity; of these latter, again, some are due to compulsion, the others to nature. Consequently all actions that are not due to a man himself are due either to chance or to nature or to compulsion. . . . Those things happen through compulsion which take place contrary to the desire or reason of the doer, yet through his own agency. . . . All actions that *are* due to a man himself and caused by himself are due either to habit or to rational or irrational craving. Rational craving is a craving for good, that is, a wish—nobody wishes for anything unless he thinks it good. Irrational craving is twofold, namely, anger and appetite. Thus every action must be due to one or other of seven causes: chance, nature, compulsion, habit, reasoning, anger, or appetite.

—Aristotle, Rhetoric, 1,10

III. Relations of hypothetical and disjunctive propositions

They have all the relations that simple propositions have, and the rules governing these relations are practically the same.

Analogy: One who understands the grammatical structure of the simple sentence has only to apply the same principles to the more complicated but not altogether new patterns of the compound-complex sentence.

A. Conjunction. Although hypothetical and disjunctive propositions are themselves relations of simple propositions, they are capable of being conjoined. The conjunction may be a bare conjunction, or a material conjunction.

B. Opposition

1. Of hypothetical propositions

Although, as has been said, every hypothetical proposition, taken by itself, is, strictly speaking, affirmative, by varying the consequent, one can construct A E I O forms of hypotheticals which, in relation to each other, differ in quality and in either quantity or modality. The square of opposition of hypotheticals may be constructed of either quantitative or of modal A E I O forms. Examples:

a. Quantitative forms

A If an animal is striped, it is always a zebra.
E If an animal is striped, it is never a zebra.
I If an animal is striped, it is sometimes a zebra.
O If an animal is striped, it is sometimes not a zebra.

b. Modal forms

A If a man's heart stops beating, he will necessarily die.
E If a man's heart stops beating, he will necessarily not die.
I If a man's heart stops beating, he may die.
O If a man's heart stops beating, he may not die.

The modal forms are better suited to hypothetical propositions. The quantitative forms in the example above do not convey the relations as well as the modal forms would.

2. Of disjunctive propositions

Their opposition also can be expressed in either quantitative or modal forms.

a. Quantitative forms

A Every number is either odd or even.
E No number is either odd or even.
I Some numbers are either odd or even.
O Some numbers are not either odd or even.

b. Modal forms

> A A triangle must be either equilateral or isosceles or **scalene.**
> E A triangle cannot be either equilateral or isosceles or **scalene.**
> I A triangle may be either equilateral or isosceles or scalene.
> O A triangle may not be either equilateral or isosceles or **scalene.**

C. Eduction

1. Of hypothetical propositions. All seven forms may be derived:

> Original: If a tree is a pine, it is necessarily an evergreen.
> a. Obverse: If a tree is a pine, it is necessarily not a **non-evergreen.**
> b. Partial contrapositive: If a tree is a non-evergreen, it is necessarily not a pine.
> c. Full contrapositive: If a tree is a non-evergreen, it is necessarily a non-pine.
> d. Full inverse: If a tree is a non-pine, it may be a non-evergreen.
> e. Partial inverse: If a tree is a non-pine, it may not be an evergreen.
> f. If a tree is an evergreen, it may be a pine.
> g. Obverted converse: If a tree is an evergreen, it may not be a non-pine.

Note. A *sine qua non* hypothetical proposition is one whose antecedent is that without which the consequent will not follow. Its antecedent is the only reason of its consequent; and its consequent cannot follow from any other antecedent.

Therefore a *sine qua non* hypothetical proposition, like a definition, is convertible simply. Example: If a substance turns blue litmus paper red, it is an acid. If a substance is an acid, it turns blue litmus paper red.

The seven eductions of a *sine qua non* hypothetical proposition can, therefore, like those of a definition, be derived in one continuous process of alternate obversion and conversion, and the eighth operation returns the original.

The ignorant assumption that a hypothetical proposition is convertible when it is not is illustrated by an incident narrated by Saint Thomas More:

> Witness: This doctor said to me that if Hunne had not sued the premunire he should never have been accused of heresy.
> Doctor: I said indeed, that if Hunne had not been accused of heresy he would never have sued the premunire.
> Witness: Lo, my lords, I am glad you find me a true man.
> Lord: I have espied, good man, so the words be all one, it makes no matter to you which way they stand; but all is one to you, a horse mill and a mill horse, drink ere you go, and go ere you drink.
> Witness: Nay, my lords, I will not drink.
> And therewith he went his way, leaving some of the lords laugh-

ing to see that as contrary as their two tales were, yet when he heard them both again, he took them both for one because the words were one.   *—The Dialogue concerning Tyndale*

2. Of disjunctive propositions

A strict disjunctive proposition which expresses the results of a logical division is, like a *sine qua non* hypothetical proposition and a definition, convertible simply. Therefore its seven eductions can be derived in one continuous process of alternate obversion and conversion and the eighth operation returns the original. Example:

Original: A material substance must be either a gas, a liquid, or a solid.
  a. Converse: A substance that is either a gas, a liquid, or a solid must be a material substance.
  b. Obverted converse: A substance that is either a gas, a liquid, or a solid cannot be a non-material-substance.
  c. Partial inverse: A non-material-substance cannot be either a gas, a liquid or a solid.
  d. Full inverse: A non-material-substance must be neither a gas, a liquid, nor a solid.
  e. Full contrapositive: A substance that is neither a gas, a liquid, nor a solid must be a non-material-substance.
  f. Partial contrapositive: A substance that is neither a gas, a liquid, nor a solid cannot be a material substance.
  g. Obverse: A material substance cannot be neither a gas, a liquid, nor a solid.
  h. Original: A material substance must be either a gas, a liquid, or a solid.

D. Syllogism

1. The hypothetical syllogism. There are two types:
   a. The pure hypothetical. This is seldom used and so is of little practical importance. All three propositions are hypothetical:

      If goods become scarce, prices will advance (other things being equal).
      If prices advance, our savings cannot buy as much as at present.
      If goods become scarce, our savings cannot buy as much as at present.

   b. The mixed hypothetical syllogism. This is extensively used and is therefore important. The major premise is a hypothetical proposition and the minor premise is a simple proposition.

Rule for the mixed hypothetical syllogism: The minor premise must either posit the antecedent or sublate the consequent of the major premise. Fallacies: (1) to sublate the antecedent; (2) to posit the consequent.

To posit the antecedent is to restate it as a fact, retaining the same quality: if it is negative in the major premise, it should be negative in the minor; if it is affirmative in the major, it should be affirmative in the minor.

To sublate the consequent is to restate as a fact its contradictory; this requires a change of quality: if it is affirmative in the major premise, it should be negative in the minor; if it is negative in the major, it should be affirmative in the minor.

Note. The rule has reference only to what the minor premise does to the major. Whenever the minor premise posits the antecedent, the conclusion posits the consequent. And whenever the minor premise sublates the consequent, the conclusion sublates the antecedent. This is correct and does not conflict with the rule.

There are two moods of the mixed hypothetical syllogism: the constructive, which posits, and the destructive, which sublates. Only two forms are valid.

1) The valid constructive mood posits the antecedent. Example:

If a man is not honest, he is not a fit public officer.
This man is not honest.
∴ This man is not a fit public officer.

2) The valid destructive mood sublates the consequent. Example:

If all students were equally competent, each would acquire the same amount of knowledge from a given course.
But each does not acquire the same amount of knowledge from a given course.
∴ All students are not equally competent.

Note. When the consequent is sublated, the conclusion should be the contradictory, not the contrary, of the antecedent.

c. Equivalent fallacies of mixed hypothetical and simple syllogisms.

1) The fallacy of sublating the antecedent in a mixed hypothetical syllogism is equivalent to the fallacy of an illicit process of the major term in a simple syllogism. Example:

If a man drinks poison, he will die.	Fallacy:
This man has not drunk poison.	Sublating the ante-
∴ He will not die.	cedent

Equivalent simple syllogism:

Whoever drinks poison will die.	M a P	Fallacy:
This man has not drunk poison.	S e M	Illicit process of
∴ He will not die.	S e P	the major term

2) The fallacy of positing the consequent in a mixed hypothetical syllogism is equivalent to the fallacy of an undistributed middle term in a simple syllogism. Example:

If a man drinks poison, he will die.	Fallacy:
This man died.	Positing the con-
∴ He must have drunk poison.	sequent

Equivalent simple syllogism:

Whoever drinks poison will die.	P a M	Fallacy:
This man died.	S a M	Undistributed mid-
∴ He must have drunk poison.	S a P	dle term

Note. If the hypothetical proposition is a *sine qua non,* no fallacy can result in a mixed hypothetical syllogism; for in that circumstance the minor premise may posit or sublate either the antecedent or the consequent. Similarly, if one of the premises of a simple syllogism is a definition, neither an illicit process nor an undistributed middle will occur, even if the special rules of the figures are disregarded.

d. By applying the rule of the mixed hypothetical syllogism, we can show formally the ground for the rules governing the syllogism as a formula of inference. We may state each of the rules in a formally correct mixed hypothetical syllogism, thus:

1) If the premises of a correct syllogism are true, the conclusion must be true.

In this correct syllogism the premises are true.

∴ The conclusion is true.

This mixed hypothetical syllogism is correct, for the minor premise posits the antecedent. It would be incorrect to sublate the antecedent; therefore if the premises are not true, the value of the conclusion is formally unknown (see page 169).

2) If the premises of a correct syllogism are true, the conclusion must be true.

The conclusion of this syllogism is not true.

∴ The premises are not true.

This mixed hypothetical syllogism is correct, for the minor premise sublates the consequent. It would be incorrect to posit the consequent; therefore if the conclusion is true, the value of the premises is formally unknown (see page 169).

The point may be demonstrated further by constructing two more correct mixed hypothetical syllogisms, the minor premise of the one positing the antecedent, that of the other sublating the consequent of the following major premise, which states the second important rule: If the conclusion of a correct syllogism is false, at least one of the premises must be false. In the same way one could prove the rules of opposition which work in only one direction, e. g., If A is true, E is false.

2. The disjunctive syllogism

This is a syllogism in which the major premise is a disjunctive proposition and the minor premise is a simple categorical proposition positing or sublating one of the alternatives.

a. There are two moods of the disjunctive syllogism:

1) *Ponendo tollens,* in which the minor premise posits one alternative and the conclusion sublates the other. Example:

S is either P or Q. This woman's long-unheard-from husband is either living or dead. (Stated before making investigation.)

S is P.   He is living. (Stated after long investigation.)

∴ S is not Q.   He is not dead. (And she cannot marry again.)

2) *Tollendo ponens,* in which the minor premise sublates

one alternative and the conclusion posits the other. Example:

S is either P or Q.   The soul is either spiritual or ma-
                              terial.
S is not Q.   The soul is not material.
∴S is P.   The soul is spiritual.

Note. This mood is valid only when the disjunctive proposition is of the strict type, its alternatives being collectively exhaustive and mutually exclusive.

b. Fallacies of the disjunctive syllogism

1) There is only one purely formal fallacy, which will seldom occur; it is present when both the minor premise and the conclusion both posit and sublate each alternative. Example:

John is either a pig or not a pig. (Only two alternatives.)

John is not a pig. (You say, removing one alternative.)

∴John is a pig. (The only alternative left.)

This appears at first sight to exemplify the second formula above. But notice that the minor premise sublates the first alternative and posits the second and does both these things simultaneously. The conclusion simultaneously posits the first alternative and sublates the second.

The root of the error lies in the ambiguity of *not* in the major premise; as worded, it may be understood with *is* or with *pig*, either with the copula or with the term. The ambiguity can be removed by a clearer statement in which the negative is clearly attached to *pig* and the alternatives are dichotomous. Thus:

John is either a pig or a non-pig.

John is not a pig.

∴John is non-pig.

Analogy: In billiards or in croquet it is permissible to move two balls with one stroke. But to move both alternatives by one statement is not permissible in the disjunctive syllogism. Each stroke, each proposition, must affect only one alternative at one time.

2) The material fallacy of imperfect disjunction, which

has also a formal aspect, occurs when the alternatives are either (1) not mutually exclusive; or (2) not collectively exhaustive. Example of the latter:

Roses are either red or white.

The roses he sent are not red.

∴The roses he sent are white.

3. The dilemma

This is a syllogism which has for its minor premise a disjunctive proposition, for its major premise a compound hypothetical proposition, and for its conclusion either a simple or a disjunctive proposition.

The dilemma, correctly constructed, is a valid and useful form of reasoning, as all but the first of the four following examples and also some of the examples in the exercises at the end of this chapter illustrate. In actual use, a part of the argument is usually only implicit.

If the disjunctive offers three alternatives, the argument is more correctly called a trilemma; if many, a polylemma.

The dilemma is constructive if the minor premise posits the two antecedents of the major; destructive if it sublates the two consequents.

a. There are four moods of the dilemma:

1) The simple constructive. Example:

The accused lives either frugally or lavishly.

If he lives frugally, his savings must have made him wealthy; if he lives lavishly, his expenditures prove him to be wealthy.

∴The accused is wealthy.

Empson, a tax-gatherer of Henry VII of England, used this argument to prove that everyone whom he haled into court could and should pay higher taxes to the king.

2) The complex constructive. Example:

Either the Christians have committed crimes or they have not.

If they have, your refusal to permit a public inquiry is irrational; if they have not, your punishing them is unjust.

∴You are either irrational or unjust.

Tertullian, the Christian apologist, used this argument

in an appeal to the Roman Emperor Marcus Aurelius, who was regarded as both a philosopher and an upright man, to stop the persecution of the Christians.

3) The simple destructive. Example:

If a student has earned graduation with the honor *summa cum laude*, he must have shown both talent and diligence.

But (his grades indicate that) either this student has not shown talent or he has not shown diligence.

∴This student has not earned graduation with the honor *summa cum laude*.

In the simple destructive dilemma, the two consequents of the major premise are conjoined by *both* and *and* instead of being disjoined by *either* and *or*. They are therefore not alternatives; if they were, to sublate one or the other of them in the minor premise would not necessarily involve sublating the antecedent in the conclusion, as is required in a destructive dilemma.

4) The complex destructive. Example:

If this man had been properly instructed, he would know that he is acting wrongly; and if he were conscientious, he would care.

But either he does not know that he is acting wrongly or he apparently does not care.

∴Either he has not been properly instructed or he is not conscientious.

Example of a trilemma (which might represent an argument of priest hunters in sixteenth-century England):

This priest can avoid capture only by flight, by combat, or by suicide.

If there is no exit but the one we guard, he cannot escape by flight; if he has no weapons he cannot combat our armed forces; if he values his eternal salvation, he will not commit suicide.

∴He cannot avoid capture.

b. Fallacies of the dilemma: (1) false major premise; (2) imperfect disjunction in the minor premise; (3) a shifting point of view.

There are three methods of attack in exposing these three sources of error:

1) Taking the dilemma by the horns

This method of attack is used when the major premise is false, that is, when the nexus affirmed between antecedent and consequent in the major premise does not hold in fact. Example:

If this man were intelligent, he would see the worthlessness of his arguments; if he were honest, he would admit that he is wrong.

But either he does not see the worthlessness of his arguments; or, seeing it, he will not admit that he is wrong.

∴ .Either he is not intelligent or he is not honest.

In attacking this dilemma, the controversialist would deny the nexus of the first part of the major premise by asserting that he is intelligent, and thereby recognizes his arguments not as invalid, but as valid.

2) Escaping between the horns

This method of attack is used when the minor premise presents an imperfect disjunction in that the alternatives stated are not collectively exhaustive. The discovery of an unmentioned alternative offers an escape from the conclusion, between the horns. Example:

If I tell my friend that her new dress is unbecoming, she will be hurt; if I tell her that it is becoming, I shall tell a lie.

But I must either tell her that it is becoming or that it is unbecoming.

∴ .I must either hurt my friend or tell a lie.

Here escape between the horns, the alternatives presented in the minor premise, is easy. I can refrain from making any comment on the dress; or, better, I can remark on some point that I can really commend, such as the color, the material, etc., avoiding any statement that will be either untruthful or offensive.

3) Rebutting the dilemma

This method of attack is used when both the dilemma open to rebuttal and the rebutting dilemma contain the dilemmatic fallacy, which is both a formal and a material fallacy. Sometimes it represents a mere change of emphasis, as from optimism to pessimism. It is occasioned by a shifting point of view, characteristic also of the paradox. (Example of a paradox: "Whosoever shall save his life shall lose it; he that shall lose his life for My sake shall save it." [St. Luke 9:24.] Here *life* means alternately "life of the body or senses" and "life of the soul." If these qualifications are inserted, the statement loses its apparent contradictoriness and becomes perfectly intelligible.)

The method of rebuttal is to accept the alternatives presented by the minor premise of the original dilemma, but to transpose the consequents of the major premise and change them to their contraries. Hence a conclusion exactly opposite to the conclusion of the original dilemma is derived.

Formal rebuttal is a rhetorical device, a mere manipulation of the material in order to show up the weakness of an opponent's position; the very fact that a rebuttal to a given dilemma can be constructed shows that the dilemmatic fallacy of a shifting point of view is present in both dilemmas and that neither one is valid.

A famous ancient example is the argument between Protagoras and Euathlus, his law pupil. According to the contract between them, Euathlus was to pay half his tuition fee when he completed his studies and the other half when he had won his first case in court. Seeing that his pupil deliberately delayed beginning the practice of law, Protagoras sued him for the balance of the fee.

Protagoras' argument:

> If Euathlus loses this case, he must pay me by the judgment of the court; if he wins it, he must pay me in accordance with the terms of the contract.
>
> But he must either win it or lose it.

∴ He must pay me in any case.

Euathlus' rebuttal:

> If I win the case, I need not pay, by the judgment of the court; if I lose it, I need not pay, by the terms of the contract.
>
> But I must either win it or lose it.

∴ I need not pay in any case.

Empson's "fork" (page 195) is another example of a dilemma open to rebuttal.

A dilemma is open to rebuttal only when there is room for a real shift in the point of view, not merely a shift of the position of the terms. For example, a child might be faced with the following dilemma:

I must take either castor oil or bitter cascara.

If I take castor oil, I shall suffer an ugly taste; and

if I take bitter cascara, I shall suffer an ugly taste.

∴I shall suffer an ugly taste in either case.

This dilemma is not open to rebuttal. There is no room for a real shift from pessimism to optimism. The following is not a rebuttal, but only a meaningless shifting of the terms:

If I take the bitter cascara, I shall escape the ugly taste of castor oil; and if I take the castor oil, I shall escape the ugly taste of bitter cascara.

But I must take either bitter cascara or castor oil.

∴I shall escape an ugly taste in either case.

If this dilemma really constituted a rebuttal to the first one, any dilemma could be rebutted. But such is not the case. Even though a dilemma open to rebuttal and its rebuttal are both fallacious, neither of them is so patently empty an argument as this second dilemma about the medicine.

QUESTIONS

1. What is a hypothetical proposition? What is the antecedent? the consequent? the nexus? Distinguish between a reason and a cause.
2. Distinguish the hypothetical proposition from the simple proposition; from the simple categorical proposition.
3. State the formula of each of the two types of hypothetical propositions; illustrate each. State the formula for the reduction of each of these types to a simple proposition; illustrate each.
4. Justify the treatment of the hypothetical proposition as a distinct logical form instead of a mere verbal conjunction of simple propositions by showing a distortion of meaning suffered by some hypothetical propositions when reduced to categorical form, and *vice versa*.
5. When is a hypothetical proposition true? false? Is the proposition which denies a hypothetical proposition ever itself a genuine hypothetical? Show by illustration that a hypothetical proposition which, taken by itself, is false may be true if understood as the contradictory of another hypothetical proposition which is false.

6. In what sense is a hypothetical proposition always affirmative?
7. What is a disjunctive proposition? State the formula for each of the three types; illustrate each.
8. Reduce a disjunctive proposition to a hypothetical; reduce that to a simple proposition. Write the three formulas involved.
9. When is a disjunctive proposition true? false? State and illustrate three methods of denying a disjunctive proposition. Is any one of these denials a genuine disjunctive proposition?
10. In what sense is a disjunctive proposition always affirmative? Justify the treatment of the disjunctive proposition as a distinct logical form.
11. Give an example of quantitative A E I O forms of a hypothetical proposition; of modal A E I O forms. Which are better suited to hypothetical propositions?
12. Give an example of quantitative and of modal A E I O forms of a disjunctive proposition.
13. What is a *sine qua non* hypothetical proposition? Illustrate. Write all its eductions.
14. Write all the eductions of a hypothetical proposition that is not a *sine qua non*.
15. What kind of hypothetical proposition and what kind of disjunctive proposition have, along with definition, the prerogatives resulting from simple convertibility? What are these prerogatives?
16. Write all the eductions of a strict disjunctive proposition.
17. Describe and illustrate two types of the hypothetical syllogism. Which is of greater importance?
18. State the rule determining the formal validity of the mixed hypothetical syllogism; the fallacies resulting from their violation. To what fallacies of the simple syllogism are these fallacies equivalent? Illustrate. If the hypothetical proposition is a *sine qua non*, do the rules of the mixed hypothetical syllogism apply?
19. What is meant by *posit? sublate?* Describe and illustrate the valid constructive mood of the mixed hypothetical syllogism; the valid destructive mood.
20. By applying the rule of the mixed hypothetical syllogism, show formally the ground for the rules governing the syllogism as a formula of inference.
21. Describe the disjunctive syllogism. Name and illustrate each of its two moods. Name and illustrate its one formal fallacy. Illustrate the material fallacy of imperfect disjunction.
22. Describe the dilemma. Name and illustrate each of its four moods. Is the dilemma a valid form of reasoning?
23. Name and illustrate the three sources of error likely to occur in a dilemma: show how to attack each. Which is the weakest method of attack? Why? Construct a rebuttal to Empson's "fork" on page 195.

EXERCISES

State the type and mood of each of the following arguments, expand any that are abridged, and determine the validity of each; if invalid, name the fallacy. Consider also whether the propositions are true. Re-state the mixed hypothetical syllogisms in their equivalent simple forms, on page 192.

1. If a poem is an epic, it is a narrative. "The Death of the Hired Man" is a narrative poem. Therefore it is an epic.
2. If a man does not forgive his enemies, he does not act as a true Christian. This man does not forgive his enemies. Therefore he does not act as a true Christian.
3. If a liquid is an acid, it contains hydrogen. Water contains hydrogen. Therefore water is an acid.
4. If a man is honest, he will try to pay his just debts. That man does not try to pay his just debts. Therefore he is not honest.
5. If a dress is woolen, it will shrink when washed in boiling water. This dress is not woolen. Therefore it will not shrink when washed in boiling water.
6. The patient will either die or get well. The patient did not die. Therefore he will get well.
7. If a car runs out of gasoline, it will not go. This car will not go. Therefore it has run out of gasoline.
8. The wind is blowing from either the west or the south. It is not blowing from the south. Therefore it is blowing from the west.
9. If the loose particles of metal mixed with sawdust and gravel in this box are iron, a magnet will draw them out. A magnet did draw them out. Therefore they are iron particles.
10. She married either a football coach or a college graduate. She married a football coach. Therefore she did not marry a college graduate.
11. If you have not a college degree, you cannot get a position as teacher in the schools of this city. You have a college degree. Therefore you can get a position as teacher in the schools of this city.
12. To live within your means, you must either curtail your expenditures or increase your income. You cannot increase your income. Therefore you must curtail your expenditures.
13. If the mining of coal is reduced, the price will be raised. The price has been raised. Therefore the mining of coal has been reduced.
14. If a college student is talented he can learn easily; if he is not, he can learn with difficulty. But every college student is either talented or not. Therefore every college student can learn either easily or with difficulty.
15. Her father either did die or will die. He did not die. Therefore he will die.
16. If this student had been inattentive, he could not have learned from the instructor how to solve the problem; if he had been dull, he could not have figured it out for himself. But either he learned from the instructor how to solve the problem or he figured it out for himself. Therefore either he was not inattentive or he is not dull.
17. Being told that a certain person maintained that there is no distinction between virtue and vice, Samuel Johnson replied: If the fellow does not think as he speaks, he is lying; and I cannot see what honor he can propose to himself from having the character of a liar. But if he does really think that there is no distinction between virtue and vice, why, sir, when he leaves our houses let us count our spoons.—Boswell.
18. *Agamemnon.* . . . Iphigenia, my virgin daughter,
    I to Diana, goddess of this land
    Must sacrifice. This victim given, the winds
    Shall swell our sails, and Troy beneath our arms

Be humbled in the dust; but if denied,
These things are not to be.—Euripides, *Iphigenia at Aulis*, ll. 89-94.

19. If this Christian does not deny his religion he will suffer physical tortures;
    if he does, he will suffer torture of conscience. But he will either deny it or
    not. Therefore he will suffer either physical torture or torture of conscience.

20. The prisoner is either guilty or not guilty. He is guilty (jury's verdict).
    Therefore he is not guilty.

21. Either death is a state of nothingness and utter unconsciousness, or it is a
    migration of the soul from this world to another. If you suppose that there
    is no consciousness, death will be an unspeakable gain, for eternity is then
    only a single night and is like to the sleep of him who is undisturbed even
    by dreams, and not only a private man but even a great king will judge that
    better than other days and nights. If death is the journey to another place
    where all the dead are, where the pilgrim is delivered from the professors
    of justice in this world to find true judges there, where a man may converse
    with Orpheus, Hesiod, Homer, Ajax, Odysseus, and numberless others, death
    will be a gain. Therefore there is great reason to hope that death is a good.
    —Socrates in Plato's *Apology*

22. The graceless Helen in the porch I spied. . . .
    For Ilium burnt, she dreads the Trojan sword;
    More dreads the vengeance of her injured lord.—Vergil, *Aeneid*, II, 775-81.

23. To balance the budget, Congress must either increase taxes or borrow money.
    If it increases taxes, the people of the United States must pay now. If it
    borrows money, the people of the United States must pay later. Therefore
    to balance the budget, the people of the United States must pay either now
    or later.

24. An Athenian mother sought to dissuade her son from entering politics by
    means of the following argument: If you act justly, your fellow politicians
    will hate you; and if you act unjustly, the gods will hate you. But you must
    act either justly or unjustly. Therefore you will be hated in either case.

25. If college football players are not to suffer an intellectual loss, their absence
    from classes must be curtailed; if they are not to suffer defeat, their practice
    time must be increased. But either their absence from class cannot be cur-
    tailed or their practice time cannot be increased. Therefore they will either
    suffer an intellectual loss or they will suffer defeat.

26. If a man sins, he must both know that an act is evil and willingly do it.
    But this man either did not know that this act was evil or he did not willing-
    ly do it. Therefore this man did not sin.

27. If the course of study in a college is easy, poor students will flock to it; if
    it is difficult, superior students will find there an intellectual challenge; if it
    is of medium difficulty, it will attract the mediocre. But it will be either
    easy or difficult or of medium difficulty. Therefore it will attract either poor
    or superior or mediocre students.

28. Foolish moral writers will tell you that whenever you do wrong you will
    be punished, and whenever you do right, rewarded; and foolish immoral
    writers will tell you that if you do right you will get no good, and if you
    do wrong dexterously, no harm.—John Ruskin, *Fors Clavigera*.

29. *Henry V*. If we are marked to die, we are enough
    To do our country loss; and if to live,

The fewer men, the greater share of honor.
God's will! I pray thee wish not one man more.
—Shakespeare, Henry V, 4.3.20

30. If a girl expects to become a concert singer, she must both have a good voice and undergo rigid training. But this girl either has not a good voice or she is unwilling to undergo a rigid training. Therefore she will not become a concert singer.

31. *Camillo.* What case stand I in? I must be the poisoner
Of good Polixenes; and my ground to do't
Is the obedience to a master . . .
Promotion follows. If I could find example
Of thousands that had struck anointed kings
And flourished after, I'ld not do't . . . I must
Forsake the court. To do't or no, is certain
To me a break-neck.—Shakespeare, *The Winter's Tale*, 1.2.352-63.

32. If the doctor did not know that the operation would hasten the death of the patient, he is incompetent; if he did, he ought to be prosecuted. But either he knew it or he did not know it. Therefore either he is incompetent or he ought to be prosecuted.

33. If you stored these furs in your garage, knowing that they were stolen, you were an accomplice to the theft; if you stored them, not knowing it, you were easily taken in. But you stored them either knowing or not knowing that they were stolen. Therefore you are either an accomplice to the theft or you are easily taken in.

34. If the colonel obeys the general's orders, he will lose the battle; if he disobeys, he will be subject to court martial. But he must either obey or disobey the orders. Therefore he must either lose the battle or be subject to court martial.

35. This student's effort to learn medicine will be either successful or unsuccessful. If it is successful, he will earn the degree M. D.; if it is unsuccessful, he should not have it, for it would be a false label plastered on a potential social menace. Therefore this student will either earn the degree M. D. or he should not get it.

36. If you were intelligent, you would have understood the directions; if you were in earnest you would have followed them. But either you did not understand the directions or you did not follow them. Therefore you were either not intelligent or not in earnest.

37. If a student violates an important rule, he is expelled from that college; if he fails in his studies, he is asked to withdraw. But my brother either was not expelled from college or he was not asked to withdraw. Therefore he either did not violate an important rule or he did not fail in his studies.

CHAPTER IX

FALLACIES

The proper attitude in argument is expressed by Socrates:

What sort of man am I? I am one of those who would be glad to be refuted when saying a thing that is untrue, glad also to refute another if he said something inexact, not less glad to be refuted than to do it, since I deem it the greater blessing, in proportion as it is a greater good, to be released from that which is the greatest evil than to release another from it.—Plato, *Gorgias*.

In so far as an argument is fallacious, it is not logical. But as logic is concerned with truth, it is incidentally concerned with the negation of truth, namely error—falsity and fallacies.

A fallacy is a violation of logical principle disguised under an appearance of validity. It is an error in process; falsity is an error in fact. Fallacy arises from an erroneous relation of propositions; falsity, from an erroneous relation of terms. A premise may be false; reasoning may be fallacious.

To discover a fallacy is to discover the reason why the mind was deceived into regarding error as truth. To classify fallacies is to attempt to find common ground for such deception. But a given argument may be fallacious for more reasons than one, and hence it may exemplify more than one fallacy. Consequently, a classification of fallacies is neither exhaustive nor mutually exclusive.

A fallacy is either formal, or material, or both simultaneously.

I. Formal fallacies

These arise from violation of rules governing the formal relations of propositions, and have been treated where these formal relations have been treated. The fallacies of opposition are violations of the rules of opposition; the commonest one is to assume of contraries that when one is false the other is true, instead of unknown. The fallacies of eduction are: illicit obversion; illicit conversion. The fallacies of the syllogistic relation are: undistributed middle term; illicit process of the major term or of the minor term; four terms; four propositions; two negative premises; two partial premises; merely seeming mediated opposition; sublating the antecedent or positing the consequent in the minor premise of a mixed hypothetical syllogism; simultaneously positing and sublating both alternatives of a disjunction; imperfect disjunction; the dilemmatic fallacy.

The nature of the formal fallacies can be most clearly illustrated in empty formulas rendered invalid and consequently fallacious by disregard of the rules of the formula. Examples:

d	d	Fallacy:	d	u	Fallacy:	d	u	Fallacy:	M e S	Fallacy:
S e	M	Illicit	S a	M	Undis-,	M a	S	Illicit	P e M	Two negative
d	u	process	d	u	tributed	d	d	process	S e P	premises
M a	P	of the	P a	M	middle	M e	P	of the	S a Mᵃ	Fallacy:
d	d	major	d	u	term	d	d	minor	Mᵇ a P	Four
S e	P	term	S a	P		S e	P	term	S a P	terms

II. Material fallacies

These fallacies have their root in the matter—in the terms, in the ideas and in the symbols by which the ideas are communicated. They vitiate an argument that may be formally correct.

Aristotle grouped them in two classes: six fallacies *in dictione*, occasioned by ambiguity of language, and seven fallacies *extra dictionem*, occasioned by a hidden assumption not conveyed in the language. They were devices used in oral controversy in Athens by the sophists, who sought, not truth, but victory over their opponents by these merely apparent refutations. These fallacies continue to be used, however, to deceive others and sometims even to deceive oneself.

A. Fallacies *in dictione*

These arise from ambiguity of language, whether of words or of construction. They have their root in the grammar (the language) that seeks to symbolize the logic (the thought), and they may all be regarded as special instances of the fallacy of four terms. This fallacy is simultaneously a formal and a material fallacy because it both violates a rule of the form and lies in the matter. Six types of fallacies *in dictione* may be distinguished.

1. Equivocation. This fallacy is occasioned by the ambiguity of a word which symbolizes two or more different terms.

Feathers are light.
Light is the opposite
　of darkness.
∴ Feathers are the opposite
　of darkness.

Here *light* names, as it were, two different buildings, *x* and *y*; *x* means light, "not heavy," and *y* means light, "not dark."

2. Amphiboly. This fallacy is produced by ambiguity of syntax or grammatical structure, such as a misplaced, a squint-

ing, or a dangling modifier, ambiguous reference of pronouns, or ambiguity of word order. Such ambiguity is especially likely to occur in an uninflected language like English.
It is always an error in grammar, but, strictly speaking, it
occasions the fallacy of four terms in logic only when the
ambiguous proposition becomes a premise in a syllogism.

a. The prophecy in Shakespeare's *2 Henry VI* (1.4.33):

> The duke yet lives that Henry shall depose.

Translated into an inflected language, like Latin, this
passage would lose its ambiguity. The argument would
become syllogistic if the duke should interpret it by adding the minor premise, "I am this duke," and conclude,
"Therefore I shall depose Henry." Or, if he should give
the alternate meaning to the major premise and conclude,
"Therefore Henry shall depose me."

b. He told his brother that he had won the prize. (Who
won it?)

c. Feed a cold and starve a fever.

Here *feed* is subjunctive. The sentence is a warning
and means: If you feed a cold, you will have a fever to
starve. As commonly interpreted, however, *feed* is taken
to be imperative, and a meaning just the opposite of the
one intended is derived.

d. *Clown.* I was a gentleman born before my father, for the king's
son took me by the hand and called me brother; and then the
two kings called my father brother.
> —Shakespeare, *The Winter's Tale,* 5.2.150

The clown has been using the words *gentleman born*
to mean "born a gentleman."

3. Composition. This fallacy occurs when a middle term is
used distributively in the major premise and collectively in
the minor premise; or when a term is used distributively in
its own premise and collectively in the conclusion. Example:

> No men are Catholics and Protestants. (Collective use.)
> Catholics and Protestants are Christians. (Distributive use.)
> .˙.No men are Christians.

Here are present simultaneously four fallacies, one material and three formal:

a. Composition. *Catholics and Protestants* is used distributively in the major premise and collectively in the minor.

(The minor premise is false if these terms are affirmed separately, true if they are affirmed together.)

b. The formal fallacy of four terms, for composition is a fallacy *in dictione*.

c. The formal fallacy of four propositions, for the major premise is a conjunction of two propositions: Catholics are Christians. Protestants are Christians.

d. The formal fallacy of an illicit process of the major term.

4. Division. This fallacy, just the reverse of composition, occurs when a middle term is used collectively in the major premise and distributively in the minor premise, or when a term is used collectively in its own premise and distributively in the conclusion. Example:

Nine and seven are sixteen. (Collective use.)

Sixteen is an even number.

∴.Nine and seven are even numbers. (Distributive use.)

In addition to the material fallacy of division, there are present here also the formal fallacies of four terms and four propositions.

It is this fallacy of division that produces such erroneous conclusions as: A single straw broke the camel's back. A single Justice of the Supreme Court determined the constitutionality of a law in a five-four decision.

Since division is merely the reverse of composition, these two fallacies can be distinguished only by noticing in which proposition the term is used collectively and in which distributively.

5. Accent. This fallacy occurs when a meaning different from that intended is conveyed through a special emphasis on certain letters, syllables, words, or ideas. Emphasis of words can be produced orally by stress or indicated in written language by italics or other visible device. Such misleading emphasis may occur in syllables of the same word or in words of the same sentence. Examples:

a. A master said to his servant: "Go heat this capon's leg," who immediately did eat it. Then his master, being angry, said, "I bade you heat it, with an *h*." "No, sir," said the servant, "I did heat it with bread."

This misunderstanding of a word, peculiar to a certain class of Englishmen, is given as an example of this fallacy by Thomas Blundeville in *The Art of Logic* (1599).

b. The servants incensed the king.

    Here the alternative pronunciations, in′censed and incensed′, convey strongly contrasted meanings, and imply different conclusions if a premise is added.

c. The early Christians called the Blessed Virgin theo′tokos, meaning "she who brought forth God." Nestorius, by a change of accent, called her theoto′kos, meaning "she who is brought forth by God," and denied the divinity of Christ.

d. He is my friend.

    Here not only does the meaning change as the emphasis is made to fall successively on each of the words, but an ironical emphasis will convey a meaning which actually contradicts the statement spoken in an ordinary manner.

    Note. This form of the fallacy of accent must not be confused with amphiboly. In this sentence there is no doubt as to the syntax of any word, whereas there always is in amphiboly.

e. Quotations taken out of context are sometimes gross examples of the fallacy of accent; e. g., The Bible says: (1) There is no God. (2) Every man is a liar.

    It is a fact that these propositions are in the Bible, but in their context the meaning is altogether different: "The fool hath said in his heart: There is no God." (Psalm 13, verse 1.) "I said in my excess: Every man is a liar." (Psalm 115, verse 11.)

f. To introduce italics into quoted material without stating that one has done so may be an instance of the fallacy of accent.

g. In extended discourse, by overemphasizing certain aspects of a subject and either slighting or completely neglecting other related aspects, one may, without actual misstatement, convey a very false idea of the subject in its entirety. This is called special pleading or propaganda and is a very frequent source of misrepresentation. Examples:

    1) The coloring of the news through overemphasis of some facts and underemphasis or omission of others, especially at the time of a political campaign.

    2) In a certain history textbook, after eulogizing the achievements of Roger Bacon, the author remarked

that Bacon had been left to die in poverty. He created a very false impression through a statement perfectly true in itself, by ignoring the fact that in becoming a Franciscan friar, Roger Bacon freely chose both to live and to die in poverty.

6. Verbal form. This is the fallacy of erroneously supposing that similarity in the form of language signifies a corresponding similarity in meaning.

a. This fallacy occurs, for instance, when identity of the prefix or suffix of words leads one to conclude erroneously that they are therefore analogous in meaning; e. g., that *inspiration* and *inexplicable* are both negative terms, and that if *in* means *not* in the one, it must mean *not* in the other.

1) An outstanding instance of such confusion is recorded in *Word Study* (April, 1947):

Frank L. Jones, president of the Greater New York Safety Council, reports that many people think that the *in-* in *inflammable* means "noninflammable", and his Council and other groups have been urging for some time that manufacturers and dealers use *flammable* to avoid such misunderstandings.

2) John Stuart Mill commits this fallacy when he argues:

The only proof capable of being given that an object is visible is that people actually see it. . . . The only proof that a sound is audible is that people hear it. . . . In like manner, the sole evidence it is possible to give that anything is desirable is that people do actually desire it.

Since the whole force of the argument lies in the assumption of a strict analogy between *visible, audible,* and *desirable,* the argument falls when it is understood that whereas, according to the dictionary, *visible* and *audible* mean "capable of being seen" or "heard," or "actually seen" or "heard," *desirable* means "worthy of desire" or "that which ought to be desired."

b. This fallacy may also arise from similarity of phrases, particularly verb phrases. Example:

He who sleeps least is most sleepy.

He who is most sleepy sleeps most.

∴ He who sleep least sleeps most.

Here the verb phrases *sleeps least* and *sleeps most* appear to be contraries; but if the tenses are more carefully discriminated, we have the following valid syllogism (true of normal, healthy persons):

He who has slept least is most sleepy.

He who is most sleepy will sleep most.

∴.He who has slept least will sleep most.

c. This fallacy also includes an illicit transition from one category to another, as in the following, from substance to relation:

A boy who has six marbles and loses one no longer has what he once had.

He who no longer has the six marbles he once had, has not necessarily lost six marbles.

∴.He who no longer has what he once had, has not necessarily lost it.

Objects collectively considered are related as members of a given group. If one is lost all that remain have lost the relation, a member of six, even though, as independent substances, they have not been lost.

B. Fallacies *extra dictionem*

Common to these seven fallacies is a hidden false assumption not warranted by the language in which the ideas are expressed.

1. Fallacy of accident

This fallacy arises from the false assumption that whatever is predicable of a subject (usually the middle term) is predicable of its accident (the minor term), and in the same sense; or that whatever is predicable of a term understood in one aspect, e. g., specifically or concretely, is predicable of the same term understood in another aspect, e. g., generically or abstractly, or *vice versa*.

Every predicate, except that in a definition or an identical proposition, is accidental to its subject in the sense that it is by accident that the given subject and the predicate should be related in the given proposition: e. g., A lion is an animal. A square is equilateral. It is an accident that an animal should be a lion rather than a mouse or a horse; or that an equilateral figure should be a square rather than a triangle or an octagon. This situation exists whenever the extension of a predicate affirmed is greater than the extension of the subject; in other words, when the proposition is convertible only *per accidens*, that is, by limitation; hence the name.

Any one of the three terms of a syllogism may be the source of the fallacy of accident, but most often it is the middle term. Example:

To communicate knowledge is commendable.

To gossip is to communicate knowledge.

∴ To gossip is commendable.

Here knowledge is understood in the generic sense in the major premise and in a specific and even in a trivial sense hardly worthy of the general name, in the minor premise. Therefore, while it is commendable to communicate knowledge understood in its essential, abstract, and general meaning, it is not commendable to communicate trivial or even mischievous information.

Aristotle remarks that the fallacy of accident results when we fail to distinguish the sameness and otherness of terms, or when we substitute an accident for an essential attribute.

According to Renaissance logicians, the fallacy of accident occurs when anything belonging to the substance of something is attributed also to some accident of that substance. Thomas Wilson (1551) gives the following examples and explanations:

(1) Fish is not the same that flesh is.

Flesh is food.

∴ Fish is not food.

In the first proposition I understand the substance of flesh, and in the second proposition I mean the accident that is in both flesh and fish. Therefore my argument is not lawful, because I referred both the substance and the accident to one and the same subject.

(2) This man is a witty fellow.

This man is lame.

∴ This man has a lame wit.

This is evidently false, because the accidents of the body are referred to the substance of the mind.

Aristotle gives an example similar to Wilson's first; and another somewhat similar to Wilson's second:

This dog is a father.

This dog is yours.

∴ This dog is your father.

The fallacy of accident may seem much like that of equivocation; but whereas the fallacy of equivocation involves a shifting of terms, the fallacy of accident involves a shifting of usage of the same term. To shift from one first imposition to another first imposition on the same word is to shift from one term to another and this is the fallacy of equivocation. But to shift from a generic to a specific usage of the same term or from the first imposition of a term to second or zero imposition, or from first to second intention is a shift in usage, and this is the fallacy of accident. Examples:

(1) Feathers are light.
    Light is an adjective.
.˙.Feathers are adjectives.

Here we have the fallacy of accident, the same term understood in two different aspects, here in two different planes of discourse; for *light* has the same meaning, although not the same usage, in both propositions. It is only *light* meaning "not heavy" that is an adjective.

To return to our analogy, the argument does not shift from one "building" to another as in equivocation, where there are two entirely different terms symbolized by *light* (see p. 205), but from one floor to another floor of the same building. In this syllogism, *light* shifts from the first floor of *x* building to the second.

Floor	*x building*
Attic _____	second intention: logic
Second _____	second imposition: grammar
First _____	first imposition and first intention: reference to real being
Basement _____	zero imposition: phonetics and spelling

Shift of imposition: from first to second

(2) Feathers are light.
    Light is a noun.
.˙.Feathers are nouns.

Here we have simultaneously two fallacies, accident and equivocation, for in the major premise, *light*, there classified grammatically, is "the opposite of darkness" (*y* building); this is not the same term as that symbolized by *light*, meaning "not heavy" (*x* building) in the minor premise. The argument moves from first floor of *x* building to second floor of *y* building represented as follows:

logic
grammar
reality
phonetics and spelling

logic
grammar
reality
phonetics and spelling

Shift of imposition (accident) and also equivocation

Every term can be used in either of the two intentions; and every word can be used in each of the three impositions. Therefore, following our analogy, every distinct meaning of a word is like a separate building, each having the four floors indicated.

Particularly enlightening species of the fallacy of accident are those that involve a shift from one plane or plateau of discourse to another by a change of intention or of imposition. The ordinary plane of discourse is that of first intention and first imposition. There are three others: that of second intention, of second imposition, and of zero imposition. A valid argument can be maintained if each term is used consistently in any one of these planes of discourse, but if the same term is shifted from one plane to another, the argument is invalid.

a. Shift of imposition. This fallacy involves the false assumption that what is true of a word understood in one imposition is true of the same word understood in other impositions. Example:

A banana is yellow. Yellow is an adjective. Therefore a banana is an adjective.

Here *yellow* is understood in first imposition in the minor premise and in second imposition in the major.

The parts of speech and other grammatical concepts are terms of second imposition in the sense that when used as predicates, that is, as modes of conceiving their subjects, they cause their subjects to be understood in second imposition, that is, as grammatical entities. (See pp. 36-39.) But that the terms of grammar may themselves be understood in all of the impositions is illustrated by:

1) Fallacious syllogisms in which the part of speech itself is shifted from one imposition to another in the premises:

a) *Carry* is a verb. *Verb* is a noun. Therefore *carry* is a noun.

b) *Hippopotamus* is a noun. *Noun* is a monosyllable. Therefore *hippopotamus* is a monosyllable.

In *a*, *verb* shifts from first to second imposition in the premises. In *b*, *noun* shifts from first to zero imposition in the premises.

2) Valid syllogisms in which the term of grammar is understood in first or in zero imposition throughout, and in which, consequently, the argument is not erroneously shifted from one plane of discourse to another.

a) *Sing* is a verb. A verb has tense. Therefore *sing* has tense.

Here *verb* is understood in the first imposition in both premises, and *sing* is understood in second imposition in the minor premise and in the conclusion.

b) *Adjective* is often mispronounced. A word often mispronounced is often misspelled. Therefore *adjective* is often misspelled.

Here *adjective* is understood in zero imposition both in the minor premise and in the conclusion.

The terms of phonetics and of spelling or orthography are terms of zero imposition in the sense that when used as predicates, that is, as modes of conceiving their subjects, they cause their subjects to be understood in zero imposition, that is, as mere sounds or notations. But that the terms of phonetics and of orthography may themselves be understood in all of the impositions is illustrated by:

1) Fallacious syllogisms in which the term of phonetics or orthography is itself shifted in imposition in the premises:

Cat is a notation. *Notation* has three syllables. Therefore *cat* has three syllables.

Here *notation* is understood in first imposition in the minor premise and in zero imposition in the major.

2) Valid syllogisms in which the term of phonetics or orthography is understood in first or in second imposition throughout and in which, consequently, the argument is not shifted from one plane of discourse to another:

a) *Indivisibility* is a polysyllable. A polysyllable may be divided between lines. Therefore *indivisibility* may be divided between lines.

b) *Invisibility* is a notation. A notation is visible. Therefore *invisibility* is visible.

In these syllogisms, *polysyllable* and *notation* are understood in first imposition in both premises; *indivisibility* and *invisibility* are understood in zero imposition in the minor premise and in the conclusion.

c) *Notation* is a noun. A noun may be the object of a preposition. Therefore *notation* may be object of a preposition.

Here *notation* is understood in second imposition in both the minor premise and in the conclusion.

b. Shift of intention. This fallacy involves the false assumption that what is true of a term understood in first intention is true of the same term understood in second intention, and *vice versa*. Examples:

1) A lion is an animal. Animal is a genus. Therefore a lion is a genus.

2) A square is equilateral. Equilateral is a differentia. Therefore a square is a differentia.

In these syllogisms, *animal* and *equilateral* are understood in first intention in the minor premise and in second intention in the major.

The predicables are terms of second intention in the sense that when used as predicates, that is, as modes of conceiving their subjects, they cause their subjects to be understood in second intention, that is, as concepts, as mental entities. (See p. 39.) But that the predicables themselves may be understood in both the intentions is illustrated by:

1) Fallacious syllogisms in which the predicable itself is shifted from first to second intention in the premises:

a) Animal is a genus. Genus is a predicable. Therefore animal is a predicable.

b) Mirthful is a property. Property is a predicable. Therefore mirthful is a predicable.

In these syllogisms, *genus* and *property* are understood in first intention in the minor premise and in second intention in the major.

2) Valid syllogisms in which the predicable is understood in first intention in both premises and in which, consequently, the argument is not shifted from one plane of discourse to another:

   a) Animal is a genus. A genus is divisible into species. Therefore animal is divisible into species.

   b) Mirthful is a property. A property is a term convertible with its subject. Therefore mirthful is a term convertible with its subject.

   In these syllogisms, *genus* and *property* are understood in first intention (that is, predicatively) in both premises; *animal* and *mirthful* are understood in second intention (that is, reflexively) in both the minor premise and in the conclusion.

c. An argument may shift in both imposition and intention. This is best illustrated by a sorites: Man is rational. Rational is a differentia. Differentia is a polysyllable. Polysyllable is a noun. Therefore man is a noun.

Here the conclusion is true, and every premise, considered separately, is true; but each of the implicit conclusions is false, and the reasoning is utterly fallacious, for the argument shifts through four planes of discourse.

2. Confusion of absolute and qualified statement (or *secundum quid*)

This fallacy arises from the assumption that a proposition true in certain respects or with certain qualifications is true absolutely or without those qualifications, or *vice versa*.

This fallacy, which is a common cause not only of deliberate deception but even of self-delusion, is occasioned by the smallness of the difference involved, for the qualification seems to add so little to the meaning that the statement is accepted absolutely. As a tool of deception, it consists in getting assent to a statement with a qualification and then proceeding as if the statement had been conceded absolutely, or *vice versa*.

The qualified statement may be true of a particular thing or person, or with respect to a particular place, time, manner, relation (as of part to whole), comparison, etc. What

is true in one respect may not be true in another respect.
Examples of this fallacy:

a. A public executioner may justly put a certain criminal to
death. Therefore every man may do so.

b. Christ cast out the buyers and sellers from the temple, because their act was evil. Therefore buying and selling is
evil.

c. Manual labor well done is praiseworthy. Therefore it is
good to do it on Sundays.

d. A negro has white teeth. Therefore a negro is white.

e. God said: "Thou shalt not kill"; therefore killing animals
for meat is wicked.

f. Francis Bacon was a good writer. Therefore he was a good
judge.

g. To suffer death unjustly is preferable to suffering death
justly. Therefore what takes place unjustly is preferable
to what takes place justly.

h. *Pandarus.* [Helen] praised [Troilus'] complexion above Paris'.
Cressida. Why, Paris hath color enough.
Pandarus. So he has.
Cressida. Then Troilus should have too much. If she praised him
above, his complexion is higher than his. He having color enough,
and the other higher, is too flaming a praise for a good complexion.
I had as lieve Helen's golden tongue had commended Troilus for
a copper nose.
—Shakespeare, *Troilus and Cressida,* 1.2.107

Cressida makes *above,* which qualified with respect to
beauty of color, qualify with respect to intensity of color.

i. Whoso drinketh well sleepeth well; whoso sleepeth well, sinneth
not; whoso sinneth not shall be blessed. Therefore whoso drinketh
well, shall be blessed.
—Thomas Blunderville, *The Art of Logic* (1599)

The second proposition is true with respect to the time
while a man sleeps; he may sin when he is awake.

3. Fallacy of consequent

This fallacy arises from the assumption that because a consequent follows upon its antecedent, the antecedent must
likewise follow upon the consequent. In other words, it involves the implicit assumption that an A proposition is convertible simply, when it is not. The fallacy of consequent
also arises from the assumption that from the contrary of the
antecedent the contrary of the consequent must follow, but

this also results from assuming simple convertibility.

The fallacy of consequent can be most readily understood as the material fallacy present whenever one commits the formal fallacy of either positing the consequent or sublating the antecedent in a mixed hypothetical syllogism whose major premise is not a *sine qua non* and therefore is not convertible simply. If it is a *sine qua non*, it is convertible, and no fallacy can result. It will be remembered (see page 192) that a mixed hypothetical syllogism can be reduced to a simple categorical syllogism, that the formal fallacy of positing the consequent is equivalent to the formal fallacy of an undistributed middle term, and that of sublating the antecedent, to an illicit process of the major term.

In categorical propositions, the predicate may be regarded as a consequent of the subject. Thus in "Man is an animal" being an animal follows from being a man, but being a man does not follow from being an animal; hence the proposition is not convertible simply.

Accordingly the following categorical syllogisms illustrate the two forms of the fallacy of consequent as well as the hypothetical syllogisms do:

a. A man is an animal. Bucephalus is an animal. Therefore Bucephalus is a man.
b. A man is an animal. Bucephalus is not a man. Therefore Bucephalus is not an animal.
c. If it rains, the ground is wet. The ground is wet. Therefore it rained.
d. If it rains, the ground is wet. It did not rain. Therefore the ground is not wet.

The fallacy of consequent is a frequent source of error in enthymemes. It is the material fallacy which falsifies the major premise of expansion *b* of the second enthymeme analyzed on page 154.

In argument, the fallacy of consequent leads a disputant to think he has refuted his opponent when he has shown the unsoundness of the reasons advanced in favor of the point urged; but this amounts to the fallacy of sublating the antecedent, for, as we noted on page 192, although the conclusion does follow from true premises, one cannot disprove a conclusion by showing that its premises are false; it may be supported by other, true premises. Nor does a disputant necessarily gain assent to his premises by getting his opponent to concede the truth of his conclusion, for to suppose that the truth of the premise follows from the truth of the conclusion is the fallacy of positing the consequent in the minor premise.

4. Arguing beside the point or ignoring the issue (or *ignoratio elenchi*)

This fallacy arises from falsely assuming that the point at issue has been disproved when one merely resembling it has been disproved; the point really at issue is consequently ignored.

Ignoratio elenchi means ignorance of the nature of refutation. To refute an opponent, one must prove the contradictory of his statement; and this is done only when the same predicate—not merely the name but the reality—is denied of the same subject in the same respect, relation, manner, and time in which it was asserted. To establish some other conclusion is to dodge the issue and to argue beside the point. For example, one attempting to refute the proposition "The popes are infallible" might think he has done so when, by citing the deeds of certain wicked popes, he has established the proposition "The popes are not impeccable." He has not, however, denied the same predicate as was affirmed in the proposition he attempted to refute. Moreover, it is not in the same respect, for infallibility has respect to freedom from error in teaching truth in matters of faith and morals to the universal church, and impeccability has respect to acting according to conscience in matters of personal conduct.

One also ignores the issue and argues beside the point who, when accused of dishonesty, replies that many others are doing the same thing, falsely assuming that when the number of dishonest persons is very large, *ipso facto* each ceases to be dishonest.

An argument that deals with the point at issue is *argumentum ad rem*. Arguments that evade the issue are given special names to signify on which irrelevant grounds they are based.

a. *Argumentum ad hominem.* This is to confuse the point at issue with the persons concerned. Attacks on the character and conduct of persons and personal abuse or praise are substituted for reasoning about the point at issue. Examples:

1) To argue that because there are wicked Catholics, the Catholic religion cannot be true.

2) To argue that, because a certain lawyer has defrauded his relatives by getting a larger share of the inheritance than was really intended by the testator, his arguments alleging that a certain bank official is an embezzler are worthless.

It is, however, legitimate to argue that, because a witness is known to have lied in a number of instances, or to have accepted bribes, his present testimony ought not to be readily accepted.

b. *Argumentum ad populum.* This fallacy arises from substituting an appeal to the passions and prejudices of the people for logical reasoning on the point at issue. Examples: The appeal to religious prejudice in the Presidential Campaign of 1928; the appeal to race-hatred by the persecutors of the Jews in Nazi Germany; the appeal to class prejudice by the Communists.

c. A special type of this fallacy is called *argumentum ad misericordiam.* It is used by many criminal lawyers to divert the jurors' minds from the real question, guilty or not guilty, by moving them to pity and to a favorable verdict because the defendant is, for instance, if a woman, beautiful, or young; or, if a man, needed by his family.

d. *Argumentum ad baculum.* This is the appeal to the "big stick." The issue is ignored in an attempt to inspire fear of the consequences of adopting a proposed opinion or program, or of allowing a movement branded as dangerous to gain strength. Examples: The threat of social ostracism or loss of a position might deter a person from embracing what he believes to the true religion. Or one may point out personal loss involved in upholding public interest.

e. *Argumentum ad ignorantiam.* This is the use of an argument that sounds convincing to hearers because they are ignorant of the weakness of the argument and of the facts that stand against it. Examples: A theory, such as that of evolution, is declared established because it has not been actually disproved—nor has it been proved. Miracles are

declared impossible; but ignorance about how they can occur does not disprove the fact that they do occur. High
rent is given as an excuse for charging high prices to those
who have not noticed that cut-rate drug stores, dime stores,
and other thriving low-price stores occupy the very high-
est-rent spots.

f. *Argumentum ad verecundiam.* This is an appeal to the
prestige or respect in which a proponent of an argument
is held as a guarantee of the truth of the argument. This is
unwarranted when reasoning about an issue is required,
and only the authority of its upholders or opponents is
given consideration. It is perfectly legitimate to supplement reasoning with authority (*argumentum ad auctori-
tatem*), but it is fallacious to substitute authority for reasoning in matters capable of being understood by reason.
This fallacy is particularly pernicious when the authority
cited is not an authority on the matter under discussion.
Example: Edison was an authority on the practical uses of
electricity but not on theology; to cite his opinion about
the non-existence of God as definitive is a gross instance
of this fallacy.

5. False cause

This fallacy consists in assigning as a reason for a conclusion a proposition which was not offered by the opponent as
his reason, and which is irrelevant. It is an attempt to show
the absurdity of an opponent's statement by joining to it
another premise of one's own concoction to reach a conclusion really at variance with the opponent's position and ridiculous or even impossible. It often amounts to setting up a
straw man, knocking him down, and then foolishly thinking
one has demolished his adversary. Example:

a. Mr. Smith urged against Mr. Jones, who holds that
younger men should replace eighty-year-olds as college
professors, that this is ridiculous, because in that case children of two or three years would make the best professors.

This conclusion, however, does not follow from Mr.
Jones's statement, but from one that Mr. Jones did not
make and would not admit, namely: "The younger a person is the better suited is he to be a college professor."
What Mr. Jones does hold is this: "Persons who are eighty

or older are well past the zenith of their powers and should be replaced by younger persons but not by those so young as not yet to have attained to the use of their faculties, much less their fullest development."

The fallacy of false cause is present also when something accidental to a thing is held to determine its nature, character, or value, for that which is not a cause is then held to be a cause. Examples:

b. The devastating wars in Europe have occurred because Christianity is a failure.

Chesterton has answered this charge:

> The Christian Ideal has not been tried and found wanting. It is something that has been found difficult: and left untried.
> —"The Unfinished Temple"

c. Football games are evil, because some gamble away much money on the results.

A thing is not evil merely because some persons abuse it. In such instances, the cause of the evil is not in the thing itself, but in those who make it an occasion for gratifying their own evil propensities.

Note. Post hoc ergo propter hoc is an inductive fallacy that is sometimes loosely identified with the deductive fallacy of false cause. The latter makes a false assumption about a reason, which is a cause of knowing; the former about a cause of being. The inductive fallacy *post hoc ergo propter hoc* results from the false assumption that whatever happens before a given event is the cause of that event. The error is increased by imperfect observation; instances in which the event occurs without the alleged antecedent cause pass unnoticed. Example: A black cat crosses my path. The next day the bank in which I have deposited my savings fails. I conclude that the black cat caused my misfortune. I have failed to notice how often a black cat has crossed a person's path and no ill-luck has followed. But even if it always followed, it would not therefore be a cause of the misfortune, for it could not be.

6. Begging the question

This is the fallacy of assuming in the premises the very proposition to be proved, namely, the conclusion—or a proposition wide enough to include the one to be proved. The con-

clusion assumed in the premises is usually hidden under synonyms, so that the identity of the propositions is less obvious.
Examples:

a. The tautological argument: The soul is immortal because
   it will live forever.

b. The shuttle argument: "That boy is insane." "Why do
   you think so?" "Because he murdered his mother." "Why
   did he murder her?" "Because he is insane."

   It may be a fact that the boy is insane and that may be
   the reason why he murdered his mother, but to reason
   without begging the question, other evidence of his insan-
   ity must be offered.

c. Arguing in a circle. This differs from the shuttle argument only by the addition of one or more propositions,
   which causes the argument to go around in a circle instead
   of merely shuttling back and forth: "The Church is infallible." "How can you prove that?" "The Bible says so."
   "What if the Bible does say so?" "The Bible is the inspired
   word of God." "How do you know that?" "Because the
   Church has so declared." "What if it has?" "The Church
   is infallible." "How can you prove that?" "The Bible
   says so."

   The fallacy of the preceding reasoning in a vicious circle
   is avoided by proving the authenticity of the Bible as a
   historical document; this breaks the circle.

d. The question-begging epithet is probably the most common instance of this fallacy. It is a phrase or a single word
   that assumes the point to be proved. It is a favorite device
   in coloring the news. Examples: The repeated reference
   to a tax bill as "the wealth-confiscation bill"; to a labor
   bill as "the slave labor bill."

7. Complex question

   This fallacy is somewhat similar to that of begging the
question. The latter assumes in the premises the proposition
to be proved, and the former assumes in the question part
of what belongs wholly to the answer.

   The fallacy of complex question occurs when, in answer
to a compound question, one demands a simple answer, whereas the correct answer would divide the question and answer
it part by part. Cross-examiners often employ this device to

trap a witness into contradicting himself, thereby weakening the value of his testimony in favor of the opposite side. Examples of this fallacy: Why did you steal my watch? When did you stop flirting? Where did you hide the body of the man you murdered? How much time have you wasted studying impractical subjects like philosophy and music? The attaching of unwelcome riders to a bill which the President favors forces him to answer simply the question: Shall he sign it, and thereby accept the rider, or shall he veto it and thereby sacrifice the bill which he otherwise favors?

QUESTIONS

1. Distinguish: fallacy; falsity; formal fallacy; material fallacy. May an erroneous argument exemplify two or more of these at one time?
2. Name the formal fallacies of: opposition; eduction; the syllogism. Illustrate six of the formal fallacies of the syllogism by fallacious formulas.
3. What error is common to all the fallacies *in dictione?* to the fallacies *extra dictionem?*
4. Name and distinguish the six fallacies *in dictione;* memorize one illustration of each given in this chapter.
5. Name and distinguish the seven fallacies *extra dictionem* and the sub-divisions thereof; memorize one illustration of each given in this chapter.
6. What is the fallacy *post hoc ergo propter hoc?* Illustrate. Is it a fallacy of deduction?
7. By what means can a term be shifted to different planes or plateaus of discourse? What fallacy results from such shifting? How many planes of discourse do we distinguish? How does this fallacy differ from equivocation?

EXERCISES

Analyze the following arguments, expanding, if necessary, those that are abridged. Name the type (see pp. 177, 204). If the argument is fallacious, it is necessary to explain clearly wherein the fallacy lies and to name it. If there are two or more fallacies present, name each one.

1. The heart is an organ. An organ is a musical instrument. Therefore the heart is a musical instrument.
2. The freshmen gave fifty books to the college library. Jane and Helen are freshmen. Therefore Jane and Helen gave fifty books to the college library.
3. A bird flies. Flies are insects. Therefore a bird is an insect.
4. Speaking of the silent is impossible. John is silent. Therefore speaking of John is impossible.
5. *Desdemona.* Do you know, sirrah, where Lieutenant Cassio lies?
   Clown. I dare not say he lies anywhere.
   Desdemona. Why, man?
   Clown. He's a soldier; and for one to say a soldier lies is stabbing.
   —Shakespeare, *Othello,* 3.4.1

6. These two men are philosophers and scientists. Philosophers and scientists often disagree. Therefore these two men often disagree.

7. Tom was being beaten with that with which I saw him being beaten.
I saw him being beaten with my eyes.

8. *Cesario.* Save thee, friend, and thy music! Dost thou live by thy tabor?
Feste. No, sir, I live by the church.
Cesario. Art thou a churchman?
Feste. No such matter, sir. I do live by the church; for I do live at my house, and my house doth stand by the church.

—Shakespeare, *Twelfth Night*, 3.1.1

9. John Smith is either a Republican or a Democrat. He is not a Democrat. Therefore he is a Republican.

10. No men are Senators and Representatives. Senators and Representatives are Congressmen. Therefore no men are Congressmen.

11. John Lewis is a baseball umpire, for the paper says he called a strike.

12. The moving train stopped. The train that stopped is standing still. Therefore the moving train is standing still.

13. "Last Monday it rained; (Jenny had to hang the wash indoors)."
"That isn't true; the sun was shining."

14. *Tom.* She writes that she is my friend. *Dick.* That means she is not your friend, Harry. *Harry.* No, it means that she is not Tom's enemy.

15. To love nothing is impossible.

16. You will be happy either in this world or in the next. You are happy now. Therefore you will not be happy in the next world.

17. "That is a salt-water lake." "No, it is a fresh-water lake."

18. Government is necessary to the welfare of society. Dictatorship is government. Therefore dictatorship is necessary to the welfare of society.

19. If a man marries, he suffers from the cares of family life; if he does not marry, he suffers from loneliness. But he must either marry or not marry. Therefore he will suffer in either case.

20. The woman who spoke hurriedly left the platform.

21. Dick is not what Tom is. Tom is a man. Therefore Dick is not a man.

22. The seated man stood up. The man who stood up is standing. Therefore the seated man is standing.

23. Helping a friend is being kind to him. Writing essays for a friend is helping him. Therefore writing essays for a friend is being kind to him.

24. A mouse is small. Small is an accident. Therefore a mouse is an accident.

25. If the number is not even, it is odd. It is even. Therefore it is not odd.

26. A boy I know will receive the honor.

27. The books in this library number three hundred thousand volumes. Shakespeare's works are books in this library. Therefore Shakespeare's works number three hundred thousand volumes.

28. A citizen need not take seriously the duty of voting; one vote more or less will have no influence in an election.

29. That student must have made no effort to learn, because his marks are low.

30. The watch ticks. Ticks hold feathers. Therefore a watch holds feathers.

31. The receiver of stolen goods should be punished. You have received stolen goods and should therefore be punished.

32. It is not right for you to enter a religious order, for if everyone did so, the race would die out.
33. "*Isolate* is correctly pronounced with a short *i*." "That isn't true; it is correctly pronounced with a long *i*."
34. He who is incapable of even planning a crime is surely not a master-criminal. This drunken man is incapable of even planning a crime. Therefore this drunken man is surely not a master-criminal.
35. No women are patriots, for they are not soldiers.
36. Jane is good. Jane is a singer. Therefore she is a good singer.
37. Not to be abed after midnight is to be up betimes; . . . To be up after midnight, and to go to bed then, is early; so that to go to bed after midnight is to go to bed betimes.—Shakespeare, *Twelfth Night*, 2.3.1-9.
38. Why, if thou never wast at court, thou never sawest good manners; if thou never sawest good manners then thy manners must be wicked; and wickedness is sin, and sin is damnation. Thou art in a parlous state, shepherd.
    —Shakespeare, *As You Like It*, 3.4.21.
39. "Do you know that Henry is tall?" "Yes." "Do you know that he is a lawyer?" "No." "Then you claim to know him and not to know him."
40. To increase production in a state, men of different natures should perform different work. Now there is an opposition in nature between bald men and hairy men. Therefore if bald men are cobblers, hairy men should not be cobblers.—Plato, *Republic*.
41. Said Morgenthau in effect: (1) to have peace, the world must de-industrialize Germany; (2) to keep Germany de-industrialized, the world must have a strong will for peace.—*Time*, October 15, 1945, p. 23.
42. All the angles of a triangle are equal to two right angles; the angle x is an angle of this triangle; therefore it is equal to two right angles.
43. If a small state is on the losing side in a war, it can be utterly annihilated. If it is on the winning side, it has no means of enforcing the principles for which it fought. Therefore it should, if possible, remain neutral.
    —Eamon de Valera. Quoted in *Time*, March 25, 1946, p. 36.
44. Not only are the masses of laborers the slaves of the bourgeois class, and of the bourgeois state; they are daily and hourly enslaved by the machine, by the overseer, and, above all, by the individual bourgeois manufacturer himself.—Karl Marx, *The Communist Manifesto*.
45. It was good to persecute the Christians, because the blood of martyrs was the seed of the Church.
46. "Why doesn't Mary speak to Jane?" "Because Jane won't speak to her." "Why doesn't Jane speak to Mary?" "Because Mary doesn't speak to her."
47. Acquiring property is good. This thief is acquiring property. Therefore this thief is doing good.
48. That general caused the damnation of many soldiers, because he sent them into battle, and many had been guilty of grave sins.
49. Men thrive on meat and potatoes. This typhoid patient is a man. Therefore he will thrive on meat and potatoes.
50. Democracy has failed in the United States, because there are boss-ridden cities and states.
51. A good man may be a bad plumber. Therefore a good man may be bad.

52. If a man remains under water thirty minutes, he will die. This diver remained under water thirty minutes. Therefore he will die.

53. It is foolish to believe that men have souls, for we have carefully dissected scores of bodies and have found no trace of a soul.

54. Cake is sweet. Sweet is an adjective. Therefore cake is an adjective.

55. The flowers in this garden form an attractive design. These pansies are flowers in this garden. Therefore they form an attractive design.

56. Detective stories are excellent literature because they are preferred by learned professors of mathematics.

57. These strikers are lazy, for they are determined not to work.

58. "Should we begin your subscription to this magazine with the January or the March number?" "I haven't said that I want it at all."

59. Have not you seen, Camillo, . . . or thought (for cogitation Resides not in that man that does not think) My wife is slippery?"

    —Shakespeare, *The Winter's Tale*, 1.2.267-73.

60. This man cannot be a criminal, for he has never been in prison.

61. We must have a new idea of God to harmonize with the great discoveries of modern astrophysics, because Harry Elmer Barnes has said so and he is a noted lecturer and writer on sociology.

62. If a person is sleeping, he can't hear a sermon. This man couldn't hear the sermon. Therefore he must have been sleeping.

63. Hauptmann ought not to have been executed, because he had a wife and young son to take care of.

64. Proletarians of the world unite! You have nothing to lose but your chains and all the world to gain.—Karl Marx.

65. There are more automobile accidents on Sundays than on other days, and many of the persons hurt are those who had attended religious services that day. Consequently, to attend religious services is to increase the danger of being injured or even killed.

66. The sun must move around the earth, for the Bible says that at Josue's prayer the sun stood still.

67. Detraction is telling the truth. Therefore it is praiseworthy.

68. We charge King Charles II with having broken his coronation oath and we are told he kept his marriage vow.—Macaulay.

69. You are foolish to believe that miracles can occur, for science cannot account for them.

70. Prohibition did not succeed because it did not have the support of public opinion; and the people did not support it because it was a failure.

71. Man is an animal. Animal is a genus. A genus is divisible into species. Therefore man is divisible into species.

72. You housewives who must do the family marketing should oppose labor unions, because union labor will lead to higher prices.

73. I do not wish to have a doctor, for I notice that all who died in this town this winter had a doctor.

74. We ought to abolish democracy and establish fascism, for it is admitted that democracy is inefficient and conducive to graft, and fascism is a form of government in which these defects are at a minimum.

75. When did you decide to stop posing?

76. It is ridiculous to worship the God of the Christians, for one ought not worship an old man with a beard.

77. This boy has undoubtedly been in Professor Smith's class, because he has had a thorough course in logic.
78. If one's hands are bandaged, one cannot play the piano. This girl's hands are not bandaged. Therefore she can play the piano.
79. She bought raw meat yesterday. What she bought yesterday she ate today. Therefore she ate raw meat today.
80. Nellie is a good seamstress. Therefore she is a good woman.
81. The hostess knows all the guests at the party. All the guests at the party are masked. Therefore the hostess knows all who are masked.
82. She must not have kept to her diet, for she is ill.
83. The obstacle is a rock. Rock is a verb. Therefore the obstacle is a verb.
84. To increase wages is to raise prices. To raise prices is to increase the cost of living. To increase the cost of living is to decrease real income. Therefore to increase wages is to decrease real income.
85. The boy who was walking slowly recited the poem.
86. Neither sixteen credit hours of college work, nor four hours a day of secretarial work, nor eight hours a week as laboratory assistant, nor waiting table three times a day, nor the editorship of the school paper, nor the duties of class treasurer, nor participation in dramatic activities will jeopardize a student's health. Therefore a student can safely undertake all of these.
87. A fur coat is comfortable to wear in winter. Therefore it is comfortable in summer.
88. This statue is a work of art. This statue is mine. Therefore it is my work of art.
89. The end of the world will come this year or it will not. It will not, you say. Therefore it will come this year.
90. He who swears that he will break his oath, and then breaks it, is a keeper of his oath.
91. No reason can be given why the general happiness is desirable except that each person, so far as he believes it to be attainable, desires his own happiness. This being a fact, we have not only all the proof that the case admits of, but all which it is possible to require, that happiness is a good, that each person's happiness is a good to that person, and the general happiness, therefore, a good to the aggregate of all persons.—J. S. Mill, *Utilitarianism*.
92. Mrs. Smith purchased chairs, tables, clocks, lamps, drapes, pictures. Every one of these is beautiful and artistic. Therefore these furnishings will make Mrs. Smith's living room beautiful and artistic.
93. If protective tariffs produce a scarcity of goods, they are injurious; if they do not, they are useless. But they must either produce a scarcity of goods or not. Therefore they are either injurious or useless, and ought to be abolished.
94. We are going to defend ourselves like good Spaniards and show that the men of Lapeza know how to die or to conquer. Therefore he who does not die defending his honor will be declared an unworthy Spaniard—a traitor to his country—and he shall die as he deserves, hanged to an oak on the hillside.—Alarcón, "The Alcalde Who Was a Charcoal Burner."
95. The eel like Johnny slipped away unnoticed.
96. Plato in his *Phaedo* proves the immortality of the soul from its simplicity. In the *Republic* he proves the soul's simplicity from its immortality.

CHAPTER X

A Brief Summary of Induction

Logic is the normative science which directs the operations of the intellect so as to attain truth.

As metaphysics, or ontology, deals with *all things as they are* in their most abstract, their most general, and, therefore, their one common aspect, being, so logic deals with *all that is thought* in its most general aspect, truth.

The requirements of truth are:

1. What is thought must represent what is. (This is the norm of conception and of induction.)
2. Thoughts must be consistent among themselves. (This is the norm of deduction.)

The first requirement is concerned with the material of reasoning; the second, with the reasoning itself. Both are necessary.

Deductive or formal logic is the only logic in the sense that it alone discovers the rules by which we think and reason correctly. But the material of thinking, the terms and propositions, must come ultimately from our experience by means of conception and induction. These processes therefore are preliminary to reasoning.

Analogy: Raw cotton is necessary to the manufacture of muslin, organdie, and lace. But it is the machines that produce the difference between these kinds of cotton goods. It is with the machine and its operation that manufacturing is specifically concerned. The production and acquisition of raw material are not, strictly speaking, problems of manufacturing; they are preliminary, and prerequisite, to it.

I. Knowledge, that is, whatever information the mind possesses, is derived from either the operation of one's own powers or from faith.
  A. The operations of one's own powers. The sense powers acquire an immediate perception of external objects, and the intellectual powers act on data provided by the senses.
    1. Sense powers
      a. These comprise:
        1) External senses: sight, hearing, touch, taste, smell
        2) Internal senses: the imagination, which produces and retains phantasms; the memory, which recalls and recognizes them as previously experienced; the common or central sense, which discriminates, coordinates, and

synthesizes the sensations; and instinct, by which a sentient being estimates an object as conducive to its physical well being or not conducive.

  b. The mode of operation of the senses
    1) Intuitive. This is the direct or immediate perception of the proper sensibles—color, sound, etc.
    2) Indirect. This is the indirect perception of the common sensibles, which may be perceived by more than one sense. For example, motion, rest, figure, and size may be perceived through both sight and touch; number, distance, direction, duration, and rhythm, through sight, touch, and hearing.
       Note. The constructive or fictive imagination can combine phantasms. Examples: mermaid, satyr, centaur, griffin.

  2. Intellectual powers
    a. These comprise: the intellect, which seeks truth, the rational memory, and the will, which seeks good.
    b. The mode of operation of the intellect
      1) Intuitive (abstraction: conception, induction)
         Examples of intellectual intuition:
         a) Metaphysical: Every effect must have an adequate cause.
         b) Logical: Contradictory propositions cannot both be true.
         c) Mathematical: Things equal to the same thing are equal to each other.
         d) Moral: Good ought to be done and evil avoided.
         e) Psychological: My consciousness testifies that my will is free.
      2) Inferential. This includes both immediate and mediate or syllogistic inference.

B. Faith. This includes all that I know from the testimony of another. This other may be:
  1. Human: parents, teachers, companions, books, magazines, newspapers, radio, etc.
  2. Divine: God communicating a revelation directly; or by miracles authenticating the message of His agent—angel, prophet, apostle, etc.

The topics of invention (see page 123) draw material for reasoning either from the exercise of one's own powers (the first sixteen topics) or from faith (the testimony of others).

Psychology, the philosphy of mind, explains the process by which concepts and judgments are obtained from the real world. Induction, like conception, is abstractive, intuitive; but whereas conception is the abstraction of the essence, and its product is a concept expressed in a term, induction is the drawing forth and perception of a relation, and its product is a judgment expressed in a proposition. Neither process is one of merely counting or adding instances; neither is a generalization from particulars, or an inference of any sort; both are intuitions of truth drawn from reality.

The basis of conception and of intuitive induction is the same: God made only individuals, but made them, as we see them in nature according to type. The essence is that which makes an individual a member of his species, or type; consequently, the concept, which is the intellectual apprehension of the essence present in the individual, is equally applicable to every member of the species. Similarly, a necessary general proposition which expresses the intellectual apprehension of a fundamental relation such as cause and effect present in the individual precisely as a member of his species must be present in every other member of the same species.

II. Induction is not a form of inference; it is a form of intuition.
   A. Every general proposition serving as a premise in a syllogistic inference is either:
      1. The conclusion of a preceding syllogism or series of syllogisms made up only of general propositions. For there is no correct formula of inference by which a general proposition can be derived as a conclusion from empirical premises, which alone express our knowledge of particular facts. (See page 149, *Rule 10*.)
      2. An induction or intuition drawn from nature.

      Therefore every general proposition is derived either directly or ultimately from induction. Induction is a mental act, but not an inference. It is preliminary and prerequisite to inference; it is an intuition of truth (either general or empirical; see page 232).
   B. There are three distinct kinds of induction, none of which is inferential:
      1. Enumerative induction is the assertion of a numerically definite plural empirical proposition as a result of observing

facts and counting instances. Example: Fifty-three persons were killed in automobile accidents in that city last year.

This is the least important kind of induction, hardly worthy to be called such. Its chief value lies in contributing ascertained facts to be used in deduction or in other kinds of induction.

A statistical deduction is a conclusion in a syllogism whose minor premise is an enumerative induction and whose major premise is a statistical or mathematical law, usually expressed in a formula. The conclusion is the statement of a numerically definite probability. Example: An insurance company bases its rates on the scientifically calculated probable number of deaths in a particular group—designated by age, occupation, locality—in a year. Vital statistics provide the minor premise for this statistical deduction, and a mathematical formula for the calculation of probability is the major. The conclusion is a statement of numerically definite probability, sufficiently accurate to be the basis of a sound business enterprise, for insurance companies have shown remarkable stability during depressions.

2. Intuitive induction is the psychological act of asserting a self-evident proposition as true. This is by far the most important kind.

   a. If the self-evident proposition is empirical, it is a datum of sense-knowledge, and is relative to the sentient individual making the intuitive induction. Example: The grass is green. A blind person could not make this induction.

   b. If the self-evident proposition is general, it is a principle of intellectual knowledge, and is relative to human reason, and to the knowledge of the terms possessed by the individual making the intuitive induction. Example: The whole is greater than any of its parts.

3. Dialectical or problematic induction is the psychological act of asserting a proposition, whether general or empirical, as a possibility, without any calculation of its probability. It is an intuition of the compatibility of the terms. Examples:

   a. A regular polygon may have a million sides.

   b. This child may become the President of the United States.

C. Nature and purpose of induction

Induction is the legitimate derivation of general propositions from individual instances. It is a method for the discovery of truth, not a process of proof, or reasoning about truth.

The physical order is, however, too complex to permit the mental act of intuitive induction without much preliminary work. Scientific methodology, or the methods of science, are concerned with this preliminary work. They are systematic procedures for the investigation of natural phenomena. Their aim is to separate what is essential or typical from what is accidental or fortuitous, and to present to the mind precise, relevant, simple data. The mind then abstracts the inductive judgment by an intuitive act as simple and spontaneous as that by which it abstracts the concept directly from sense data.

Scientific methodology is not a mental act at all, but a safeguard to precision in the investigation of nature. It is preliminary to induction from complex phenomena just as induction itself is preliminary to deduction. Induction and deduction are distinct, but in practice they go hand in hand.

Each of the special sciences aims to abstract from the complex natural phenomenon laws governing that aspect of nature with which it is concerned. For example, mathematics is concerned only with quantity, physics with motion, anatomy with the structure of living organisms, economics with man's activities in making a living.

Analogy: Petroleum is a complex natural substance, from which are abstracted by fractional distillation diverse substances. Among them are gasoline, benzine, naptha, kerosene, vaseline, paraffin, artificial asphalt, mothballs. The distinctive characteristic of each of these products is due to (1) the abstraction of part from the whole (compare the special sciences, each of which deals only with a selected phase of nature) by means of fractional distillation (compare induction), and in some instances by means of (2) a process of manufacture (compare deduction) which transforms the natural product by means of machinery (compare the mind). Thus the final products owe their being to nature's gifts modified by man's ingenuity.

The aim of every science is the knowledge of facts through their causes. This is true of both deductive and inductive sciences. In deduction we know the fact, the conclusion, through its causes, the premises. In induction, we apprehend the cause common to a number of observed facts; this is a principle, a middle term, by which their relation can be understood.

We shall consider first the nature of causality, then the uniformity of causation, and lastly how scientific method aids in discovering causes.

D. Causality

Since induction is concerned mainly with the investigation of causes, it is important to understand:

1. The distinction between a cause, a condition, and a special type of condition called a determining agent.

   a. A cause is that which has a positive influence in making a thing to be what it is. To the sum of its causes, it owes every one of its characteristics.

      A cause is not a mere antecedent in a time sequence. For instance, day and night follow each other, but they do not cause each other. The assumption that the antecedent in a time sequence is a cause is the inductive fallacy *post hoc ergo propter hoc*. (See page 222.)

   b. A condition is that which in any way enables a cause to act in producing the effect, but to which the effect owes none of its characteristics. Examples: Light is a condition requisite to the carving of a statue; food, to the health and competence of the sculptor; scaffolding, to the decoration of the ceiling of a church.

   c. The determining agent is a condition which sets in motion the causative factors. It differs from other conditions in being the origin or occasion of the effect. Examples: The mosquito which transmits the yellow fever germ; the flea which transmits the bubonic plague.

      Science often seeks the determining agent rather than one of the four metaphysical causes.

2. The four metaphysical causes. These, according to Aristotle, explain every material effect. They are: the efficient, the final, the material, and the formal cause.

   a. Two are extrinsic to the effect, the causes of its becoming what it is, e. g., a statue.

      1) The efficient cause: the agent, and the instruments; e. g., the sculptor, and the hammer and chisel.

      2) The final cause: the end or purpose that moved the agent; e. g., desire to honor a national hero, the particular design the artist conceived, love of art, fame,

money, etc. The final cause is first in intention, last in execution.

b. Two are intrinsic to the effect, the causes of its being what it is.

1) The material cause, that out of which it is made, e. g., marble, bronze, wood.

2) The formal cause, the kind of thing into which it is made, e. g., Lincoln, Napoleon, Bucephalus.

Note. To know an object through its formal cause is to know its essence. Thus the formal cause of man is his soul animating his body, his rational animality. The material cause is that particular matter which constitutes his physical being; it continually varies through metabolism but is supported and unified by the formal cause, the soul in the body. Thus, despite metabolism, the man remains the same man throughout his life, through the persistence of the formal cause.

E. The uniformity of causation

This is a postulate of all natural sciences, a physically, not a metaphysically, necessary assumption of the scientist who studies the material universe. (See page 104.) It is not capable of proof but only of illustration.

The postulate may be stated thus: The same natural cause, under similar conditions, produces the same effect.

This generalization needs to be limited in two important ways:

1. It is not applicable to a being with free will in those of his activities subject to control by his free will. Thus a man is free to lift his arm or not to lift it, to choose to think upon one subject rather than upon another. But he has no such free control over the circulation of his blood, his digestion, falling from a height when support is removed, etc.

2. The uniformity of causation requires the normal concurrence of the First Cause. Thus miracles represent a deviation from the uniformity of nature, attributable to the free will of the First Cause .(See page 104.)

Note. The postulate of the uniformity of causation should not be confused with the philosophical principle of causality, namely: Whatever comes into being must have an adequate cause. The latter is a philosophical axiom, knowable by intuitive induction. Philosophical axioms are metaphysically necessary truths. The postulates of science are not and, accordingly, have not so high a degree of certainty.

F. Scientific induction as a method of discovering truth embraces the following five steps:

1. Observation. This is asking questions of nature, in order to get facts, the data of induction. Because of the complexity of nature, observation must be selective, analytic. Care should be taken to obtain facts free from inference. Ordinary observation is supplemented by:

   a. Scientific instruments, e. g., telescope, microscope, microphone, camera, barometer, thermometer, delicate balances.

   b. Statistics, or enumeration. This is the substitution of exact counting for random observation, e. g., a statistical study of the recurrence of depressions, of the causes of death, of the number of marriages and divorce, of the diffusion of hereditary traits among offspring.

      Simple observation, aided by the use of scientific instruments and of statistics, is almost the only means available to such natural sciences as systematic zoology and astronomy, and to some of the social sciences.

   c. Experiment. This is observation under conditions subject to control. Its advantage lies in the opportunity it offers to simplify, to analyze, to repeat at will: to ask questions of nature, one at a time, by varying conditions, one at a time.

      A science which can employ experiment advances much more rapidly than one which cannot. The rapid progress of physics, chemistry, bacteriology, nutrition, are due in large measure to experiment.

2. Analogy. Likeness observed in different classes of phenomena suggest to the alert scientific mind the probability of a causal relation. Analogy is a fertile source of hypotheses. Example: The periodic table of the chemical elements had its inception in analogy; and it presents analogies which have occasioned other scientific discoveries.

3. Hypothesis. This is a scientific guess at general laws, to explain phenomena which appear to be causally related. Hypotheses guide observation and experiment. Subsequent investigation either verifies or disproves them.

4. Analysis and sifting of data. Scientific methodology.

Roger Bacon (1214?-1294) and Francis Bacon (1561-1626) developed a theory of induction. John Stuart Mill (1806-1873) formulated five canons or general methods of science, and popularized them. They are:

a. The method of agreement. If two or more instances of the phenomenon under investigation have only one circumstance in common, the circumstance in which alone all the instances agree is the cause or the effect of the given phenomenon.

Note. In Mill's formulas the capital letters stand for antecedents, the small letters for consequents. Each group stands for an instance.

Formula: ABC — abc; ADE — ade. Hence A is causally related to a.

Example: W. S. Jevons describes how the cause of the irridescence of mother-of-pearl was discovered:

A person might suppose that the peculiar colours of mother-of-pearl were due to the chemical qualities of the substance. Much trouble might have been spent in following out that notion by comparing the chemical qualities of various irridescent substances. But Sir David Brewster accidentally took an impression from a piece of mother-of-pearl in a cement of resin and beeswax, and finding the colours repeated upon the surface of the wax, he proceeded to take other impressions in balsam, fusible metal, lead, gum arabic, isinglass, etc., and always found the irridescent colours the same. He thus proved that the chemical nature of the substance is a matter of indifference, and that the form of the surface is the real condition of such colours.

b. The method of difference. If an instance in which the phenomenon under investigation occurs, and an instance in which it does not occur, have every circumstance in common save one, that one occurring only in the former, the circumstance in which alone the two instances differ is the effect or the cause or an indispensable part of the cause of the phenomenon.

Formula: ABC — abc; BC — bc. Hence A is causally related to a.

Examples: Sore eyes and retarded growth of rats which have no Vitamin A in their diet. A bell struck in a vacuum makes no sound; if air is admitted, it does; hence the vibration of air is seen to be causally related to the production of sound.

c. The joint method of agreement and difference. If two or more instances in which the phenomenon occurs have only one circumstance in common, while two or more instances in which it does not occur have nothing in common except the absence of that circumstance, the circumstance in which alone the two sets of instances differ is the effect or the cause or an indispensable part of the cause of the phenomenon.

Formula: ABC — abc, ADE — ade, BDM — bdm, CEO — ceo. Hence A is causally related to a.

Examples: The use of diphtheria antitoxin to create immunity from diphtheria; the presence of the hydrogen ion in all acids.

d. Method of residues. Subduct from any phenomenon such part as is known by previous inductions to be the effect of certain antecedents, and the residue of the phenomenon is the effect of the remaining antecedent.

Formula: ABC — abc. But it is known that A causes a and B causes b; then C must cause c.

Examples: Exact determination of the weight of a pint of milk in a quart bottle requires that the weight of the bottle and of a pint of air be subtracted from the whole. Discovery of argon in the air; of the planet Neptune.

e. The method of concomitant variations. Whatever phenomenon varies in any manner whenever another phenomenon varies in some particular manner is either a cause or an effect of that phenomenon or is connected with it through some fact of causation.

Formula: $A^1BC — a^1bc$, $A^2BC — a^2bc$, A^3BC, $—a^3bc$. Hence A is causally related to a.

Examples: Effect of changes of temperature on a column of mercury—hence the thermometer; tides and the moon; law of supply and demand, affecting price.

5. Verification of the hypothesis

Francis Bacon not only anticipated the substance of Mill's canons, but indicated the succeeding steps in the discovery of scientific law. The form of which he speaks is the formal cause of the effect in question.

Every form which is present when the property in question is absent, or absent when the latter is present, or which does not increase or decrease concomitantly with the latter, is to be rejected as not being the form causally connected with the latter. . . . Where you cannot (as in mathematics) see that a proposition must be universally true, but have to rely for the proof of it on the facts of your experience, there is no other way of establishing it than by showing that facts disprove its rivals.

Hence the steps in verification:

As in forming a concept, abstraction withdraws the attention of the intellect from what is not essential so that it may intuit what is essential, so elimination withdraws its attention from what is not causally related so that it may intuit what is causally related.

e. Elimination is accomplished by means of deductive reasoning from a disjunctive proposition. The minor premises of the eliminative syllogisms are empirical propositions stating the result of observation of the facts under investigation. The major premises are the canons of the general scientific methods.

The cause of X is either A or B or C or D.

(1) But A is present when X is absent.
   The cause of X cannot be present when X is absent.
   Therefore A is not the cause of X.

(2) B is absent when X is present.
   The cause of X cannot be absent when X is present.
   Therefore B is not the cause of X.

(3) C does not vary concomitantly with X.
   The cause of X does vary concomitantly with X.
   Therefore C is not the cause of X.

But the cause of X is neither A nor B nor C (as is shown above).

Therefore the cause of X is probably D.

Note 1. The alternatives of the disjunctive syllogism should not be a mere enumerative catalogue of possibilities. The alternatives should be selected by scientific insight into the probable antecedents, not by a random gathering of irrevelant facts. (Compare analogical inference, page 164.)

Note 2. Mere elimination provides no certitude. The conclusion of the disjunctive syllogism merely represents the degree of simplification that scientific method can achieve. After the rival alternatives have been disproved, the data, the facts of nature, thus divested of some of their complexity, stand naked, as it were, before the mind's eye.

b. Intuitive induction. If the mind sees positive reasons for asserting that the cause of X is D, there is certitude. If not, the analysis of the data was probably incomplete, and the alternatives were not exhaustive; an unknown antecedent, not listed, may be the cause of X.

c. Application and demonstration by deduction

The certitude resulting from the intuitive induction of a general law must be demonstrated by syllogistic inference.

1) A regressive syllogism is the link between induction and deduction. It is a theoretical verification of the hypothesis by deduction.

The seeking for the cause of natural phenomena, for a law that governs them, is a seeking for a middle term, which is the formal cause of the relation of the terms in the conclusion of a syllogism.

In contrast to the definite process by which the premises lead to the conclusion, this seeking for the middle term is an indefinite, inverse process, for S and P may be related by many M's. The conclusion may be supported by many reasons. (See page 157.)

Analogy: In mathematics, we proceed definitely from multiplier and multiplicand to the product, but the inverse process is indefinite. Example:

(1) Given: 6×6. What is the product? Definite answer: 36.

(2) Given: 36. What are the factors? Indefinite answer, a series of alternatives: plus 6 squared; minus 6 squared; 2×18; 3×12; 4×9; —2× —18; —3×—12; —4×—9.

Induction is a similar indefinite, inverse process, until it is verified by deduction and application.

In our observation of nature we intuit the empirical proposition S is P. But S is P because it is M. The whole problem of the discovery of laws of nature is the problem of discovering M. The effect P proves the presence of the cause M. Here M must be not only the antecedent of P but the only antecedent, a property or a definition. Hence M is P must be convertible simply to P is M. In other words, science is seeking the verification of an hypothesis which can be expressed in a hypothetical proposition that is reciprocal: If S is M, it is P; and if S is P, it is M. When this reciprocal relationship is found, it may be stated in a regressive syllogism in the first figure: S is P. P is M. Therefore S is M. The theoretical verification of the hypothesis, stated fully, then is: If S is M, it is P. But S is M. Therefore S is P.

2) A demonstrative syllogism. This is a practical verification of the hypothesis by deduction.

As a final step in its verification, the hypothesis must be applied over and over again to the facts of nature, and thereby have its truth demonstrated. The hypothesis becomes the major premise in a syllogism whose minor premise is an empirical proposition derived by intuition from the observation of nature. The conclusion which follows from a correct syllogistic formula employing these premises is, then, an empirical proposition which is an inference from the hypothesis being tested. If this process is repeated again and again, with different, typical, and widely selected data as the minor premises of the testing syllogisms, and if, in every case, the empirical conclusion inferred conforms to the observed facts of nature, then the hypothesis is verified and it is demonstrated to be a law of nature. Herein, then, by combining deduction with induction, we verify before the tribunal of human reason the general law with which induction furnished us.

Thus we have, through deduction, consistency in the conceptual order, and through induction, the assurance that this conceptual order truly represents the real order. (See page 227.)

III. Place of philosophy (love of wisdom) in the field of knowledge
Our rationality urges us to analyze, relate, organize, synthesize, and so to simplify our knowledge.

Philosophy represents the greatest unity and simplicity to which unaided human reason can attain.

The progress toward unity may be represented thus:

4. Experience (facts, e. g., stone falls, chair falls, etc.)

3. Science (laws, e. g., law of gravity.)

2. Philosophy (principles, e. g., every effect must have an adequate cause.)

1. Beatific vision. (Unity of Perfect Truth; the all in the One. Theology and faith prepare us for the beatific vision after death.)

These four steps in the synthesis of knowledge are the special provinces of:

A. History. Its primary function is to chronicle the facts of experience.

B. Science. Its primary function is to organize facts under their proximate causes, laws.

C. Philosophy. Its primary function is to discover ultimate causes. It accepts the findings of the special sciences as its data, and treats of the ultimate principles and characteristics which constitute the order of the universe as a whole.

    1. Speculative philosophy is concerned with knowledge of the real order for the sake of knowledge.

    According to the three classes of objects to be understood, the mind employs three kinds of abstraction, and distinguishes three great fields of knowledge:

    a. Physics in the wide sense meaning all the special sciences that deal with the material world; they abstract from individual conditions and are concerned with general laws and the universal type.

    b. Mathematics abstracts for consideration only quantity.

    c. Metaphysics abstracts only being as being.

    2. Practical or normative philosophy regulates actions according to some standard.

    a. Logic deals with thought; it directs the intellect to truth.

    b. Ethics deals with action; it directs the will to good.

    c. Aesthetics deals with expression; it directs the intellect, the senses, and the emotions to beauty and its contemplation.

    Abstraction is the basis of science and of philosophy. Each special science adopts as its sphere of investigation one general characteristic, and ignores all others. It is only by this means that man can make progress in knowledge. (See page 54.) A complex being, for example, man, is made the object of distinct special sciences, such as biology, psychology, anthropology, ethics, economics, politics, each of which studies only a chosen aspect. Even chemistry, physics, mathematics, contribute to our knowledge of man. No one science gives us the whole truth. All together give us one truth, a composite picture, limited, of course, by the inadequacies of the human mind.

It is very important to realize the selectivity of the special sciences—to understand that each represents but one aspect of reality. To know one aspect as a part of a greater complex whole is to know a part of the truth. But to think that one such aspect is the whole is to distort truth into gross error. This is the danger of specialization. Philosophy, which harmonizes the findings of the special sciences, comes closest to giving us the whole truth, insofar as we can know it by reason alone.

D. Theology. Its primary function is to supplement human knowledge with knowledge to which unaided human reason could not attain. This is Revelation, which comprises both speculative and practical knowledge, chiefly of God, who is the First Cause of all that science and philosophy study, and the Last End of man, who studies them.

QUESTIONS

1. How is induction related to deduction? Explain by an analogy.
2. How do the topics of invention correspond to the sources from which we derive our knowledge?
3. By which cognitive power and by which mode of its operation do you know: smoothness; that an apple is round; consistency; that two parallel lines can never meet; that a room is large and octagonal; thunder; that a straight line is the shortest distance between two points; that two and two are four; that snow is cold; a centaur; fragrance; saltiness; that if two straight lines intersect, the vertical angles are equal; goodness; that an orange is juicy; fairies; blue; that coffee is hot; that a locomotive far to the left of you is approaching; that some time has passed; stickiness?
4. Are the following known to you by the exercise of your cognitive powers or by faith: Chicago; the Atlantic Ocean; China; King George VI of England; Franklin D. Roosevelt; that an equilateral triangle is equiangular; that all acids contain hydrogen; that Arcturus is forty light-years from the earth; that mercury is a liquid which does not make your hands wet; that you were

born on the day you give as your birthday; that Caesar conquered Gaul; that you were baptized; that you received confirmation; that if **hydrogen** is passed over copper oxide, pure copper and water can be seen; that God exists; that the Holy Eucharist is the Body and Blood of Christ; that you have five fingers on each hand; that there are white corpuscles in your blood; that the Hudson River flows into the Atlantic Ocean?

5. Show that induction cannot be a form of inference. Show that as a mental act it is, like conception, intuitive.

6. Distinguish and illustrate three kinds of induction.

7. Distinguish: a cause, a condition, a determining agent. Give an example of each.

8. Distinguish the postulate of the uniformity of causation and the principle of causality.

9. Outline in detail the five steps involved in scientific induction.

10. State Mill's canons. Illustrate. Are these preparatory to induction or do they constitute induction?

11. Explain in detail the method of verifying an hypothesis. At what point do deduction and induction meet?

12. Outline the subdivisions of philosophy.

13. Explain the relationship between history, science, philosophy, and theology.

14. Why does each special science select for study only one aspect of reality? What danger resulting from this fact must be avoided?

CHAPTER XI

COMPOSITION AND READING

I. A brief survey of the development of rhetoric, logic, and poetic

The art of rhetoric originated in Sicily, when a democracy was established in Syracuse in 466 B. C. and Corax and his pupil Tisias assisted those who had been dispossessed of property to convince the judges that they had a just claim to its restoration. Corax put together some theoretical precepts based principally on the topic of general probability, called *eikos*, (see Aristotle, *Rhetoric*, 2.24.9) and Tisias developed it further, as Plato shows in *Phaedrus*. Gorgias, the Sicilian, came to Athens in 427 B. C., introduced the art of rhetoric into many parts of Greece, and had many disciples, among whom the most admirable and famous was Isocrates, the orator and teacher. Gorgias, Protagoras, Prodicus, and Hippias emphasized the graces of style, figures of speech, distinction of synonyms, correctness and elegance in the choice of words, and rules of rhythm. Gorgias aimed to teach how to convince independently of any knowledge of the subject. He admittedly taught persuasion, not virtue. Plato and Aristotle condemned the sophists Gorgias, Protagoras, and others for their superficiality and disregard of truth in teaching how to make the worse appear the better cause.

Aristotle himself constructed a well-balanced system of the arts of discovering and communicating truth, and his treatises on these subjects profoundly influenced his own and succeeding ages. He systematized rhetoric and made it an instrument of truth. He explicitly claimed to be the founder of the art of logic. His *Poetics* is the beginning of real literary criticism.

Logic and rhetoric are concerned with the discovery and communication of truth directly from the mind of the author to the mind of the hearer or reader. Poetic is a very different mode of communication, indirect, through the imitation of life in characters and situations whose experience the reader or listener shares imaginatively as if it were his own; yet it rises out of knowledge as well as feeling, and logic and rhetoric are employed in the communication of the whole, which goes beyond them.

A. Aristotle divided logic, according to its subject matter, into scientific demonstration, dialectic, and sophistic, treated in the works named below.

1. *Analytics, Prior* and *Posterior.* Scientific demonstration has as its subject matter premises that are true and certain.

   In this field there are not two sides to a question, but only one. The reasoning is merely expository, as in geometry, moving step by step to the conclusive demonstration of what was to be proved.

2. *Topics.* Dialectic has as its subject matter opinion, not certain knowledge; therefore the premises are merely probable.

   In this field there are two sides to a question, and there is reasonable support for opposing views, both only probable, neither certain, although each person engaging in the discussion may be personally, even ardently, convinced of the truth of his views. Yet he cannot justly regard them as having the quality of geometric proof, because each must recognize that the matter under discussion is not intrinsically clear, and that his opponent's view is not so manifestly false as the proposition that two and two make five. The argument is conducted in a spirit of inquiry and love of truth. If, in the course of the discussion, one disputant sees that his opponent's view is true and that which he has advanced is false, he may be justly said to have won the argument, because he has gained truth, which, he now sees, his opponent had at the start.

   Plato's *Dialogues* are the perfect examples of dialectic.

3. *Sophistical Refutations* (treatise on material fallacies). Sophistic has as its subject matter premises that seem to be generally accepted and appropriate, but which really are not.

   In this field, usually that of opinion, the sophist seeks, not truth, but only an appearance of truth, achieved by the use of fallacious arguments designed to put down the opponent in contentious dispute. He who wins by such methods has not won truth. On the contrary, he has made error appear to have triumphed over truth, and nobody has won truth by means of the argument.

   It is a sad commentary that many persons today attach to the word argument only the sophists' conception, entertain the sophistic notion of "winning" an argument, and ignore the fine and constructive pursuit of, or understanding of,

truth to be gained by the only forms of argument worthy
of the name, and most worthy of men, namely the first two.

B. Rhetoric, according to Aristotle, is the counterpart of dialectic,
and the rhetorical enthymeme is the counterpart of the dialectical syllogism. Both these arts deal with opinion, with probability, not certainty, and therefore these two arts, and they alone,
are capable of generating arguments on two or more sides of a
question. Dialectic deals with philosophical and general questions, proceeds by question and answer, employs technical language, and is addressed to philosophers. Rhetoric deals with
particular questions, such as political action, proceeds by un-
interrupted discourse, employs usually non-technical language,
and is addressed to a popular audience.

Rhetoric is defined by Aristotle as the art of finding in any
given subject matter the available means of persuasion. The
modes of persuasion are three, and since, as Aristotle remarks,
one must know, not only what to say, but how to say it effectively in words and in a well disposed order, his basic treatment
may be outlined thus:

1. Persuasion is achieved by means of:
   a. *Logos*: one should convince the minds of the hearers or
      readers by proving the truth of what one is saying.
   b. *Pathos*: one should put them into a frame of mind favor-
      able to one's purpose, principally by working on their emo-
      tions.
   c. *Ethos*: one should inspire in them, by courtesy and other
      qualities, confidence in one's character, competence, good
      sense, good moral character, and good will.
2. Style should be characterized by good diction, good grammatical structure, pleasing rhythm, clear and appropriate
   language, effective metaphor, etc.
3. Arrangement is the order of parts: introduction, statement
   and proof, conclusion.
   The five traditional parts of rhetoric were invention (finding arguments for persuasion), arrangement of the parts of a
   composition, style, memory of a speech, and the proper use
   of voice and gesture in delivering it.

C. Poetic, as Aristotle understands it, is imitation, an imitation of
life, in which the author does not speak to the reader directly,
but only through his characters. He lets them speak and act,

and the reader or listener identifies himself imaginatively with them. The use of verse is not essential.

Because poetic communication is mediate, through the interposition of the characters and the situation in the story, it is more subject to misinterpretation than direct or expository communication. If, for example, one does not recognize irony, burlesque, or satire, one will understand just the opposite of what is intended by the author. It is necessary to learn how to interpret poetic communication. Often it is the easiest, most natural, and most effective means of communication, e. g., the parable of the prodigal son; but sometimes it is difficult to understand, e. g., the parable of the unjust steward (St. Luke 16: 1-9).

In the *Poetics*, Aristotle discusses tragic drama and the epic, both plotted narrative. He distinguishes six formative elements or qualitative parts of drama: (1) plot, (2) characters, (3) the thought of the characters, (4) diction, or style, (5) music, (6) spectacle (production in the theatre, scene, costumes).

The specific function of tragedy is to produce in the audience a purification of the emotions through pity and fear, evoked principally by the tragic suffering of the hero. To produce this effect, the tragic hero must be a man, not perfect, but on the whole good, for whom one feels liking and sympathy, whose misfortune is brought upon him, not by vice or depravity, but by an error of judgment or a flaw in his character.

It will be noticed that character (*ethos*), thought (*logos*), arousing the emotions (*pathos*), and style are basic in both rhetoric and poetic.

Poetic is the imitation of an action by which agents to whom we ascribe moral qualities achieve happiness or misery. Their thought and character are shown as the causes of their actions which result in success or in failure. Moreover, at any time, anywhere, a man of this kind will probably, or even necessarily, say or do this, under circumstances like this. Yet this man, even while typical of many others, is realized in this story vividly and imaginatively as an individual one has known, whose joys and sorrows one has shared. Therefore poetic stands in a unique position between history and philosophy. It is more philosophic and of greater import than history because it is universal, not singular, and represents what might be, not merely what has been. By it one gathers the meaning of things as the insight of an artist perceived it. It is more moving than philosophy because the universal is realized intensely in the individual portrayed and the appeal is to the whole man, to the imagination, the feelings, and the intellect, not to the intellect alone.

II. The short story

Poetic, as Aristotle conceived it, is plotted narrative dramatically imitating action in human life, whether in epic or drama. Consequently, poetic is realized also in the novel and the short story.

Because the short story is the shortest form of plotted narrative, the form probably most widely read by college students, and the form to be written in a course in college composition, we shall focus our more detailed study of plotted narrative on it, although the principles are applicable, both in reading and in writing, to the novel, the drama, and the epic as well. In the following discussion, emphasis is sometimes on reading, sometimes on writing.

A. The plot, not the characters, is the first and the essential element in poetic, just as order or design, not color, is in painting. The characters reveal themselves in the action.

A plot is a combination of incidents so closely connected by cause and effect that not one of them may be transposed or withdrawn without disjoining and dislocating the whole. This causal connection constitutes unity of action, the one unity essential to every poetic work.

A plot, says Aristotle, must have a beginning, a middle, and an end. The beginning is that which is not necessarily after, or caused by, something else, but which causes that which follows it; the middle is that which is caused by what precedes it and is the cause of what follows it; the end is that which was caused by what precedes it, but does not cause something to follow after it. In other words, a plot has a rising and a falling action in a sequence of cause and effect.

The topics cause and effect (see p. 123) are the tools for analyzing poetic, just as division is the tool for analyzing rhetorical, in the sense of expository or direct, communication of ideas.

The plot is the story. Every plot is a narration of events, but not every narration of events is a plot. A plot is a narration of selected events causally connected, rising out of a conflict and the resulting obstacles to be overcome, all of which creates suspense which is not satisfied until the end. Thus plotted narrative has logical and artistic unity which unplotted narrative lacks, for in unplotted narrative the end is simply a cessation of the story, which could be continued indefinitely beyond that point; in plotted narrative there is actual dissatisfaction unless the end is known and there is a sense of finality when it is known—no desire to have the story go on and on.

The plot of a short story involves a single situation: one central character is facing a problem, and the plot is its solution. The problem or conflict is the driving desire or purpose of the main character, who, encountering obstacles, either overcomes them (happy ending), or is overcome by them (tragic ending); both are solutions.

Therefore the simplest analysis of any plotted narrative is in terms of character, problem, and solution. This analysis may be made of the main plot and of subplots, if there are any, as there are in some dramas and novels.

1. Parts of the action: (1) the situation or exposition; (2) the complication or rising action; (3) the resolution or falling action. The basic analysis of plotted narrative discovers:
   a. The beginning of the action
   b. The turning point (the logical climax)
   c. The denouement or final outcome (the emotional climax)

   Example from drama: In Shakespeare's *Hamlet*, the beginning of the action is where the ghost tells Hamlet that he is his father, murdered by the king, and asks Hamlet to avenge this wrong. The turning point is where Hamlet, thinking it is the king, whose reactions to the play within the play have revealed his guilt, kills Polonius instead. The denouement is where Hamlet kills the king with the poisoned weapon which the king had prepared for him, and from which he, too, dies.

   These three points in the action, it will be noticed, are what Aristotle called the beginning, the middle, and the end of a plot. (See page 249.)

   The parts of a plot may be diagramed thus, with the three important points of the action marked a, b, c.

2. Problems of action
   a. Plausibility. This is absolutely essential to a story. It is

the achievement of illusion and inward consistency. No matter how imaginative or even fantastic a story may be, it must create illusion; it must seem real.

Means to secure plausibility:

1) Natural, adequate motivation (the reasons why the characters act as they do)

2) Skillful, adequate forecast. Forecast includes motives, and also details of setting, appearance, incident, etc., which make later events seem plausible.

3) Vivid, concrete, realistic detail (as in *Robinson Crusoe*)

4) First person angle of narration (more convincing)

5) Unfamiliar setting: time and place that the reader cannot check on

6) Doubting characters convinced; reader also (as in Munro's "Tobermory")

7) Tone (Let's play there are fairies, or go to a world very different from ours, as in *Alice in Wonderland*)

b. Where to begin the story—at the beginning, the middle, or near the end of the series of events that constitute the story. It is often better to plunge *in medias res,* into the midst of the events, as Homer does in the *Iliad* and the *Odyssey,* and to tell what happened earlier (restrospective action) at points where the incidents will have greatest significance. For example, in the *Odyssey* the story of Odysseus' pursuit of the boar which tore his leg is told in Book XIX, where the scar causes his old nurse to recognize him, although the incident occurred earlier perhaps than any other related in the story.

Retrospective action may be introduced by letters, by dialogue, by reminiscent reverie. In *A Tale of Two Cities* the letter which Dr. Manette wrote during his imprisonment in the Bastille, before the story opened, is introduced with intense dramatic effect at Charles Darnay's second French trial near the end of the novel. The conversation between Sidney Carton and the Sheep of the Prisons (Solomon Pross) near the end of the novel clarifies the facts about the mysterious funeral of Roger Cly and Jerry Cruncher's muddy boots (bits of forecast) introduced near the beginning.

Retrospective action is very important in building a story; it is a means to secure artistic unity, dramatic effect, compactness.

1) Prospective action is that which moves forward chronologically: the order of narration corresponds to the order of events.

2) Retrospective action is that which moves backward chronologically: the order of narration differs from the order of the events narrated. The action is retrospective whenever an incident which occurred before another is told after it. In moving pictures this device is called a flashback.

A story *cannot* begin with retrospective action, although it may begin with reminiscence; these two are not identical. Whatever the reader is told first in a story cannot have occurred before something he has already been told in this story.

The stories which develop the Fothergill Plot (see John Berdan, *Fourteen Stories from One Plot*) illustrate a variety of effects produced by beginning the story at different points. There are five incidents in the plot common to all the stories. Some of the stories begin with the first, others with the second, third, or fourth incident.

c. Division into dramatic scenes and non-dramatic narration

1) Dramatic scenes create an experience for the reader to share imaginatively, through dialogue, reverie, detail, of action, and vivid picturing details. A scene is obligatory if it is psychologically necessary to present it dramatically in order to satisfy the reader's interest in certain points and to make the story or the character convincing and plausible.

Dialogue should: (1) forward plot; (2) reveal character; (3) be natural.

Dialogue cannot be created by merely putting words into quotation marks and adding *he said, she said*, etc. It must have the quality of speech and must fit the character and situation.

2) Non-dramatic narration merely gives the reader information through the author's explanation and sum-

mary of events. In most good stories there is little of this.

d. Angle of narration. Some problems to consider:

1) Third person is more flexible, and most readers seem to prefer it. First person is more vivid. To tell a story in first person through the major character may cause him, or her, to appear egotistical. To tell it in first person through a minor character, e. g., Dr. Watson in the Sherlock Holmes stories, is one way to avoid this difficulty.

2) Focus. From whose point of view is the story to be told? Whose story is it to be?

Sometimes the choice of an unusual angle of narration gives a fresh and interesting turn to an otherwise ordinary story; e. g., the threatening break-up of a home told from the laundryman's or grocer boy's point of view, or a college romance told from a cab driver's point of view, in either first or third person.

An interesting effect is sometimes produced, but usually in a work longer than a short story, by telling the same story or a part of a story more than once, each time from the point of view of a different character, e. g., Browning's *The Ring and the Book*.

3) Frame or parenthetical device, a story within a story, e. g., Dostoevski's "The Thief," Kipling's "The Man Who Would Be King."

4) Objective (events and speech only) or subjective (thoughts of characters told). If subjective, the story may tell the thoughts of one character only (giving a better focus) or of more than one character (omniscient author).

e. Forecast. This hints but does not reveal; it effects suspense and plausibility.

f. Suspense. This is interest created by: motivation; forecast; choice of the point for beginning the story. Suspense is not surprise.

g. Transition. Modern writers often favor abrupt transitions. Milton is outstanding for his plausible and smooth transitions in *Paradise Lost*.

h. Technique of presentation: Let the characters act out the story. Sometimes a story is told through letters, diary, dream. Any one of these will employ one or more of the four techniques: (1) dialogue; (2) reverie; (3) picturing details; (4) explanation and summary. Usually all of these are combined; explanation should be used sparingly.

The structure of a story, either one that has been read or one to be written, may be presented as follows. The theme is the underlying idea of the plot expressed in general terms in one sentence. (See page 259.) Asterisks indicate dramatic scenes.

(See page 259.)

THE PIECE OF STRING
by
Guy de Maupassant

Character: Maître Hauchecorne
Problem: To clear himself of suspicion of theft.
Solution: He did not succeed in clearing himself but died, vainly protesting his innocence.
Theme: He who protests too much is not believed.
Beginning of the action: Hauchecorne picked up a piece of string, and an enemy saw him.
Turning point: Accused by his enemy of picking up a wallet that had been lost, he told the truth, but his story was not believed even after the lost wallet was found and returned; it was thought that an accomplice returned it. (He was freed from the legal charge but not from the suspicion of his fellow townsmen.)
Denouement: Worn out by vain efforts to make himself believed, he wasted away and died, still not believed.

Retrospective Action	Prospective Action
	1. Seeing on the ground a piece of string, Maître Hauchecorne picked it up. He noticed that Maître Malandain was watching him.
2. He and Malandain had once had a quarrel and had borne each other malice ever since.	
	*3. While Hauchecorne was at Jourdain's inn, the town crier announced that Maître Houlbreque had lost a pocketbook containing 500 francs and business papers.
	*4. The corporal of gendarmes came to the inn and called for Hauchecorne, who went with him.

Retrospective Action (cont.)

Prospective Action (cont.)

*5. Brought before the mayor, Hauchecorne was accused of stealing the pocketbook.

6. Malandain had brought the charge against him.

*7. Hauchecorne denied the charge, and asserted he had merely picked up a piece of string, which he drew from his pocket.

8. No one believed him.

9. Searched at his own request, Hauchecorne was dismissed with a warning.

10. Hauchecorne told the story of the string to all he met. No one believed him. They laughed.

11. Hauchecorne went home to his own village and made the rounds telling his story, which no one believed. He brooded over it all night.

12. Next day, a farm hand returned the missing pocketbook.

13. He had found it, and being unable to read, had taken it to his master.

*14. Hauchecorne repeated to everyone he met the story of the string, triumphantly adding as proof of his innocence the fact that the purse had been returned.

*15. He realized that people thought his accomplice had brought it back. The crowd jeered at him.

16. Struck to the heart by the injustice of the suspicion, Hauchecorne continued to tell his tale, adding proofs, but the more artful his arguments the less he was believed.

17. Jokers would lead him on to tell the story.

18. Exhausting himself in useless efforts to vindicate himself, he wasted away, his mind grew weak, and he died, vainly protesting his innocence.

B. Characters
  1. Classes depending upon the degree of characterization
     a. Lay figure: not characterized, merely a figure needed in
        in the plot, e. g., Orestes in *Iphigenia at Aulis*; Iris and
        Chryseis in the *Iliad*, the minor wooers in the *Odyssey*,
        Hawthorne's David Swan, Luchesi in "The Cask of Amon-
        tillado," Mme. Forestier in "The Necklace"
     b. Type: like other members of his class, but different from
        other types, e. g., a typical miser, lawyer, young girl;
        Euryclea, Mme. Loisel
     c. Individual: typical, yet distinctive among members of his
        class, e. g., Shylock, Sidney Carton, Iphigenia
  2. Motivation: the reason why the characters act as they do;
     hence the basic link between characters and plot. Adequate
     motivation is the principal means to create plausibility and
     suspense.
  3. Methods of revealing character
     a. Direct: traits described by the author or by other charac-
        ter (less effective because it merely gives the reader infor-
        mation about the character)
     b. Indirect: moral qualities revealed by what the character
        thinks, says, or does, conveyed by presenting details and
        letting the reader judge for himself what the trait is (more
        effective because it creates an experience for the reader
        who thereby imaginatively meets the character and perhaps
        even identifies himself with the character)

        A detail suggests much more than it actually states, for
        from it the reader spontaneously builds up a vivid image
        of the whole. The use of detail is the principal means to
        make the reader see everything with the vividness of an
        eye witness, to make the story tell itself without the in-
        trusion of the author, to make it a poetic communication
        creating illusion. Examples:
        1) Detail of mental analysis or reverie

           a) A strange elation took possession of him. He felt himself
              already back in the glamorous past—young and free, with
              life and romance before him instead of behind.
                                                        —Kaye-Smith

           b) Everything whirled through his head pell mell. He had the
              sensation of falling down a precipice. The bottom seemed to
              to have dropped out of everything.—Sramek.

c) She tried to recall the slight giddiness of the dancing and the firm pressure of his arm against her. She remembered his face when he was bending towards her, making efforts to look serious and grave, but somehow so boyish.

—P. DuBos

2) Detail of speech

You're vot I call a bird in de hand, an' it ain't fur you to be givin' orders—it's fur me. An' anyway I guess we ain't a goin' to be able to make a trade—leastwise not on yore terms. But we'll do business all right, all right—anyhow I will.—Cobb

3) Detail of action

a) Larry, crying a shrill warning, sprang between Sullivan and the open furnace.—Greene

b) Mrs. Reed, impatient of my now frantic anguish and wild sobs, abruptly thrust me back and locked me in, without further parley.—C. Brontë

4) Detail of gesture

a) The thin hands, picking at the fastenings of a spacious bag, trembled and twitched.—Brush

b) He still slowly moved his finger over his upper lip, and still his eyes dwelt dreamily on the glowing grate.

—C. Brontë

c) She could skim the State Street windows and come away with a mental photograph of every separate tuck, hem, yoke, and ribbon.—Wharton

d) . . . in whose parents' presence all free conversation ceased and even the neighbors' children kept their eyes on the tablecloth.—Canby

5) Detail revealing emotion

a) The lady's eyes grew moist, but the hot tears did not fall. They trembled in her voice.—Van Dyke

b) A flash of ice, a flash of fire, a bursting gush of blood went over him, and then he stood transfixed.—Stevenson

c) My skin went tight and cold and my heart fluttered.

—Zane Grey

d) He hesitated, and felt an excitement in the pit of his stomach as a man does when he is faced with an important decision; his heart thumped.—R. Ayre

6) Detail of experience—cold, heat, touch, smell, taste, sound, sight—causing the reader to share imaginatively the experiences of the characters

a) Detail of touch (this includes temperature and the kinetic sense—movement and muscular strain)

i. Once in the road, he had the gale in his face, and the wet snow on his mustache and eyelashes instantly hardened to metal. The same metal seemed to be driving a million blades into his throat and lungs.—Wharton

ii. Their hands clasped in the brief tight greeting of the West that is death to the hand-shake microbe.

—O. Henry

b) Detail of smell

Around him flowed a faint odor, damp, dusty, of cardboard, paint, tin, caught there in the cellar holding him.

—Hull

c) Detail of taste

. . . licking their fingers with that absorbed inward look that comes only from whipped cream.—Mansfield

d) Detail of sound

It was a low, dull, quick sound—much such a sound as a watch makes when enveloped in cotton.—Poe

e) Detail of sight

Their bark was speckled with the vivid alternate splendor of ebony and silver, and was smoother than all save the cheeks of Eleonora. . . . And life arose in our paths; for the tall flamingo, hitherto unseen, with all gay glowing birds, flaunted his scarlet plumage before us.—Poe

7) Detail of allusion (See page 31.)

a) Her professional self was a sort of gold-paying Letitia Hyde to a very delicate Miss Jekyll.—Wilkinson

b) The ladies would not thus rival Atalanta if they but knew that any one were at leisure to observe them.

—Hawthorne

8) Detail of incident

a) Bill was pasting court plaster over the scratches and bruises on his features.—O. Henry

b) He followed the trail of the other man who dragged himself along, and soon came to the end of it—a few fresh-picked bones where the soggy moss was marked by the foot-pads of many wolves.—Jack London

c) After a time the bell for rest time clanged out and was followed by footsteps, voices, shutting of doors, and then quietness.—Attenborough

d) Captain Mercadier—twenty-six years of service, twenty-two campaigns, and three wounds—had just retired on his pension.—Coppée

9) Detail picturing places

a) Mrs. Jellyby, sitting in quite a nest of waste paper, drank coffee all the evening, and dictated at intervals to her eldest daughter.—Dickens

b) The sick man that crawled, a sick wolf that limped, two creatures dragging their dying carcasses across the desolation and hunting each other's lives.—Jack London

10) Detail picturing people—appearance (features, dress)

    a) A Dresden China girl with a heart-shaped face.—Brush

    b) The child was limp, like a hothouse plant, and everything about him seemed extraordinarily soft and tender: his movements, his curly hair, the look in his eyes, the velvet jacket.—Chekhov

    c) A tall, debonair, and rather dangerously handsome man to whom six o'clock spelled evening clothes.—Ferber

C. Thought. The thought and moral qualities of the characters, says Aristotle, are the natural causes of the action, or plot. Thought and action reveal character. Thought expressed in language is that part of poetic which is common to both logic and rhetoric, for the characters employ these arts to prove or disprove, to arouse emotion, or to maximize and minimize things.

1. Particularly important thoughts are the general statements or sententious utterances (general propositions, apothegms, proverbs) which express a universal view or judgment or philosophy of life. *Hamlet* owes much of its philosophical quality to the large number of such utterances in it. Examples:

    a.   . . . to the noble mind
    Rich gifts wax poor when givers prove unkind.
                  —Shakespeare, *Hamlet,* 3.1.100

    b.   . . . the good, when praised,
    Feel something of disgust, if to excess,
    Commended.—Euripides, *Iphigenia at Aulis,* ll. 1054-56

    c. Even his character grew firmer, like that of a man who has made up his mind, and set himself a goal.—Gogol, "The Cloak"

    d. Could we know all the vicissitudes of our fortunes, life would be too full of hope and fear, exultation or disappointment, to afford us a single hour of true serenity.—Hawthorne, "David Swan"

2. Theme. This is the underlying thought of the whole story stated in one sentence. It is usually a conviction about life, which might have been the subject of an essay or a sermon, but which has been expressed instead in a poetic communication, a story, drama, or novel. Examples:

    a. A man should not be allowed to perish altogether.
                  —Dostoevski, "The Thief"

    b. All that glitters is not gold.—Maupassant, "The Necklace"

    c. Revenge is sweet.
    —Poe, "The Cask of Amontillado" and Aeschylus, *Agamemnon*

    d. Sacrifice for the public good exalts the sorrow it entails.
                —Euripides, *Iphigenia at Aulis*

D. Diction or style

In poetic or fictional composition the most important characteristic of style is that, as far as possible, it puts the actual scenes before the reader's eyes. The use of detail in doing this has already been illustrated. At the very time when he is constructing his plots, and, especially when delineating his characters, the writer is engaged in finding the appropriate expression for his conceptions. Specific words and metaphors give liveliness. The principles of good expository composition are also applicable to fiction. (See pages 278 ff.)

The tone or mood is important in fiction. The author's attitude toward his material may be serious, earnest, realistic, romantic, flippant, cynical, satiric; the work may be a burlesque, a fantasy, etc.

Of the two remaining elements of drama discussed by Aristotle, music is not essential today, as the songs of the chorus were in Greek drama; music is dominant, however, in opera. Spectacle is essential to the production of drama; it includes costumes and scenery.

Setting, imaginatively realized, is often important in fiction. It includes place, time, customs, circumstances, background, milieu. Generally these should be given in detail (of sight, sound, touch, etc.) through the characters, and naturally growing out of incidents throughout the story rather than in long descriptions at or near the beginning. The setting may create atmosphere, e. g., sordid, gloomy, sinister, gay (a very important element in Poe, Hawthorne, Bret Harte). Local color may be created by, for instance, dress, customs, characteristics of crowds, the use of dialect.

E. The work as a whole

The distinctive value of the world's great stories is that they lead the reader to share imaginatively the rich and varied experience of individual characters confronted with problems and conditions of life common to men in all ages. They present potentialities and norms of living made significant by the best writers. For example, they may show men and women suffering as a result of their own desire to have an excess of what is good for them or of what is not good, even sinful. They show how false conceptions of happiness lead to misery. A story that portrays evil is morally sound if it shows evil as evil, yet does not so portray the evil as to make it a source of temptation to a normal reader. Good stories appeal to the human in us. We may love, detest, admire, pity, scorn, or ridicule.

Ask yourself: What vision of life, what insight, is gained from this story? What problems has the author stated and solved? What has he left unsolved? Does the story present the problem of conflicting duties, the claims of public good against those of private good, human rights against property rights, adjustment to environment, clashes of culture, etc.? Has the story brought to life fictional or historical personages worth knowing? Are they individualized? alive? Are they normal and fine persons or are they perverted? Are they heightened above life to an ideal conception? Are their actions and dialogue appropriate? Which are the most interesting persons? Why? Which persons and incidents in the story does the author seem to approve? to disapprove? What seems to be his philosophy of life? What is the dominant idea, the single impression, left by the story? Does it present other times, other places, other civilizations and cultures? Is the style distinguished? What are the literary relationships and influences that affect the story? What was the author trying to do in this work? Did he succeed in doing it? Was it worth doing?

Dostoevski's "The Thief," for example, answers the question, who is my neighbor? Am I my brother's keeper? Yes. Is it right to let a man perish altogether? No, not even if he seems worthless, an incorrigible drunkard, lazy, ungrateful, a thief, a liar. Not even if I am poor and have very little to share with anyone, and he has no particular claim on me, such as kinship or friendship. He is a human being and I must not let him perish. That claim is sufficient. This story gives a vision of life. It asserts on the lowest level, in universal terms, the inescapable kinship of all human beings and the duty of brotherly love.

In reading, think critically, analytically, not vaguely. Develop a critical vocabulary that expresses real thought and discrimination.

Growth in the apprehension of poetic communication follows from a true understanding of its specific nature, and from exercise in analysis and criticism. At first, critical reading may be laborious and slow, but later it will become easy, spontaneous, and richly rewarding. It differs from uncritical reading as dim or blurred vision differs from clear, distinct vision, or as the naked eye's perception of a drop of blood as simple and homogeneous differs from the discriminating perception of it as complex and heterogeneous when seen through the magnifying power of the microscope.

III. Figurative language

According to the ancient conception, expressed by Cicero and Quintilian, figurative language includes any deviation, either in thought or expression, from the ordinary and simple modes of speaking. This would include the language of ordinary persons moved by excitement to adopt short cuts and turns of expression which give their speech liveliness and vividness not ordinarily found in it.

Cicero and Quintilian distinguished about ninety figures of speech, and Renaissance rhetoricians about two hundred in all. They divided them into tropes and schemes. Schemes were fashionings of language or thought deviating from the ordinary. They were divided into grammatical and rhetorical schemes. Grammatical schemes included devices which today are treated as means to improve style through grammar: variety of structure, parallel and antithetical structure, balance, rhythm, emphasis, elliptical structure, and the use of one part of speech for another, e. g., nouns used as verbs. Rhetorical schemes of repetition were frequently used to emphasize parallel structure, balance, and rhythm. They included repetition of letters in alliteration and repetition of words. Rhetorical schemes of thought corresponded to the threefold means of persuasion *logos, pathos,* and *ethos* (see page 247). One hundred and twenty-two of the two hundred figures corresponded to the topics of logic (see page 123) and the forms of reasoning. We have already seen that litotes is the rhetorical counterpart of logical obversion (see page 135). Other rhetorical schemes corresponded to the enthymeme, the disjunctive and hypothetical syllogisms, and the dilemma.

The modern concept of figures of speech is almost limited to those which ancient and Renaissance rhetoricians called tropes. A trope is the turning of a word from its ordinary and proper meaning to another not proper, in order to increase its force and vividness. It is an imaginative, in contrast to a matter-of-fact, use of words. For example, "The knife is rusty" is a matter-of-fact use of *rusty*. "Their minds are rusty" is a figurative use of *rusty* turning it to a meaning not proper to it, but nonetheless forceful.

The value of tropes lies in their power to convey ideas vividly in a condensed and picturesque style. Their abundant use in newsmagazines and newspapers, especially in sport columns, testifies to their brevity and utility. They are means to achieve a clear, forceful, lively style. The most important trope is the metaphor.

Renaissance rhetoricians distinguished from four to ten tropes; Quintilian, fourteen. We shall distinguish eight tropes (simile, metaphor, onomatopoeia, personification, antonomasia, metonymy, synecdoche, and irony) and shall notice from which topic of invention each is derived.

A. The first three of these tropes are based on similarity.

1. A simile is not, strictly speaking, a trope, since the similarity is expressed and no word is turned to a meaning not proper to it. Its resemblance to metaphor is so basic, however, that this technical distinction will be ignored here.

   A simile expresses through *like, as,* or *resembles* an imaginative comparison between objects of different classes. Examples:

   a. Senators and representatives rose like corn in a popper, introducing legislation.—*Time,* January 27, 1947, p. 19

   b. This habitual exorbitance goes far towards accounting for the compelling tone which resounds through all of O'Neill's work like the ringing of red iron on an anvil.
      —*Time,* October 21, 1946, p. 76

   c. Hence much reading [without sufficient thinking upon it] deprives the mind of all elasticity, as a weight continually pressing upon it does a spring.—Schopenhauer, "On Thinking for Oneself"

2. A metaphor boldly states, without using a word of comparison, the identification of similar objects of different classes. Examples:

   a. All this caused the Federal Reserve Bank of New York, the Sanhedrin of financial theologians, to say in its July report. . . .
      —*Time,* July 14, 1947, p. 79

   b. For there is no chemistry to equal that which works in the marriage of catastrophe with a courageous heart.
      —*Time,* October 21, 1946, p. 75

   c. All these major disputes were deadlocked. They waited for a magic wage formula, or a settlement in steel to unlock them.
      —*Time,* September 23, 1946, p. 41

3. Onomatopoeia is the use of words or rhythms whose sound imitates the sense. Examples:

   a. And the plopping of the waterdrops . . .—Amy Lowell
   b. The moan of doves in immemorial elms
      And murmuring of innumerable bees . . .—Tennyson
   c. But when loud surges lash the sounding shore,
      The hoarse, rough verse should like the torrent roar;
      When Ajax strives some rock's vast weight to throw
      The line too labors, and the words move slow.—Pope

B. Personification and antonomasia are based on the relation of subject and adjuncts.

  1. Personification is the attribution of life, sensation, and human qualities to objects of a lower order or to abstract ideas. Examples:

     a. The mists, like ghosts, were stealthily withdrawing in every direction into the woods.—Thoreau
     b. I would hate that death bandaged my eyes, and forebore,
       And bade me creep past.—Browning
     c. Life's but a walking shadow, a poor player
       That struts and frets his hour upon the stage
       And then is heard no more.—Shakespeare
     d. Here lies his head upon the lap of earth.—Gray

  2. Antonomasia is of two kinds: (1) a proper name is substituted for a quality associated with it and used much like a common name; (2) a phrase descriptive of attributes is substituted for a proper name.

     a. Some call him [Azikiwe] the Negro Gandhi, the jungle George Washington . . . the Bertie McCormick of the Niger Delta, a coconut grove Jim Farley, and one of the few people in the world who got a high opinion of the U. S. from washing dishes in a Pittsburgh waffle foundry . . .—*Time*, June 9, 1947, p. 28
     b. The sage of Monticello became the third President of the United States.

C. Metonymy is a trope based on subject and adjunct and also on cause and effect.

Metonymy substitutes subject for adjunct, adjunct for subject, cause for effect, or effect for cause, including each of the four causes, efficient, final, material and formal (see page 234). An author, for instance, is the efficient cause of his writings. Examples:

     a. . . . to have thy prison days prolonged through middle age down to decrepitude and silver hairs, without hope or respite . . .
                                  —Lamb

b. Their regular hours stupefy—not a fiddle nor a card after eleven!
—R. Sheridan

c. The days are evil.—Saint Paul

d. Awake, the morning shines.—Milton

e. Calais was peopled with novelty and delight.—Hazlitt

f. May my hands . . . never more brandish revengeful steel.
—Shakespeare

g. I had been in youth . . . a great reader of Livy.—De Quincey

h.   . . . altar, sword, and pen,
Fireside, the heroic wealth of hall and bower,
Have forfeited their ancient English dower
Of inward happiness.—Wordsworth

i. Though we walk in the flesh, we do not make war according to the flesh.—Saint Paul

If an effect is signified by a remote cause, the figure was called metalepsis, a kind of metonymy. Example:

Tuberculosis fighters are convinced that the absolute weapon against the disease is only a few million dollars off.
—*Time,* June 30, 1947, p. 79

D. Synecdoche is a trope based on division. It substitutes the part for the whole, the whole for the part, species for genus, or genus for species. Examples:

a. The news that Daisy Miller was surrounded by a half dozen wonderful mustaches checked Winterbourne's impulses to go straightway to see her.—Henry James

b. The world praised him.

c. Give us this day our daily bread.

d. Like to a pair of lions smeared with prey—Shakespeare

E. Irony is a trope based on contraries. By naming one contrary it intends another. Examples:

a. *Gabriel.* [*to Satan*] Courageous chief,
The first in flight from pain, hadst thou alleged
To thy deserted host this cause of flight,
Thou surely hadst not come sole fugitive.—Milton

b. *Richard III.* [*to himself*] Simple, plain Clarence! I do love thee so
That I will shortly send thy soul to heaven.—Shakespeare

F. Faults to be avoided in using figures of speech

1. Mixed figures. Example: The flower of our youth is the foundation on which we will build until our light will shine out to all the world.

2. Cliché—trite, stereotyped figure of speech. Examples: brave as lions, cunning as foxes, raven tresses, lily hands, alabaster neck.

     3. Far-fetched or lacking good taste. Example: He is as de-
pendable as a Big Ben alarm clock.

IV. Poetry and versification

    Poetry may be divided into narrative, didactic, and lyric poetry.
Narrative poetry includes drama, epic, ballad, and romance; what
has been said of plotted narrative applies to these species in so far
as they are plotted. Didactic poetry is not poetic in Aristotle's sense
of imitating action; rather, it is expository. It merits the name
poetry if it has the requisite qualities of thought, style, and rhythm,
which will be discussed presently. Outstanding examples are Lu-
cretius' *De Rerum Natura* and Pope's *Essay on Criticism.* Lyric
poetry includes the song, hymn, sonnet, ode, rondeau, and many
other special verse forms. It expresses the poet's feelings, impressions, and reflections rather than an objective incident, although
an incident may occasion the reflections. The drama developed
from the lyric, and there are many songs and lyric passages in
plays, particularly in Greek and Renaissance plays. Probably most
persons today think of poetry primarily as lyrical.

    Aristotle distinguishes poetry from other modes of imitation ac-
cording to the means employed. Music employs rhythm and harmony; dancing, rhythm alone; and poetry, rhythm and language.
Meters in language are species of rhythm.

    The classical and neo-classical ideal is that poetry should be ob-
jective, should appeal to the intellect and should achieve beauty
through form perfectly ordering matter that has intrinsic dignity
and elevation. The romantic ideal is that poetry should be subjective, should appeal to the feelings and should achieve beauty
through the free and spontaneous play of imagination and fancy
on material that may be either picturesquely strange or homely
and commonplace. A considerable number of modern poets emphasize a sense of fact and seek to achieve distinction by the use
of sharp, concrete, often obscure diction and imagery, and new,
sometimes harsh, rhythms. A blend of the characteristics of these
three groups is found in the best poetry. For example, Milton's
Paradise Lost blends classical and romantic characteristics.

    Although the conceptions of poetry vary considerably, it is gen-
erally agreed that poetry is a communication of experience, of
emotion as well as thought, which embraces the universal under
the particular.

    Poetry may be defined as the expression in fitting, rhythmical language of the thought, imagination, and emotion of the poet, reflecting some aspect of beauty and truth, and capable of arousing a response in the imagination and feelings of the reader or listener.

The language of poetry is distinguished by an enhanced rhythm, although, according to Aristotle as well as Wordsworth, meter is not essential. It is further distinguished by exceptional energy, vividness, imagery, penetration, and compression, whereby much meaning is packed into few words. While achieving these qualities, a great poet has as his primary mark, so far as form is concerned, the capacity to arrange words in eloquent, inevitable, and unimprovable order and beauty; so far as matter is concerned, he must have a deep perception of truth and beauty in nature, man, and God.

Poetry communicates experience that cannot be expressed in any other way. The poet sees and feels with a depth and intensity beyond that of the ordinary man; he communicates not thought only but this experience. To read poetry is to share the experience of the poet who wrote it.

The form of poetry is of its essence to such a degree that the form is felt to be inevitable; that is, it is felt to be the only form in which that matter could be satisfactorily communicated. Hence matter and form are united in poetry more intimately than in merely logical communication.

It is true that what one person considers to be poetry another may not. This is so because one reader may find poetic experience in a work that will not evoke such a response in another reader. Poetry depends much on the psychological dimension of language, which is less objective than the logical dimension; the subjective varies from person to person. There is, however, much poetry capable of evoking poetic response in so many readers through the years that it is universally judged to be truly poetry.

The subjective character of a poetic impression is the theme of the following poem:

SONGS OF THE SONGLESS

They have no songs, the sedges dry,
And still they sing.
It is within my breast they sing,
As I pass by.
Within my breast they touch a spring,
They wake a sigh.

> There is but sound of sedges dry.
> In me they sing.
>   —George Meredith

The true opposite of poetry is matter-of-fact, as Wordsworth insists in his "Preface to the Lyrical Ballads." The opposite of prose is verse; both have rhythm, but verse has meter, and prose has not.

Consequently, poetry should not be identified with verse: poetic passages occur in novels and other prose writings; some verse is distinctly, often dully, matter-of-fact and anything but poetic. The following bits of verse are decidedly not poetry:

> Thirty days hath September,
> April, June, and November.

> Early to bed and early to rise
> Makes men healthy, wealthy, and wise.

Elements of form

A. The emphasized rhythm essential to poetry may be achieved by various means.

  1. Parallelism. This is the chief rhythmical device of Hebrew poetry. Parallelism has been called thought-rime because the commonest form is a repetition of thought in different words. If a psalm is read with the repeated parts omitted, one perceives at once that it is prosaic, in contrast.

    There are three main types of parallelism. Examples from the Psalms:

    a. Repetitive parallelism (thought repeated)

> For my life is wasted with grief; and my years in sighs. (30:11)

    b. Antithetical parallelism (thought contrasted)

> For wrath is in his indignation; and life in his good will. (29:6)

    c. Additive or synthetic parallelism (like a waltz step)

> This is the generation of them that seek him,
> of them that seek the face of the God of Jacob. (23:16)

  2. A systematic use of the caesura (a natural pause in a line, usually in or near the middle) and of alliteration (which serves to bind the fourstressed line into a rhythmic unit). These two devices create the strong rhythm of Old English poetry. Example from *Beowulf* (Gummere's translation):

> We twain had talked, in time of youth
> and made our boast,—we were merely boys,
> Striplings still, to stake our lives
> far at sea: and so we performed it.

3. Cadence. This device is based on the natural rise and fall of the speaking voice. It is the avowed principle of the writers of *vers libre* or free verse and is explained by Amy Lowell. Example: Whitman's poem on page 275.
4. Meter. This is measured rhythm which conforms to a predetermined regular pattern of stressed and unstressed syllables. It is the chief rhythmical device of the great body of English poetry.
   a. The foot is the metrical unit; it is made up of one stressed syllable and one or more unstressed syllables. A metrical foot may be:
      1) Dissyllabic
         a) Iambus (e. g., desire)
         b) Trochee (e. g., under)
      2) Trisyllabic
         a) Dactyl (e. g., silently)
         b) Anapest (e. g., interfere)
         c) Amphibrach (e. g., insisted)
   Memory Device T I A D A
   Position of the stressed syllable:

   1. T rochee .... ´⌣
   2. I ambus .... ⌣´
   3. A napest .... ⌣⌣´
   1. D actyl .... ´⌣⌣
   2. A mphibrach .... ⌣´⌣

   b. Scansion is the marking off, orally or in writing, of the feet in verse so as to make explicit the metrical structure. In English verse an ictus is more proper than a macron to mark stressed syllables, but the macron, proper to Latin and Greek verse, may be more convenient to use.

   To name the meter of a poem is to state the kind of feet, the number of feet in one verse, and irregularities such as catalexis. According to the number of feet, the the verse is called monometer, dimeter, trimeter, tetrameter, pentameter, hexameter, heptamter, octameter, etc. Example: The meter of Blake's "The Tiger" is trochaic tetrameter catalectic.
   c. Irregularities and variations
      1) Catalexis: the omission of one or two unstressed syllables at the end of a verse

2) Feminine ending: the addition of one or two unstressed syllables at the end of a verse

3) Anacrusis: the addition of one or two unstressed syllables at the beginning of a verse

4) Truncation: the omission of one or two unstressed syllables at the beginning of a verse

Note. Catalexis and feminine ending often belong to the pattern. Anacrusis and truncation never do. They are only means of adapting irregular lines to the prevailing pattern; for example, there are six anacrustic lines out of twenty-four lines in Blake's "The Tiger."

5) Spondee: a foot consisting of two stressed syllables; it is usually a substitute for a dactyl and is relatively infrequent in English.

6) Pyrrhic: a foot consisting of two unstressed syllables.

d. Rhythm, or verse phrasing, is not identical with meter. (Compare time and phrasing in music.) Poems of the same meter may be dissimilar in rhythm, for the thought pattern may not coincide with the metrical pattern, although it fits into it. (Compare in rhythm Pope's "An Essay on Criticism" and Browning's "My Last Duchess," both written in the same meter, iambic pentameter rimed in couplets.)

Poor verse, unpoetic, deserving to be called doggerel, results when the rhythm coincides too exactly with the meter. In good verse, the rhythm seldom corresponds exactly with the meter, although it harmonizes with it and may be metrically perfect. The variety within order which thus characterizes good verse is achieved not by violating the metrical pattern but by using more subtle, artistic devices: by shifting the caesura, by using run-on lines as well as end-stopped lines, phrases of light and of heavy syllables, words of varying number of syllables—in a word, by setting the thought pattern in harmony with, but not in identity with, the metrical pattern. Good verse is regular in meter but has a varied rhythm. Both Pope and Browning, cited above, write verse in which the rhythm is artistically varied. Pope uses more subtle means and the variety is less evident. Milton in *Paradise Lost* shows himself a supreme artist in writing verse that is poetry of the highest order; he is a master of subtle variations.

We may distinguish three oral readings of a poem: oral scansion, explicitly revealing the meter; a sing-song reading (such as children in the grades tend to do), revealing the presence or absence of a doggerel rhythm; the intelligent reading revealing the full meaning and beauty of the poem.

B. Rime (or rhyme) is identity of sounds at the end of two or more words, with a difference at the beginning. The riming must begin on stressed syllables.

1. Kinds of rime

a. Masculine: words having one final stressed syllable riming; e. g., reign, gain; hate, debate.

b. Feminine: words having two or more syllables riming (the first of which must be stressed); e. g., unruly, truly; towering, flowering.

Note. Feminine rime is not identical with feminine ending. Compare:

(1) Tell me not in mournful numbers.—Longfellow

This illustrates feminine rime (*numbers* rimes with *slumbers* in the third line following) but not feminine ending, for a trochee regularly ends with an unstressed syllable.

(2) Our lives would grow together
In sad or singing weather   —Swinburne

This illustrates feminine rime and feminine ending.

(3) When I am dead, my dearest   —C. Rossetti

This illustrates feminine ending but not feminine rime, for *dearest* does not rime with any word in the stanza.

2. Imperfect rime: words that are not identical in riming sounds; e. g., heaven and even; geese and bees. (But *geese* and *fleece* are perfect rimes; so are *bees* and *ease*.)

Eye rime is a name given to the imperfect rime of words that look alike, but do not sound exactly alike; e. g., seven and even; love and prove.

3. Position of the riming words

a. End rime is the riming of a word at the end of one line with a word at the end of another line. This is the most usual form.

b. Internal rime is the riming of a word in the middle of a line with another in the same line, usually at the end of it. Example:

> And the silken sad uncertain rustling of each purple curtain
> Thrilled me—filled me with fantastic terrors never felt before.
> —Poe.

C. Assonance is identity of vowel sound in the middle of two or more words in the same line, with a difference at the beginning and end. Example:

> A hand that can be clasped no more.—Tennyson

D. Alliteration is identity of sound at the beginning of two or more words in the same line. Example:

> What a *t*ale of *t*error now their *t*urbulency *t*ells.—Poe

The following do not alliterate: *s* and *sh*; *t* and *th*.

Point out the alliteration and assonance in the following sentence: Never pump pneumatic phrases into frenzies.

E. Onomatopoeia: words imitating sounds; e. g., boom, swish. (See page 263.)

F. The stanza is the unit of metrical discourse somewhat as the paragraph is the unit of prose discourse; poets may, however, let their sentences run from one stanza into another, as Tennyson does in *In Memoriam*.

Verse is metrical discourse. A verse is one line of metrical discourse. A stanza is a group of verses, that is, of lines, constituting a typical, recurrent unit of a poem; the stanza is usually characterized by a combined metrical and rime pattern.

A stanza is described by stating the rime pattern and the meter of the verses comprising the stanza. It is an important means of variation and of originality in poetic form. Metrical discourse may or may not employ rime, assonance, alliteration, etc. When adopted, rime usually becomes a part of the pattern of the poem.

Some important forms of metrical discourse are:

1. Blank verse: iambic pentameter, unrimed; e. g., Milton's *Paradise Lost*, Shakespeare's plays

2. Heroic couplet: iambic pentameter in rimed couplets; e. g., Pope's "Rape of the Lock"; Goldsmith's "The Deserted Village"; Dryden's "Absalom and Achitophel"

3. Heroic quatrain: iambic pentameter, riming abab; e. g., Gray's "Elegy"

4. The sonnet (Petrarchan or Italian form); iambic pentameter, fourteen lines in octave and sestet, riming abba abba cdecde. The sestet may vary from this somewhat, e. g., cdcdcd, or cdcdee.

5. The sonnet (Shakespearean form) composed of three heroic quatrains followed by a rimed couplet: abab cdcd efef gg

6. The Spenserian stanza has nine lines riming ababbcbcc; the first eight lines are of iambic pentameter, but the last is an alexandrine, which is iambic hexameter. It is the stanza of Spenser's *Faerie Queene* and of Byron's *Childe Harold*.

   Note. Iambic pentameter is the most important meter in English. Iambic meter is best adapted to the English language; and pentameter, neither too long nor too short, is least monotonous, for since the caesura does not divide it into halves, moving the caesura creates a pleasing variety of effect. Dactylic hexameter is the heroic or epic verse of the Greek and Latin literatures (*Iliad, Aeneid*); but it is not well adapted to the English language. Longfellow's *Evangeline* is perhaps the best-known long poem in this form.

7. The rondeau—rimes aabba aabR aabbaR. (R means refrain)

8. The triolet—rimes A B a A a b A B. (The capital letters stand for lines repeated.) Usually the lines are short, but the line may vary in length and rhythm.

9. The limerick (five line jingle) is the only indigenous English verse form.

A cinquain is free verse of twenty-two syllables arranged in five lines. (See page 268.) It is modeled on the Japanese hokku and tanka and was devised by Adelaide Crapsey. Examples of cinquains:

TRIAD

Adelaide Crapsey

These be
Three silent things:
The falling snow . . . the hour
Before the dawn . . . the mouth of one
Just dead.

GIFTS

Sister M. Eleanore, C.S.C.

What gifts
A tree can bring:
A house for life, a house
For death, a refuge for all men,
God's cross.

The following illustrate the triolet:

SERENADE TRIOLET

George Macdonald

Why is the moon
  Awake when thou sleepest?
To the nightingale's tune
Why is the moon
Making a noon
  When night is the deepest?
Why is the moon
  Awake when thou sleepest?

SONG

Adelaide Crapsey

I make my shroud, but no one knows—
So shimmering fine it is and fair,
With stitches set in even rows,
I make my shroud, but no one knows.
In door-way where the lilac blows,
Humming a little wandering air,
I make my shroud and no one knows,
So shimmering fine it is and fair.

The following illustrate the rondeau, the quatrain, and free
verse:

IN FLANDERS FIELDS

John McCrae

In Flanders fields the poppies blow
Between the crosses, row on row,
  That mark our place, and in the sky,
  The larks, still bravely singing fly,
Scarce heard amid the guns below.

We are the dead; short days ago
We lived, felt dawn, saw sunset glow,
  Loved and were loved, and now we lie
  In Flanders fields.

Take up our quarrel with the foe!
To you from failing hands we throw
  The torch; be yours to hold it high!
  If ye break faith with us who die
We shall not sleep, though poppies grow
  In Flanders fields.

THE DANDELION

John Banister Tabb

With locks of gold today;
Tomorrow, silver gray;
Then blossom-bald. Behold,
O man, thy fortune told!

EVER UPON THIS STAGE

Walt Whitman

Ever upon this stage
Is acted God's calm annual drama.
Gorgeous processions, songs of birds,
Sunrise that fullest feeds and freshens most the soul,
The heaving sea, the waves upon the shore, the musical, strong waves,
The woods, the stalwart trees, the slender, tapering trees,
The lilliput countless armies of the grass,
The heat, the showers, the measureless pasturages,
The scenery of the snows, the winds' free orchestra,
The stretching light-hung roof of clouds, the clear cerulean and the
    silver fringes,
The high dilating stars, the placid beckoning stars,
The moving flocks and herds, the plains and emerald meadows,
The shows of all the varied lands and all the growths and products.

MOONLIGHT AND MAGGOTS

Carl Sandburg

(For the departed bongo Vachel Lindsay
the yet-with-us bongo A. McLeish and
bongoes yet to come)

The moonlight filters on the prairie.
The land takes back an old companion.
The young corn seems pleased with a visit.
In Illinois, in Iowa, this moonlight is on.
A bongo looks out and talks about the look of the moon
As if always a bongo must talk somewhat so in moontime—
The moon is a milk-white love promise,
A present for the young corn to remember,
A caress for silk brown tassels to come.

Spring moon to autumn moon measures one harvest.
All almanacs are merely so many moon numbers.
A house dizzy with decimal points and trick figures
And a belfry at the top of the world for sleep songs
And a home for lonesome goats to go to—
Like now, like always, the bongo takes up a moon theme—
There is no end to the ancient kit-kats inhabiting the moon:
Jack and the beanstalk and Jacob's ladder helped them up,
Cats and sheep, the albatross, the phoenix and the dodo-bird,
They are all living on the moon for the sake of the bongo—
Castles on the moon, mansions, shacks and shanties, ramshackle
Huts of tarpaper and tincans, grand real estate properties
Where magnificent rats eat tunnels in colossal cheeses.
Where the rainbow chasers take the seven prisms apart
And put them together again and are paid in moon money—
The flying dutchman, paul bunyan, saint paul, john bunyan,
The little jackass who coughs gold pieces when you say bricklebrit—
They are all there on the moon and the rent not paid
And the roof leaking and the taxes delinquent—
Like now, like always, the bongo jabbers of the moon,
Of cowsheds, railroad tracks, corn rows and cornfield corners
Finding the filter of the moon an old friend—
Look at it—cries the bongo—have a look! have a look!

    Well, what of it? comes the poohpooh—
Always the bongo is a little loony—comes the poohpooh.
The bongo is a poor fish and a long ways from home.
Be like me, be an egg, a hardboiled egg, a pachyderm
Practical as a buzzsaw and a hippopotamus put together,
Get the acts and no monkey business what I mean.
The moon is a dead cinder, a ball of death, a globe of doom.
Long ago it died of lost motion, maggots, masticated the surface of it
And the maggots languished, turned ice, froze on and took a free ride.
Now the sun shines on the maggots and the maggots make the moonlight.
The moon is a cadavar and a dusty mummy and a damned rotten investment.
The moon is a liability loaded up with frozen assets and worthless paper.
Only the lamb, the sucker, the come-on, the little lost boy, has time for
      the moon.

    Well—says the bongo—you got a good argument.
I am a little lost boy and a long ways from home.
I am a sap, a pathetic fish. a nitwit and a lot more and worse you couldn't
      think of.
Nevertheless and notwithstanding and letting all you say be granted and
      acknowledged
The moon is a silver silhouette and a singing stalactite.
The moon is a bringer of fool's gold and fine phantoms.
On the heaving restless sea or the fixed and fastened land
The moon is a friend for the lonesome to talk with.
The moon is at once easy and costly, cheap and priceless.

The price of the moon runs beyond all adding machine numbers.
Summer moon-music drops adagio sostenuto whathaveyou.
Winter moon-music practices the mind of man for a long trip.
The price of the moon is an orange and a few kind words.
Nobody on the moon says, I been thrown out of better places than this.
No one on the moon has ever died of arithmetic and hard words.
No one on the moon would skin a louse to sell the hide.
The moon is a pocket luckpiece for circus riders, for acrobats on
     the flying rings, for wild animal tamers.
I can look up at the moon and take it or leave it.
The moon coaxes me; be at home wherever you are.
I can let the moon laugh me to sleep for nothing.
I can put a piece of the moon in my pocket for tomorrow.
I can holler my name at the moon and the moon hollers back my name.
When I get confidential with the moon and tell secrets
The moon is a sphinx and a repository under oath.

     Yes Mister poohpooh
I am a poor nut, just another of God's mistakes.
You are a tough bimbo, hard as nails, yeah.
You know enough to come in when it rains.
You know the way to the postoffice and I have to ask,
They might fool you the first time but never the second.
Thrown into the river you always come up with a fish.
You are a diller a dollar, I am a ten o'clock scholar.
You know the portent of the axiom: Them as has gits.
You devised the abracadabra: Get all you can
               keep all you get.

  We shall always be interfering with each other,
  forever be arguing—
  you for the maggots, me for the moon.
Over our bones, cleaned by the final maggots as we lie
     recumbent, perfectly forgetful, beautifully ignorant—
There will settle over our grave illustrious tombs
On nights when the air is clear as a bell
And the dust and fog are shovelled off on the wind—
There will sink over our empty epitaphs
     a shiver of moonshafts
     a line of moonslants.

V. Expository writing

Expository writing includes all kinds of writing which seek to communicate ideas directly from the mind of the author to the mind of the reader with the primary aim to inform. Clear expository composition is needed in all walks of life. It is the indispensable tool both of teaching and of being taught. Textbooks, class explanations, lectures, recitations, examinations are expository. So also are such practical matters as describing a process, giving directions, a summary, a report, business letters, social letters. Other, more literary, forms of exposition include the essay which defines a term or elaborates a general proposition, literary criticism, dramatic and art criticism, the formal and the familiar essay.

The familiar essay aims rather to please than to inform the reader. It stands between story and exposition, and, like the lyric, it is a subjective communication of thought and feeling colored by the personality and mood of the author. A commonplace, even trivial, subject is made charming, amusing or piquant when discussed in a chatty, casual, informal manner by a person who is delightfully whimsical, fanciful, belligerent, or even pompous. For example, Lamb's mood ranges from "A Dissertation upon Roast Pig" to "Dream Children." Holmes represented himself as the autocrat of the breakfast table. Stevenson wrote "An Apology for Idlers." The style of the familiar essay is an essential element and should have a quality similar to that of a story, full of feeling, imagination, and vivid detail.

The literary critical essay, although expository, may deal with poetic material. It may, like Aristotle's *Poetics* or Dryden's *Essay of Dramatic Poesy*, expound critical principles with a few illustrations for clarity; or it may apply critical principles in evaluating a particular work, as in a book review or a critical study such as a dissertation or a research paper.

The serious expository essay is exemplified in Milton's "Of Education," Newman's "Knowledge Viewed in Relation to Learnnig," Arnold's "Sweetness and Light." Division by means of a topical outline is the basic tool for analyzing all forms of exposition, just as the relation of cause and effect is the basic tool for analyzing all forms of plotted narrative.

Methods of exposition include development by means of all the topics of logic and rhetoric (see page 123), but most useful are definition, division, comparison, analogy or similitude, cause and effect.

Of first importance in expository writing is the subject matter, which should interest as well as inform the reader. This it will do if the writer has kept the reader in mind, and has helped him to understand the abstract by means of the concrete, providing examples from which the reader can make the abstraction himself and so comprehend it thoroughly. The intellect is normally reached through the imagination and therefore even in workaday prose, figurative language is an effective means to promote both clarity and interest. The writer must make himself so clear that he cannot be misunderstood even by the poorer-than-average reader. He must hold interest by avoiding monotony.

Next in order and importance is the organization of the subject matter so as to secure unity, coherence, and emphasis, three principles which govern the composition of the sentence, the paragraph, and the whole work. A topical outline showing the relation of the parts to the whole is the means to this end. The main heads should divide the whole. The subheads should subdivide each larger head. Division of any whole results in at least two parts; one subhead is literally nonsensical. Careful attention should be given to arranging all the parts in the most effective sequence. The position of greatest emphasis is at the end; next greatest, at the beginning; least, in the middle.

Clarity is the first requisite of style in expository writing. (Grammatical correctness is a pre-requisite.) Next to be sought are appropriateness, force, and beauty. Appropriateness is the adaptation of style to the subject matter, and, above all, to the reader or hearer. Vivid, specific diction and imagery, effective combination of words, especially of nouns and verbs, arresting phrases, metaphors, allusions, and compression contribute to both force and beauty. So does variety.

Variety is a cardinal principle of effective style. There should be variety in diction through the use of synonyms, in sentence length, in grammatical structure, and in rhythm. Variety in grammatical structure and rhythm are secured through omitting or adding conjunctions, through differences in word order, in sentence beginnings, in the use of simple, compound, and complex sentences, of prepositional and participial phrases, of clauses, of loose and periodic structure, of parallel and antithetical structure. These structures may be clarified and emphasized by the effective repetition of words.

In the following passage from Washington Irving the repeated *he must* emphasizes parallel structure, while each verb following it is varied, as is also the length of the clauses. Conjunctions are omitted in one clause and an extra one is added in another. The paragraph is developed by division.

The stranger who would form a correct opinion of the English character . . . must go forth into the country; he must sojourn in villages and hamlets; he must visit castles, villas, farmhouses, cottages: he must wander through parks and gardens; along hedges and green lanes; he must loiter about country churches; attend wakes and fairs and other rural festivals; and cope with the people in all their conditions and all their habits and humors.

In a periodic sentence the meaning is held in suspense until the end, as in this sentence from Carlyle's *Sartor Resartus*:

Considering our present advanced state of culture, and how the Torch of Science has now been brandished and borne about, with more or less effect, for five-thousand years and upwards; how in these times especially, not only the Torch still burns, and perhaps more fiercely than ever, but innumerable Rush-lights, and Sulphur-matches, kindled thereat, are also glancing in every direction, so that not the smallest cranny or dog-hole in Nature or Art can remain unilluminated—it might strike the reflective mind with some surprise that hitherto little or nothing of a fundamental character, whether in the way of Philosophy or History, has been written on the subject of Clothes.

In the following passage from Stewart Edward White's "On Making Camp" the rhythm reflects the boy's unorganized and scattered efforts:

Dick was anxiously mixing batter for the cakes, attempting to stir a pot of rice often eough to prevent it from burning, and trying to rustle sufficient dry wood to keep the fire going. . . . At each instant he had to desert his flour sack to rescue the coffee pot, or to shift the kettle, or to dab hastily at the rice, or to stamp out the small brush, or to pile on more dry twigs.

VI. Assignments in composition

  A. Autobiography (simple narration)

    1. Divide your autobiography into six to eight chapters. Do not attempt to include all incidents. Do not give a thin, generalized account of a long period, but write fully on a few events chosen.

      Select incidents having human interest, for example, your first circus, a visit to a farm, to your grandmother, some trouble you got into or out of, learning to swim, a trip, rather than incidents that are much the same for everyone, such as your high school graduation. Give a title to each chapter and to the whole. Select any chapter you wish and write it in detail (400-700 words). You may use simple narration, diary form, or letters. Write in an informal, easy, natural style, as you would talk. Give lively, vivid details of persons, places, incidents. Use dialogue if it fits in. Make the characters and events "come alive." Avoid what is trite, obvious, and general.

      Write a brief synopsis (10-40 words) of each of the other chapters. Put into its proper place the chapter you wrote in detail. Mark with an asterisk one other chapter which you choose to develop in detail for the next assignment.

2. Write in detail (400-800 words) another chapter of your autobiography. Profit by the comments and corrections made on your previous paper.

B. Composition to intensify reading and make it more significant

1. Select some phase of Greek or Roman literature that you have read recently, one that enters into more than one work; for example, the character of Agamemnon, Achilles, Odysseus, Penelope, Clytemnestra, Helen; the conflict between public good and private good; the concept of the gods and its effect on the characters or on the story. State in one declarative sentence the substance of what you intend to say on this selected subject. Make a skeleton outline for a talk (3 to 5 minutes) to be given to the class.

After each topic of the outline, list exact references to passages in the works which prove your point. In giving your talk, you may use the outline and may read the passages from the book. The class will comment on good and bad points in the talks.

2. Keeping in mind the comments made on the talks, improve, if you can, the outline you made for the talk. Write a paper developing it in 300-500 words of your own; quote passages to prove your points, giving exact references in footnotes. Make footnote references to Homer and Vergil by title (underlined), book, line, thus: *Iliad*, Book I, lines 84-86; to the plays by title and line, thus: *Agamemnon*, lines 1097-1102.

3. Select some phase of a play or a story as the subject for a talk in class; for example, a character or a comparison of characters, motivation and suspense, elements of satire, comic incidents and devices, tragic quality, ethical quality, customs of the times revealed, political or literary implications, philosophy of the characters or of the author expressed in the theme, situations, and sententious utterances, style (effective diction, allusion, detail, figures of speech, including litotes). Consider also the questions on the work as a whole, page 260.

4. In your anthology of literature, read any ten poems that you have never read before. List them by author and title in the order of your preference. Write an outline for a talk on the poem you placed first. Consider both its matter and its form

(see pages 266-273) but do not make your talk too technical. Try to convey to your classmates just why the poem is
significant, inspiring, beautiful.

C. Writing a short story

1. Read three stories and make a list of missing scenes in each,
that is, of incidents that are merely implied or only briefly
told about, not presented in detail and therefore not expe-
rienced by the reader.

Examples of missing scenes from Maupassant's "The
Piece of String":

(1) The quarrel between Hauchecorne and Malandain.
(2) Malandain goes to the authorities and declares that he
saw Hauchecorne pick up the lost pocketbook.
(3) The farm hand takes the pocketbook to his master
and next day brings it to the authorities in the town.
(4) Malandain comes upon the scene just after Hauchecorne has told his story to a crowd.
(5) Hauchecorne's death.

2. Write a missing scene (350-600 words) from any one of the
stories read, using detail (see page 256) so as to cause your
reader to experience the incident imaginatively. You may
begin and end with words from the story (in quotation marks)
to show just where your scene fits in. It must be plausible.
Try to make it conform as nearly as possible to the character,
tone, and setting which the author of the story has created.

3. Present in detail your plan for an original short story of
1000-3000 words. To be original a plot need not be fantastic.
Ordinary events are usually best. The source of your plot
may be your own experience or that of someone you know
well, an anecdote you have read or heard, a news item, or
pure invention. The best material is usually that drawn from
experience but modified by free invention. A plot must have
conflict—a problem, obstacles to be overcome. A plot is not
original if it is taken from a movie, radio drama, stage play,
novel, another short story, or another student. If a news item
provided the nucleus for your plot, clip it to your paper.

State: (1) source of your plot; (2) title; (3) theme; (4)
main character, problem, and solution; (5) the beginning of
the action, the turning point, and the denouement; (6) in
columns headed prospective and retrospective action, list in

detail the incidents of the plot, numbering them to show sequence (the space in the other column opposite each item should be blank); mark with an asterisk the scenes you plan to make dramatic (that is, to present through dialogue or reverie. See page 254.) If you do not plan to use any retrospective action, you will not need two columns. Usually, however, one can construct a plot in a more effective sequence by the judicious use of retrospective action.

4. Using detail, write a scene (350-600 words) from your story, any scene; it need not be the first. Regard it primarily as a character sketch presented through dialogue, action, or reverie. Do not use monologue. Give the scene a title.

Pay very careful attention to the following points in stories you read, and especially in writing your scenes and your story:

(1) Use commas to set off a word used in direct address.

(2) Use quotation marks correctly. Be especially careful in the divided quotation.

(3) In writing dialogue, test whether you have two sentences or one by omitting *he said* or a similar expression; if without it you would have two sentences, you have the same number with it. Place a semicolon or a period between the sentences.

(4) In writing dialogue, begin a new paragraph for every change of speaker. Do not end a paragraph with a comma or colon following *said* or other matter introductory to a speech. Such matter belongs in the same paragraph with the speech.

(5) *He said* can be varied by the use of more specific words. Often such explanatory phrases can be omitted, for the identity of the speaker can be made clear by the context or by detail of action.

(6) Do not omit the question mark where it belongs.

(7) The past tense is the one most suited to narration. Do not shift to the present tense without necessity.

5. Write another scene (350-600 words) from your story, profiting by comments and corrections on your previous paper.

6. Write your story (1000-3000 words). State the number of words at the end. Use detail. Let the characters tell the story.

Pay careful attention to the seven points listed in **assignment** *3*, above. Clip to your paper your approved plan with all the marks, corrections, and suggestions on it (not a clean copy of it); otherwise your story will not be accepted. You need not adhere strictly to the approved plan, but may make minor changes that will improve it. Major changes require a new approval before the story is submitted.

D. Verse-writing and description

1. Write a series of little pictures, brief poetic expressions of observations or experiences or moods genuinely your own. Do not attempt rime. Use simple concrete language that exactly expresses what you see or feel or think; strive for insight, imagination, freshness, genuineness.

2. Write at least eight lines of original verse or 250 words of good descriptive prose (see assignment *6* below). Verse is preferred but not required. Try cinquains or other free verse; or metrical forms: couplets, quatrains, or a triolet. State whether you concentrated most on the matter or the form.

3. Write at least twelve lines of original verse or 400 words of good prose description. Try quatrains or a rondeau.

4. Write at least fourteen lines of original verse or 500 words of good prose description. Try a sonnet or a rondeau.

5. Write at least fifteen lines of verse, metrical or free, or 500 words of good prose description.

Rime Aid

a	n
b, bl, br	o
c, ch, chr, cl, cr	p, ph, phr, pl, pr
d, dr, dw	q
e	r
f, fl, fr	s, sc, sh, sl, sp, spr, st, str, sw
g, gl, gr, gw	t, th, thr, tr, tw
h	u
i	v
j	w, wh, wr
k, kl, kr, kw	x
l	y
m	z

If you have not at hand something like *Webster's Collegiate Dictionary* with its vocabulary of rimes, the above should prove useful. Example:

To find words that rime with *plane*, prefix each of the

above to the sound *ane;* ignore the combinations that mean nothing in English; those remaining are the words riming with *plane*:

bane, blain, brain, Cain, cane, chain, crane, Dane, deign, drain, fain, fane, feign, gain, grain, Jane, lane, lain, sane, main, mane, pane, pain, plain, rain, reign, rein, sane, seine, Seine, skein, slain, Spain, sprain, stain, strain, swain, thane, train, twain, vain, vane, vein, wane, Zane. Besides these there are words of two or more syllables accented on the last, such as: inane, disdain, ordain, refrain, entertain, etc.

6. Write a description (300-500 words) on any subject you choose, effectively employing sense detail and figures of speech (see pages 257 and 262.)

7. Choose one subject for five descriptions: (1) for identification; (2) appearance, objective, from a changing point of view; (3) from a static point of view; (4) appearance, subjective, from an unfriendly point of view; (5) from a friendly point of view. (Suggested subjects: a house, farm, summer resort, lake, dog, sled, horse, person.)

E. The familiar essay

1. Be prepared to give a three-minute talk on one of the essays assigned for reading. Discuss it in the light of one or more points explained on page 277. As you read the essays assigned, make marginal notes of likenesses and contrasts between them in ideas and style, and incorporate these in your talks. In other words, always get out your mental hooks and eyes when you read. Also note figures of speech, allusions, sententious remarks, good definitions, fine distinctions, unfamiliar meanings of words.

2. Write a familiar essay (350-700 words) on any subject you choose. It may be an essay in definition, if you wish. See page 102. Strive especially for a vivid, condensed style. The following passages from a student's essay exemplify this:

Why, I could buy some cologne or perfume, couldn't I? The vision of the smiling saleslady with her hollow laugh and flowing, persuasive voice enters my mind just before I picture the well-stocked tray of perfume bottles which decorates my friend's dressing table. . . .

Days slip past and suddenly the little red circle on my calendar becomes yesterday. I receive a phone call from my friend who wants to thank me for the lovely present and to assure me that there is nothing she would rather have received than a box of chocolates and a dainty handkerchief.

—Jeanne Beck, "On Buying a Birthday Present"

F. Writing the preliminary research paper. Its purpose is to learn: (1) how to use a library in locating material, and to get acquainted with important library tools; (2) how to employ effective methods of selecting material wisely, of reading purposefully, and of taking notes systematically; (3) how to limit a subject, choose a thesis, organize material, and outline it; (4) how to assimilate this foreign material, and so dominate it by reorganizing it and so transform it by your own style as to make your research paper truly original; (5) how to document the paper with quotations having clear references in footnotes and a bibliography correct in form; (6) to gain such facility in the handling of this tool (approved methods of investigation and report) as to be able to use it effectually during college in term papers for all courses and in investigations in later life.

In a research paper correct form is strictly essential, just as formal dress is essential at a ball and certain other social gatherings. Therefore spare no pains to make habitual the use of correct forms in bibliography and footnotes. The forms may vary somewhat among different publishing houses. What is important is to be consistent throughout. You will use the standard forms prescribed here.

The preliminary paper is a short introduction to this type of writing, with special emphasis on technique in order to prepare for a longer piece of work.

Choose for your subject one of the essayists studied this semester.

1. If your chosen author is a British writer, read and take notes on the article about him in the *Encyclopedia Britannica* and in either the *Dictionary of National Biography, British Authors of the Nineteenth Century, Authors Today and Yesterday, Living Authors,* or *Twentieth Century Authors.* If he is an American writer, read and take notes on the article about him in the *Encyclopedia Americana* (not in the *Britannica,* although he is probably treated there) and in either the *Dictionary of American Biography, American Authors* 1600-1900, *Contemporary American Authors,* or one of the last three works listed in the preceding sentence. There will be repetition of matter; therefore whichever article is read second can be read more rapidly. Notice the character of each reference work.

Find the full name of the author of the article, usually signed by initials which are explained at the beginning of the volume. Remember that your chosen author is the subject, not the author, of the article about him. Therefore, in your bibliographical note, his name, changed to the normal order with the surname last, should be enclosed in quotation marks because it is the title of the article. See examples below. If you cannot discover who wrote the article, begin your bibliographical note with the title.

Also locate at least three magazine articles about your subject in the *Reader's Guide to Periodical Literature*, checking to see that your references are to periodicals available in the library. If you have time, read one article and take notes on it.

Submit your notes on this work as follows. Take notes lengthwise on slips 3×5 inches, one note to a slip. On the top slip write your name, section, date, and chosen author. On the next slips make a bibliographical note of each work consulted, strictly according to the following forms, using a separate slip for each note. For standard reference works alphabetically arranged you may either state the volume and page numbers or omit them.

James, E. I. "Gilbert Keith Chesterton," *Encyclopedia Britannica*, 14th ed.

"James Russell Lowell," *Encyclopedia Americana*, 1944.

Dobson, Austin. "Sir Richard Steele," *Dictionary of National Biography*, XVIII, 1017-24, 1921-22.

Robinson, Herbert Spencer. "Richard Le Gallienne," *Authors Today and Yesterday*, 1933.

Oehser, Paul H. "Pioneers in Conservation," *Nature Magazine*, XXXVIII (April, 1945), 188-90.

In the upper right hand corner of each bibliographical slip, write an abbreviated symbol to be used on each note slip taken from that work; e. g., Brit, Amer, DNB, DAB.

Do not take too many notes, especially from general reference works. The articles in periodicals are likely to be more specific and more useful.

Write in the upper left corner of each slip a topical heading, e. g., home influence, independence, love of nature, humorous description, criticism of works, which will indicate in a quick glance the content of the note. In the upper right corner, write the abbreviated symbol and page reference to show precisely the source of the material; notes without this reference are worthless. If a note will not fit on one slip, it is better to continue it on the back than on another slip.

Do not number your notes. They should be analytic and selective, and each should be comprehensible no matter how it gets mixed up later with others.Notes are written on separate slips so that later they can easily be reorganized, combined with matter from other sources, or discarded, according to the outline you will eventually make.

Take three kinds of notes on this and on later assignments (not necessarily each kind every time):

(1) Quote exactly. Use three dots to indicate parts omitted (four dots, if one is a period belonging in the quoted matter). Use brackets to enclose explanatory words you insert. State page number where quotation begins; if the quotation runs on to another page, draw a slant line before the first word on the new page, for later you may wish to quote only the last part. Example:

Humorous description   Lit. Es.

"This poor old brute .   . could never make up his mind which of his four paces . . . would be most agreeable to me. . . . He treated me to a hodge-podge of all his several gaits at once. Saint Vitus was the only patron saint I could think of."   —"In Italy," I, 138

The full bibliographical note for the work from which this quotation was selected is:

Lowell, James Russell. *Literary Essays.* Vol. I. New York: Houghton Mifflin & Co., 1892.

(2) Summarize the passage in your own words, usually condensing it very much and carefully avoiding the phrasing of the book; this will insure you against unconscious garbling when you come to write your paper. Give page reference.

(3) Write down your own ideas that come to you while reading: your thoughts stimulated by the reading, your comments and opinions, comparisons, ideas about organization. These are the most valuable notes to make. Capture these ideas while you read; otherwise they will elude

you. If they are brief comments on your reading, you will find it convenient to write them on the backs of the slips containing the matter you are commenting on; or below it, if you clearly distinguish the two.

Submit your notes so as to receive helpful criticism and guidance both as to method and content.

2. Read and take notes on your chosen author treated in either the *Cambridge History of English Literature*, the *Concise Cambridge History of English Literature* (only if he is not treated in the larger work), or the *Cambridge History of American Literature*. Also locate at least three articles about him in the *International Index to Periodicals*, checking to see that your references are to periodicals available in the library; read and take notes on at least one of them, following directions given in the preceding assignment.

Since the Cambridge histories are not arranged alphabetically, it is desirable to specify the volume and page number. Use the following forms:

> Walker, Hugh. "John Ruskin," *Cambridge History of English Literature*, XIV, 163-172.
>
> Baker, Harry T. "Hazlitt as a Shakespearean Critic," *Publications of the Modern Language Association of America*, XLVII (1932), 191-99.

(*PMLA* is also permissible for the preceding periodical both in the bibliography and footnotes, especially since it is the display title. A few other journals may be similarly abbreviated, if desired.)

3. Read and take notes on essays by your chosen author. The card catalogue in the library will direct you to books by him and to some collections in which his essays appear. Consult also the *Essay and General Literature Index*, 1900-1933, and its supplements; this includes references to essays in periodicals. For bibliographical notes use the following forms. If the date of publication is not given, write n. d. in its place.

> Repplier, Agnes. *Eight Decades*. Boston: Houghton Mifflin Co., 1937.
>
> Hazlitt, William. "On the Disadvantages of Intellectual Superiority," in *The College Book of Essays*, compiled by John Abbott Clark. New York: Henry Holt and Co., 1939, pp. 673-84.
>
> Lamb, Charles. "Dream Children" and "The Superannuated

Man," in *Western World Literature*, ed. H. W. Robbins and W. H. Coleman. New York: The Macmillan Co., 1938, pp. 999-1004.

Adams, James Truslow. "The Mucker Pose," *Harper's Magazine*, CLVII (November, 1928), 661-71.

Other library tools with which you ought to get acquainted are: *Index to Plays, Index to One Act Plays,* and *Index to Short Stories* compiled by Ina Firkins; *Catholic Periodical Index, New York Times Index, Poole's Index;* the *United States Catalogue* and its supplement, the *Cumulative Book Index;* the *Catholic Encyclopedia* and other special encyclopedias; *Cambridge Bibliography of English Literature;* the *Year's Work in English Studies.*

4. Continue reading and taking notes on essays by your chosen author, not about him. You must deal principally with his works. Read with an active mind alert to discover what you can make out of this material, what insight, what relation of ideas you can express in your preliminary paper.

5. Choose a narrow phase of your subject and formulate a title for your proposed paper, which must be expository, not narrative. Your paper must be a composition, not a compiling or a stringing together of quotations or a mere retelling of what you have read, whether narrative or expository. It must be an original creation in the sense that it intelligently reconstructs materials gathered from a variety of sources. The design must be yours: the selection of a phase of the subject, the organization of ideas, the choice of illustration or quotation to support your points. Put life, enthusiasm, and your own personality into it.

Your thesis is a single declarative sentence expressing the substance of your paper. Examples: Ruskin's writings are characterized by an intensely human quality. The essays of Hilaire Belloc reflect his positive views on Catholicism and politics. Thoreau is a capable interpreter of nature.

Your thesis should express a unification of a variety of materials new to you; it should represent a significant insight into the worthwhile reading which you have newly become acquainted with. Your ideas need not be new to your teacher or to others who have previously acquainted themselves with the same reading.

Submit the title, thesis, and skeleton outline for your preliminary paper (300-450 words). Title, thesis, and outline should correspond, for each in its way expresses in substance the whole composition. In your outline apply the principles of logical division: the main heads must equal the whole composition; the subheads must equal the larger heads which they divide; you cannot divide by less than two subheads. Divisions should not overlap. See pages 96 and 279. Give careful thought to effective sequence.

6. Write your preliminary research paper (300-450 words, exclusive of quotations). State the number of your own words. Clip to it your approved outline, not a clean copy of it; otherwise it will not be accepted. You may improve the outline in minor points, but major changes require a new approval before you submit your paper.

Your paper must be self-contained, that is, intelligible to a reader unacquainted with the subject. It must be clear and have within itself adequate support for every point made. Mere statement is not proof; rather, a statement requires proof or illustration. The necessary support for a statement is secured by well-selected quotation or by a specific instance told in your own words; for both, give footnote page reference to source. A paper should also be self-contained in not referring, for example, by a pronoun to its title or thesis; these are not within the paper but precede it and are external to what should be its self-contained completeness and intelligibility.

You must quote from more than one source, but more from works by your author than from those about him. Avoid quoting the illustrations from an author's work which are quoted in a work about him; use different illustrations of your own choosing selected by you directly from the author's own works. Do not introduce into your paper comments about works which you have not read; deal only with materials you yourself have read. You may, however, introduce comments about works you have read; these comments may disagree among themselves and you yourself may disagree with them.

Directions for footnotes:

a. Place a superior (raised) reference number at the close of a quotation or a specific citation in your paper that requires footnote reference to source. At the foot of the same page, place corresponding superior number for footnote. Write footnotes on the same line horizontally if they are short; otherwise write them one below the other. Double space between footnotes. Indent each.

b. Number your references in one consecutive series from the beginning to the end of your paper; do not begin a new series on each page.

c. Footnote references serve two purposes: to acknowledge your indebtedness; to authenticate your statements.

d. Footnotes may also be used to add information or comment which does not fit in so well in the body of the paper. Notice these in some of the works you read.

e. In footnotes, the author's given name is placed first, then his surname, followed by a comma, and then the title of the work.

f. For the first citation the reference is given in full. For later citations it is somewhat abbreviated. Examples:
First citation:

Caroline F. E. Spurgeon, *Shakespeare's Imagery and What It Tells Us* (Cambridge: Cambridge University Press, 1935), p. 263.

Later citation:

Spurgeon, *Shakespeare's Imagery*, p. 187.

g. When a bibliography is placed at the end of a book or a paper, it is not necessary to give in the footnotes the imprint of books (place, publisher, date), although sometimes such complete data are given in both places.

h. Use the following abbreviations in footnotes:

1) *Ibid.*, meaning the same work as that referred to in the immediately preceding footnote. It may refer to the whole or to a part of what preceded.

2) For reference to the same work as that of a previous, but not the immediately preceding, footnote, use *op. cit.*, meaning the work cited, usually preceded by the author's name. This abbreviation cannot be used after a second work by the same author has been introduced into the footnotes. In that case, you must repeat the title for each reference. The title may be repeated also if the reference has been so far back as to inconvenience the reader. This will hardly occur in a short paper.

3) *Loc. cit.* means the same page in the same work as was previously cited.

4) If more than one page or inclusive pages are cited, use pp., which means pages. For the following page or pages add f. or ff. to the number. Examples: pp. 27, 32; pp. 16-30; pp. 48 f.; pp. 56 ff.

5) When one cites ideas or passages running here and there through a work, *passim* is used instead of the page number. You will seldom have occasion to use it.

The following series of footnotes illustrates forms to be used not only in your preliminary paper, but also in your later paper, which will not be limited to essayists. Notice that when both volume and page are given the numbers stand alone; when only one is given they are preceded by Vol. or p.

[1]John Ruskin, "The Golden Gate," in his *Mornings in Florence,* p. 36.

[2]*Ibid.,* p. 20.

[3]Ruskin, *Modern Painters,* quoted by Hugh Walker, *Cambridge History of English Literature,* XIV, 163.

[4]Ruskin, "Traffic," in *Western World Literature,* ed. H. W. Robbins and W. H. Coleman, p. 1134.

[5]*Loc. cit.*

[6]Thomas Fowler, "Sir Francis Bacon," *Dictionary of National Biography,* I, 823.

[7]Edward T. Cook, "John Ruskin," *ibid.,* XXII, 1182.

[8]Samuel Johnson, "Observations on the State of Affairs in 1756," *Works* (London, 1825) VI, 113-15.

[9]Cook, *op. cit.,* p. 1191.

[10]R. E. Spiller, "Literary Revaluations," *Saturday Review of Literature,* X (January 13, 1934), 406.

[11]Fowler, *loc. cit.*

[12]Ruskin, "The Golden Gate," *op. cit.,* p. 35.

[13]E. De Selincourt (ed.), *Spenser's Poetical Works,* p. xxix.

[14]Plutarch, "Antonius" in his *Lives, Englished by Sir Thomas North,* IX, 96.

[15]Shakespeare, *Macbeth,* II, iii, 96-101.

The last shows the form more widely used for references to plays by act, scene, and line. Another acceptable form is: *Macbeth,* 2.3.96-101. If the reference is put in the body of the paper immediately beside or below the excerpt, it may be abbreviated thus: (*Mac.,* 2.3.96)

Directions for bibliography:

At the end of your paper, beginning on a new sheet, present your formal bibliography in one alphabetical list. Alphabetize by author's or editor's or compiler's surname placed first. If this name is not given, alphabetize by the first word of the title that is not grammatically an article. Where there are two or more entries for the same author or editor alphabetize by title, and do not repeat the author's name; instead, precede all but the first title with a blank line five spaces long in typing. Do not enter the same work twice. The entries should be in form like those illustrated above (pages 287, 289); sometimes it is stipulated that the total number of pages in the book, including introductory pages, be added at the end, thus: Pp.xiv+326.

In the bibliography (but not in the footnotes), underlining of the titles of books, but not of magazines, is optional; in manuscript it is desirable. The titles of parts of works must always be enclosed in quotation marks.

Include in your bibliography all the works you used in your investigation, not merely those you quoted in your paper.

On the front page of your paper write your title, thesis, name, date, and the number of words in your paper.

Special advice and warnings concerning the writing of a research paper:

(1) Don't garble material from your reading. You cannot make a passage your own by substituting a few synonyms for the words of another, omitting phrases or in other ways doctoring the passage so as to avoid putting it into quotation marks. Such a garbled passage is neither the author's nor yours; it is utterly dishonest. Any doctoring of a passage done with the passage before you is likely to be garbling of it.

To avoid such garbling, read the material, in not too small portions, put it aside, and express the gist of it in your own words without looking at the material. Or else quote it, choosing parts if you wish and indicating omissions by marks of ellipsis (three dots; see examples, page 288.)

To use without quotation marks and without giving

due credit matter taken from the work of another is plagiarism (a criminal offense).

(2) Weave quotations in so that they make sense in your context; adapt your structure to the quoted material or omit some part that does not harmonize. Use brackets to enclose explanatory words that you insert; marks of parenthesis indicate the author's own interruption of himself.

(3) Quote verse in lines, dropping to the next line in your manuscript for, and after, the quoted verse.

(4) In typed manuscripts, quoted passages of verse or prose occupying a number of lines may be typed single space to set them off from the rest of the material which should be double-spaced; quotation marks should then be omitted.

(5) Double quotation marks in your sources become single quotation marks within a quotation. If the material you quote runs through more than one paragraph or stanza, use double quotation marks at the beginning of each but at the close of only the last.

(6) In the body of your paper as well as in the footnotes and bibliography, consistently underline titles of wholes (books and magazines) and enclose in quotation marks titles of parts (poems, essays, encyclopedia articles, magazine articles).

(7) Distinguish, for example, *Hamlet* and Hamlet. *Hamlet* names a play; Hamlet names a character.

(8) If your paper deals with both fact and fiction, handle each appropriately; do not confuse them.

(9) Make sure that your research paper is expository, not narrative.

(10) Don't write thinly on a broad subject; treat adequately a limited subject.

(11) Don't write about an author; write about his work. Know his work first hand. Quote from his work.

(12) Prove your thesis, not some other.

(13) Make sure that your paper fits your thesis, that it is no broader, no narrower.

(14) Avoid sweeping statements. Be content to tell what you really know.

(15) Avoid jargon, verbosity, vagueness, trite expressions.

G. The research paper (1000-1750 words, exclusive of quotation)

The primary purpose of the preliminary research paper was to give you exercise in the use of important library tools and in the technique of writing a clear, straightforward, well-organized paper proving certain points, giving references in footnotes, and concluding with a bibliography. Special emphasis was placed on correctness of form.

In a more mature paper general reference works, such as encyclopedias, are not likely to be quoted. More specific works are to be preferred.

Writing a research paper involves in a notable degree the exercise of the liberal arts and is therefore an effective means of getting a true liberal education. The end of a liberal education, says Newman, is enlargement of mind, which "consists not merely in the passive reception into the mind of a number of ideas hitherto unknown to it, but in the mind's energetic and simultaneous action upon and towards and among these new ideas. . . . It is the action of a formative power, reducing to order and meaning the matter of our acquirements; it is a making the objects of our knowledge subjectively our own, or, to use a familiar word, it is a digestion of what we receive into the substance of our previous state of thought."

The virtue of the undergraduate research paper is the benefit, "the enlargement of mind," which the student gets from the experience: from the reading, thinking, organizing, writing, authenticating. To this the graduate research paper should add the virtue of contributing something to the sum of human knowledge.

In writing the present paper, you may, if you wish, keep the same subject you had for your preliminary paper and incorporate that paper, or a part of it, in this one. You will, however, probably prefer a new subject. Choose one that you will really enjoy working on, one that will be valuable and interesting to you.

Some of the following suggested subjects are suitable only for A students; some can be developed satisfactorily by B and C students. It is true that the subjects would challenge capable mature writers; but it is also true that students gain benefit from grappling with the best. College freshmen have done respectable work with these subjects. You are not limited to the subjects listed. The subject you choose must, however, be approved not only in itself but, in the judgment of the instructor, as suitable for you in the amount of time available for this work.

Particularly valuable are comparisons of a literary work, such as a play by Shakespeare, with its source, for here you see the mind and hand of a great artist at work. You see what he selects from the source, what he omits, what he amplifies, what changes he makes, how he unifies material, creates dramatic conflict and suspense, builds character, develops thought, and achieves a significant result. This study can be made only of those works whose sources are available to you in the library.

It is also interesting to see how the same subject, such as the story of Phaedra, is developed by artists of different ages and cultures, Euripides, Seneca, and Racine; or how Sophocles' *Oedipus the King* illustrates the principles set forth in Aristotle's *Poetics*.

SUGGESTED SUBJECTS

1. A Comparison of Shakespeare's *Hamlet* with Its Source
2. The same for other plays: *Antony and Cleopatra, Coriolanus, Timon of Athens, The Two Noble Kinsmen, Macbeth, King Lear, As You Like It, Twelfth Night, The Comedy of Errors, The Taming of the Shrew, Richard II, Richard III*
3. A Comparison of Beatrice and Rosalind (or Launcelot Gobbo, Touchstone, and Feste; or Desdemona, Hermione, and Imogen; or Orlando and Romeo; or Coriolanus and Timon; or Iago, Edmund, and Iachimo)
4. The Character of Henry V (or Hamlet or Macbeth or Portia)
5. Falstaff as a Comic Character
6. A Comparison of Shakespeare's *Merchant of Venice* with Marlowe's *Jew of Malta*
7. A Comparison of Shakespeare's *Antony and Cleopatra* with Dryden's *All for Love*
8. Oberon in Greene's *James IV*, Shakespeare's *A Midsummer Night's Dream*, Drayton's "Nymphidia," and Jonson's masque *Oberon*
9. Marlowe's *Tamburlaine* as an Expression of the Renaissance Spirit
10. A Comparison of Jonson's *Catiline* and Cicero's Orations against Catiline
11. A Comparison of Dekker's *The Shoemaker's Holiday* and Deloney's *The Gentle Craft*
12. A Comparison of Marlowe's *Doctor Faustus* and Goethe's *Faust*
13. A Comparison of Goethe's *Faust* and the Opera *Faust*
14. Goethe's *Faust* as a Work of Art
15. A Comparison of Terence's *Andrian* and Thornton Wilder's *A Woman of Andros*

16. A Comparison of Eugene O'Neill's *Mourning Becomes Electra* with Its Greek Prototype
17. A Comparison of Maxwell Anderson's Elizabeth with the Historical Elizabeth (or his Mary Stuart with the Historical Mary Stuart)
18. Phaedra: Euripides, Seneca, Racine
19. T. S. Eliot's *Murder in the Cathedral* Compared with the Historical Facts
20. Oedipus the King: Sophocles and Seneca
21. Sophocles' *Oedipus the King* in the Light of Aristotle's *Poetics*
22. The Character of Iphigenia in Euripides' *Iphigenia at Aulis* and *Iphigenia in Tauris*
23. The Character of Achilles (or Agamemnon) in Homer and in Greek Drama
24. The Character of Penelope in the *Odyssey*
25. The Character of Socrates in Plato's Dialogues
26. A Comparison of Hawthorne's *Wonder Book* and *Tanglewood Tales* with Their Sources in Ovid's *Metamorphoses*
27. A Comparison of Spenser's "Muiopotmus," Drayton's "Nymphidia," and Joseph Rodman Drake's "The Culprit Fay"
28. A Comparison of Medieval Epic and Romance: the *Song of Roland* and *Aucassin and Nicolette*
29. A Comparison of Milton's *Comus* with Its Sources
30. Gamaliel Bradford, the Modern Plutarch
31. The Ideal Commonwealth: Plato's *Republic* and More's *Utopia*
32. Chesterton's *Ballad of the White Horse* Compared with Its Historical Sources (or "The Battle of Lepanto" Compared with the Historical Facts)
33. Chesterton's Ability to Recreate Vividly Selected Historical Episodes ("The Donkey", "The Ballad of the White Horse," "The Battle of Lepanto")
34. Walt Whitman's Poetry in the Light of His Theories
35. The Poetry of Emily Dickinson (or Alice Meynell, or Louise Imogen Guiney, or Edna Millay, or Robert Frost, or Carl Sandburg, or Francis Thompson, or John Masefield, or Browning, or Keats, or Poe)

1. Begin reading and taking notes on your chosen subject. Read the older work or factual matter or theory first, before you read the literary work that grew out of it. Follow the same directions about note-taking, thinking, and organizing as were given for your preliminary research paper. Take notes lengthwise on slips 3 × 5 inches, one note to a slip. In order not to slow down your reading too much, note under topics merely the page numbers, marking with an asterisk those references that seem especially valuable. Select the best of these for notes before returning the book to the library. Share the books generously with others who must use the same ones you need.
2. After you have read all the necessary primary material, do some reading of critical works related to it. Use some material from periodicals.
3. Submit title, thesis, skeleton outline.

4. Write your paper (1000-1750 words, exclusive of quotation). Make this the best piece of work you ever did. Let it be the culmination of your study up to the present and show your growth in thought, in capacity to read and appreciate, to organize and relate, to be exact in form and effective in style. Follow carefully all directions on pages 291-295.

H. Brief for debate, an exercise in argumentation:

Argumentation differs from exposition in assuming that the person or persons addressed are more or less opposed to one's views and therefore need to be persuaded of what the writer or speaker believes to be the truth.

Select passages from one of the following works read in part this semester: Machiavelli's *The Prince*, Rousseau's *Discourse on the Origin of Inequality among Men*, Marx's *The Communist Manifesto*, Schopenhauer's "On the Sufferings of the World," and Nietzsche's *Thus Spake Zarathustra*. Outline the author's argument in the form prescribed for a brief, presenting a resolution or a thesis divided into three or four main issues, each with subdivisions. Consult, if you wish, books in the library, such as the *Catholic Encyclopedia* and other more specific works. Using above all your own best power to think, to reason correctly, to detect fallacies, write a brief in direct opposition, point for point, to the selected arguments of the author you chose to debate against. Indicate after your points, or at the end of your brief, or both, what works you consulted.

QUESTIONS AND EXERCISES

1. Who originated the art of rhetoric? Where? Why? When?
2. Who introduced rhetoric into Greece? When? What was his attitude toward truth? Name his most illustrious pupil.
3. Which of the arts of langauge did Aristotle first formulate as an art?
4. Briefly describe each of Aristotle's three divisions of logic according to the subject matter, and name the work in which he treated each.
5. State Aristotle's definition of rhetoric. Explain how rhetoric is related to dialectic or logic. How is it related to poetic?
6. Explain what is meant by the persuasion of *logos; pathos; ethos.*
7. What did Aristotle mean by poetic? Did he consider verse essential to poetic? Did he consider action or story essential?
8. Name the six formative elements or qualitative parts of drama distinguished by Aristotle. What did he regard as the specific function of tragedy? What, accordingly, must be the character of a tragic hero?

9. Explain the unique position which poetic occupies between history and philosophy.
10. In what sense are the short story and the novel poetic?
11. Why is plot the first and the essential element in poetic? What is a plot? What is the basic tool for analyzing all forms of plotted narrative? Why? What did Aristotle mean by the beginning, the middle, and the end of a plot? What terms shall we use for these points?
12. Analyze each play and short story you read in terms of character, problem, solution; theme; beginning of the action, turning point, denouement. See pages 250 and 254 ff.
13. What is plausibility? Is it essential to a story? Mention seven means to achieve plausibility.
14. What is retrospective action in a story? Discuss its value. Illustrate from stories you have just been reading. Can reminiscence present retrospective action? Can there be in a story reminiscence that is not retrospective action?
15. What problems should be considered in determining which angle of narration to adopt?
16. From stories and plays you have recently read give examples of forecast; motivation.
17. Mention four techniques which may be employed in telling a story. Which is the poorest?
18. From stories or plays read this semester give an example of a type character, an individual character, a lay figure.
19. What is direct characterization? indirect? Which is better?
20. What is meant by thought as an element in drama or story? What is the theme?
21. In stories you read mark the sententious utterances or general propositions. Reflect and decide whether you agree or disagree with them.
22. What is the most important feature of style needed in writing a good story?
23. Mention five attitudes of an author toward his work which may create a certain tone or mood.
24. What is meant by music in drama? by spectacle? How should setting be handled in short stories?
25. Try to make your own the searching questions for evaluating the story as a whole and apply them in your reading. (See pages 260 f.)
26. What was the conception of figurative language held by Cicero and Quintilian? How many figures of speech were distinguished by them? by the Renaissance rhetoricians?
27. What is a trope? Name eight tropes; three based on similarity; three on the relation of subject and adjuncts; one on cause and effect; one on division; one on contraries.
28. Mention four faults to be avoided in using figures of speech.
29. Classify the following expressions as either matter-of-fact or figurative (naming the figure): silver moon; velvet jacket; sunset maple; kettle sings; soup boils; dagger pierced; velvet lawn; lady sings; velvety moss; moon-faced boy; kettle boils; satin dress; pearly teeth; silver spoon; bloody sword; ape-like grin; sunset glows; oily words; beady eyes; bloody sky; cold pierced; icy stare; baby whimpers; timid star; feathery cake; umbrella elm; fan-like vase; wind whimpers; steely glance; storm snarled.

30. Classify the figures of speech in the following. Some exemplify more than one.
  (1) I heard the slush, slush, slush of his waterfilled rubbers as he strode beside me.
  (2) It is exhilarating to discoved that one's partner at bridge is just learning the game.
  (3) He sacrificed his inheritance for a pair of laughing eyes.
  (4) Will the pulpit or the screen mold the youth of our land?
  (5) The diamond dew sparkled in the morning sun.
  (6) Three little heads bobbed past the window.
  (7) Her hand was like a dry leaf.
  (8) The sun dropped into the giant jaws of the hills.
  (9) Social position became his Barabbas.
  (10) Her almond-shaped face appeared in the window.
  (11) Moscow ignored Washington.
  (12) He keeps strumming and thrumming and squeaking on his fiddle every afternoon for two hours.
  (13) A set jaw confronted John as he stepped into his father's office.
  (14) He is that delight of football coaches, a one-man team, a show-off player.
  (15) The windows of the empty house stared foolishly at me.
  (16) The rosebud mouth of the little girl was quivering with disappointment.
  (17) With a bird-like motion of her head the old maid noted her fellow passengers.
  (18) She is the Helen Wills Moody of fencing.
  (19) A hundred hoofs clattered on the stony road.
  (20) Her eyes were damp violets.
  (21) The kitten looked like a ball of cotton.
  (22) She is fond of Chopin.
  (23) As a good fire brightens a room so does kindness cheer the universe.
  (24) She gazed at the scarf of foam in the boat's wake.
  (25) Dusk, a little gray mouse, crept across the sky, nibbling at the sunset.
  (26) Fifty pairs of heels clicked in perfect rhythm.
  (27) She began reading Thackeray and Fielding.
  (28) Yes, I had a good time. I love to break through the ice and get wet, especially when there is no fire or shelter within a radius of two miles.
31. Note and classify figures of speech in your reading. In giving an example of a simile, it is necessary to present both of the similar items, for the objects must be of different classes; simple comparisons are matter-of-fact, not imaginative.
32. Into what three classes may poetry be divided? Briefly describe each. How is drama related to lyric poetry?
33. What means of imitation do the following employ: music, dancing, poetry?
34. Distinguish the characteristics of classical, romantic, and modern poetry. Which kind is the best?
35. How may poetry be defined? In what sense is it philosophical or universal? Is meter essential?
36. What is the opposite of poetry? of prose? What is the essential difference between prose and verse? How does the rhythm of prose differ from the rhythm of verse? Mark as stressed or unstressed each syllable of a prose passage, such as that quoted from Washington Irving or that from Stewart

E. White on page 279 f., to show the rhythm. How nearly does it follow a pattern?

37. Is the rhythm of verse identical with its meter? What should be their relation?

38. Briefly describe four devices to achieve the emphasized rhythm essential to poetry. Cite an illustration of each. Which device is used in the great body of English poetry?

39. Explain: foot; catalexis; feminine ending; anacrusis; truncation; spondee; pyrrhic; caesura; end-stopped lines; run-on-lines; an alexandrine; a verse; a stanza.

40. Distinguish: rime, assonance, alliteration; feminine rime and feminine ending. Illustrate each.

41. Give an example of masculine rime; feminine rime; imperfect rime.

42. What is eye rime? internal rime? internal alliteration?

43. Write the pattern of: anapest, trochee, dactyl, iambus, amphibrach. Illustrate each by a word or by a line of verse.

44. Describe and cite an example of: blank verse, heroic couplets, heroic quatrain, the sonnet, the cinquain. Which of these is free verse? Name the meter of the others.

45. State the rime pattern of the Petrarchan sonnet; the Shakespearean sonnet.

46. Which is the most important meter in English? Why? Which is the most important meter in the Greek and Latin literatures? Name one English poem written in this meter.

47. Scan the following and name the meter of each.

    (1) Of old sat Freedom on the heights
    (2) Just for a handful of silver he left us
    (3) The stars with their laughter are shaken
    (4) Hard he labored, long and well
    (5) For the moon never beams without bringing me dreams
    (6) Pardoned in heaven, the first by the throne
    (7) Oh, to be in England
    (8) What a world of solemn thought their monody compels
    (9) Menace our heart ere he master his own
   (10) The lilies and roses were slow to awaken
   (11) I arise from dreams of thee
   (12) Come hither, the dances are done
   (13) "It's bitter cold, it's bitter cold," the Color-Sergeant said
   (14) From the lake to the meadow and on to the wood
   (15) Beginning to faint in the light that she loves
   (16) But the rose was awake all the night for your sake
   (17) They are neither brute nor human
   (18) And lift the gold and silver that has mouldered there for years
   (19) For one that will never be thine
   (20) Found the one gift of which fortune bereft us
   (21) Mosses and heather
   (22) At the midnight in the silence of the sleeptime
   (23) With whom she has heart to be gay
   (24) Lived in his mild and magnificent eye
   (25) In the core of one pearl all the shade and the shine of the sea

48. Classify every word in the first stanza of Gray's "Elegy" according to the image or images it conveys as: sight, sound, touch, temperature, movement and muscular strain, smell, taste, no image. Do the same for the stanza quoted on page 46. Compare these two stanzas in poetic quality. What conclusions do you come to?

49. From poems you read quote phrases that convey vivid sense-images; figures of speech; emotion; exalted ideas.

50. Read Poe's "The Philosophy of Composition." Outline it.

51. What is expository writing? Mention fifteen kinds of composition that are expository.

52. Describe the familiar essay. Give examples.

53. What is the basic tool for analyzing expository writing?

54. Read Newman's discourse on "Knowledge Viewed in Relation to Learning." State his thesis (a one-sentence summary of the whole discourse) and make a skeleton outline.

55. Do the same for Arnold's "Sweetness and Light."

56. In all essays, ideas and style are important. Which of these seems more important in the serious expository essay? in the familiar essay?

57. Show how the principles of unity, coherence, and emphasis govern the composition of a sentence, a paragraph, and a whole composition. Which in all of these is the position of greatest emphasis? of least?

58. What is the best means to secure coherence in expository writing?

59. What is the first requisite of style in expository writing? Mention three other qualities to be sought and means to achieve them.

60. Describe fully how the principle of variety is applied in good style.

INTRODUCTORY ENGLISH: GENERAL REGULATIONS

1. Manuscript form
   (1) Use ink or typewriter (double space) for all assigned written work; paper 8½x11, plain or ruled, but not that with lines narrowly spaced. Leave adequate margins.
   (2) Do not fold papers.
   (3) On first page of every assignment, write at the left, English I; at the right, your name, and the date; in the middle of the fourth line, the title. No heading is needed on succeeding pages, but number them. In the extreme upper right corner of the first page, state the time you spent on the day's entire assignment.
   (4) Every theme must have a title. A general subject, such as character sketch or description, is not a title.
   (5) Use one side of paper only in writing themes. You are permitted to use both sides of the paper for exercises.
   (6) Papers must be neat. If, however, you make a slight error, strike out words by drawing a line neatly through those you wish to omit. Never use parentheses to indicate deletion. Parentheses are punctuation marks that have their own functions; deletion is not one of them.
   (7) Get a supply of paper clips for manuscripts of two or more pages.
2. All assigned written work is due at the beginning of the class period. It will not be accepted at the close of the period, or later in the day, or on another day. Special exceptions to this rule, for instance, on account of illness, are made by individual conference with the instructor when the occasion arises.
3. The assigned written work is due from a section which does not meet on a given day, provided that other sections do meet that day.
4. An absentee whose written work is not sent in at the beginning of the class period receives a grade of 0 for the day, unless she has a special permission to submit the work later and does so. A student who is present in class, but whose assignment is not submitted at the beginning of the class period, receives a grade of 25% for attendance.
5. An absentee from a quiz receives a grade of 0. One who is absent on account of illness may make arangements to recover the grade lost. This is usually done by taking the quiz later or by outlining the matter assigned for the quiz.
6. All term papers must be submitted at the time assigned. A student who omits one automatically loses credit for the course. Term papers required in Introductory English include: your autobiography; a short story; a preliminary research paper; a longer research paper; and others that may be announced.
7. Penalties: A loss of 5% is incurred for lack of a title, for using pencil, or for writing a theme on both sides of the paper; a loss of 2% for every failure really to know what a sentence is (run-together sentences, comma splice, or a sentence fragment); a loss of 1% for every other error in mechanics—punctuation, grammar, spelling. Penalties are deducted from the grade representing the qualitative rating which the paper would have received if the errors were not present.
8. Record on the sheets provided all errors in mechanics of composition and misspellings in all written work. Keep this record clear, neat, complete, and up-to-date—ready to submit whenever asked for. Notice what your particular failings are and work systematically to rid yourself of them. Write your name in the upper right corner of record sheets.

Symbols Used In Marking Papers

1	Don't use *like* as a conjunction; use *as, as if,* or *as though.*
2	Don't say the *reason is because;* say the *reason is that.*
3	Don't confuse *due to* (adj.) and *because of* or *on account of* (adv.)
4	Don't say *can't help but see;* say *can't help seeing.*
5	Don't use *which* to refer to an entire clause.
6	Don't make an illogical comparison; e. g., She has a face like an Indian (should be *Indian's* or *that of an Indian*).
7	Use the genitive case of a noun or a pronoun that modifies a gerund.
agr.	Lack of agreement (subject and predicate; pronoun and antecedent)
ap.	Omission or misuse of the apostrophe
cap.	Use a capital letter.
cf.	Compare
cl.	Not clear
coh.	Lack of coherence
coll.	Colloquial language undesirable here
d.	Poor choice of words
dm.	Dangling modifier; e. g., Rushing into the room, a vase fell off the table
dx.	Good choice of words
E.	Faulty emphasis
F.	Fragmentary sentence, not justifiable here
fig.	Poor use of figure of speech
fig. m.	Mixed figure of speech
fw.	"Fine writing"; do not use it.
gr.	Error in grammar
id.	Faulty idiom; e. g., *different than* (should be *different from*)
K.	Awkward
l. c.	Use a small letter.
m.	Faulty meter
N. S.	Fragmentary sentence, but permissible; should be marked *N.S.* in margin
O.	Obscure
p.	Faulty punctuation
pro.	Misuse of pronoun
pt. v.	Point of view violated
q.	Omission or faulty use of quotation marks
r.	Faulty rime
ref.	Faulty reference
rep.	Undesirable repetition
S.	Sentence error (run-together sentences or comma splice)
si.	Split infinitive; e. g., *to slowly walk* (should be *to walk slowly*)

sp.	Misspelling
stet.	Let it stand.
str.	Faulty structure
syl.	Faulty syllabication. Divide only between syllables, not within a syllable.
t.	Error in tense
taut.	Tautology; e. g., *return back*
tr.	Faulty transition
U.	Lack of unity
v.	Faulty use of verb
w.	Wordy
wk.	Weak
x.	Good
√	Poor
¶	Begin a new paragraph.
No ¶	Do not begin a new paragraph.
// str.	Use parallel structure.